D0143033

NATIVE AMERICANS IN THE NEWS

Recent Titles in
Contributions to the Study of Mass Media and Communications

Ranks and Columns: Armed Forces Newspapers in American Wars
Alfred Emile Cornebise

Clarifying McLuhan: An Assessment of Process and Product
S. D. Neill

Political Protest and Street Art: Popular Tools for Democratization in Hispanic Countries
Lyman G. Chaffee

The Best of the Rest: Non-Syndicated Newspaper Columnists Select Their Best Work
Sam G. Riley, editor

Advertising, Alcohol Consumption, and Abuse: A Worldwide Survey
Joseph C. Fisher

Beyond Agendas: New Directions in Communication Research
Philip Gaunt, editor

The Press and Politics in Israel: *The Jerusalem Post* from 1932 to the Present
Erwin Frenkel

The Disabled, the Media, and the Information Age
Jack A. Nelson, editor

Censorship of Expression in the 1980's: A Statistical Survey
John B. Harer and Steven R. Harris

The U.S. Media and the Middle East: Image and Perception
Yahya R. Kamalipour

Advertising, Alcohol Consumption, and Mortality: An Empirical Investigation
Joseph C. Fisher and Peter A. Cook

The Press in Times of Crisis
Lloyd E. Chiasson, Jr.

NATIVE AMERICANS IN THE NEWS

Images of Indians in the Twentieth Century Press

Mary Ann Weston

Contributions to the Study of Mass Media and Communications,
Number 49

Greenwood Press
Westport, Connecticut • London

Library of Congress Cataloging-in-Publication Data

Weston, Mary Ann.
Native Americans in the news : images of Indians in the twentieth century press / Mary Ann Weston.
p. cm.—(Contributions to the study of mass media and communications, ISSN 0732–4456 ; no. 49)
Includes bibliographical references and index.
ISBN 0–313–28948–4 (alk. paper)
1. Indians in the press—United States. 2. Indians of North America—Public opinion. 3. Public opinion—United States. 4. Journalism—United States—History—20th century. I. Title. II. Series.
PN4888.I52W47 1996
302.23'2'08997—dc20 95–37334

British Library Cataloguing in Publication Data is available.

Library of Congress Catalog Card Number: 95–37334
ISBN: 0–313–28948–4
ISSN: 0732–4456

First published in 1996

Greenwood Press, 88 Post Road West, Westport, CT 06881
An imprint of Greenwood Publishing Group, Inc.

Printed in the United States of America

The paper used in this book complies with the Permanent Paper Standard issued by the National Information Standards Organization (Z39.48–1984).

10 9 8 7 6 5 4 3 2

To Michael, Christopher, and Matthew,
and to the memory of Chloe.

Contents

Preface ix

1. Indians, Images, and the News Media 1
2. The 1920s: Assimilation versus Cultural Pluralism 19
3. The 1930s: In New Deal Legislation, Reform Meets Reality 49
4. World War II: Braves on the Warpath 85
5. The 1950s: Termination and Relocation 99
6. The 1960s and 1970s: Direct Action for Self-Determination 127
7. The 1980s and 1990s: Talking Back to the Media 153

Selected Bibliography 167

Index 177

Preface

This is not a book about Indians. Rather, it is about how Indians have been written about in the mainstream press. It is about perceptions—readers' perceptions fostered by newspaper and magazine articles. These stories, I submit, had and have a powerful role in shaping our views of Native Americans—and the actions we and our representatives in government take based on those views.

I do not pretend to be an "expert" on Indians. They are experts on their own cultures and lives. I have, however, learned a great deal from native people who have generously shared their insights. What I have hoped to do is to show how disparate cultures, those of Native Americans and of mainstream journalism, interacted to produce the portrayals you will read about in the pages that follow.

This work could not have been done without the help of many. I wish to acknowledge some of them here and ask the indulgence of those I omitted.

My colleagues at the Medill School of Journalism, Northwestern University gave me encouragement and understanding. Richard Schwarzlose gave advice, offered support, answered questions without hesitation, and helped me believe it could be done. Dean Michael Janeway allowed me released time from teaching obligations to research and write. Paul Lavrakas and David Protess generously provided expert advice and support. The Gannett Urban Journalism Center provided a grant that enabled much of the research on this project to go forward.

Marion Marzolf of the University of Michigan and Carolyn Martindale of Youngstown State University reviewed and offered valuable suggestions on parts of the manuscript.

Many native and nonnative people generously lent advice and insights and viewpoints. Among them are Roger Buffalohead, John Coward, Ada Deer, Paul DeMain, Lucy Ganje, Fred Hoxie, Beverly Deepe Keever, Faith Smith, James Yellowbank, and others past and present.

My intrepid graduate assistants Loren Billings, Eileen Finan, and Heather Hamill often went beyond the call of duty in tracking down articles.

The staffs of several libraries, including the Northwestern University Library, Library of Congress, San Francisco Public Library, Chicago's Harold Washington Public Library, Evanston Public Library, Arizona Historical Society, Omaha Public Library, State Historical Society of Wisconsin, University of Arizona Library, and Arizona State Historical Society, were unfailingly helpful.

Jane Edwards, formerly of the Mitchell Indian Museum, gave me the original inspiration for this work.

My son Christopher read and made insightful suggestions on the manuscript. My son Matthew found invaluable source material that might otherwise have been overlooked. My husband, Michael Weston, identified articles, read and edited many drafts, tried valiantly to teach me the difference between "which" and "that," and supplied the inexhaustible patience, compassion, and support that made this possible.

1

Indians, Images, and the News Media

In 1933 James O'Donnell Bennett, a writer for the *Chicago Tribune*, visited the Indian village at the Century of Progress world's fair, trying to reconcile the images in his mind with the Native Americans he saw there. The questions he asked in his story reflected his perplexity. "Are these men who move with such beautiful poise really majestic or only stolid? . . . Are they truly laconic or only verbally dull? Are they tractable?. . . Are they truthful? . . . Do they crave liquor? . . . Are they lazy?"[1]

In 1989 a reporter for the *Chicago Sun-Times* wrote about another Indian image causing controversy, if not perplexity. "Illinois politicians are hitting the warpath over whether Chief Illiniwek, symbol of the University of Illinois, should hang up his headdress for good."[2]

Both stories dealt with powerful and pervasive images. In the first case the reporter tried to interpret real Native Americans through the images that were familiar to him. In the second case the image—Chief Illiniwek—*was* the focus of the story, and real Indian people were nowhere to be seen. The two stories were written in the same city more than a half century apart, but the images they portrayed have existed since the time of Columbus in the pictures, stereotypes, and mythologies that whites have constructed about Native Americans.

These images in literature and popular culture—from James Fenimore Cooper to Kevin Costner, from the cigar-store Indian to the Jeep Cherokee—are familiar to anyone acquainted with American literature, movies, sports, or advertising. They have been the subject of a number of scholarly and popular investigations.[3]

Less thoroughly explored is the place of these images in journalism. News journalism, which purports to deal in fact, not fiction, which seeks to inform as well as entertain, plays by a different set of rules from popular culture or literature or advertising. Journalism has a unique position in the construction and repetition of images. It is not considered literature and is not supposed to employ imagination and fantasy as literature does, though newspaper features and magazine articles may use other literary devices. The presumed requirements of factuality, however, set journalistic accounts apart from fiction.

Furthermore, though journalism is charged with reporting on events, it is not, generally, regarded as the instigator of events or the originator of policies. The rhetoric of journalism calls on the press to recreate a reality, rather than invent it.

This is not to say that the press does not deal in images. One of the first to explore this notion was Walter Lippmann. He recognized that people construct and act upon "fictions" to explain and make the world manageable. "For the real environment is altogether too big, too complex, and too fleeting for direct acquaintance. We are not equipped to deal with so much subtlety, so much variety, so many permutations and combinations. . . . [W]e have to reconstruct it on a simpler model before we can manage with it." Lippmann also noted the dangers of "blind spots" and uncritical acceptance of stereotypes. Yet, he observed, in journalism, stereotypes provide readers a "familiar foothold" to get them into the story.[4]

While the kinds of stereotypes discussed by Lippmann can help make sense of a complex world, inaccurate ones can distort reality to the detriment of the people and issues being portrayed. This study will explore the notion that the news media have perpetuated popular images of Native Americans, images that were badly flawed—inaccurate stereotypes, in fact.[5] This repetition of inaccurate images, which runs counter to the press' ideal of fair and factual reporting, has been a consequence of the news process itself. The practices, traditions, and forms of journalism, rather than challenging the stereotypes in popular culture, have repeated and reinforced them. By doing so, the press has given these images the weight of factuality. By reporting them and incorporating them into purportedly factual accounts of events (i.e., news), the news media give them another dimension.

Readers and viewers know—on one level, at least—that savages depicted in movies or the crude "mascots" used by sports teams are fiction, fantasy, or symbol. But news is supposed to be different. Audiences are asked to take news accounts as at least a version of reality. Yet, if the Native Americans who populate that reality are inaccurately represented, how is the audience to separate the real native people, issues, and events from the popular culture images?

Given the press' self-imposed mission of providing fair and factual information, it is pertinent to explore how the news media deal with both the imagery and the reality of Native Americans. This study will examine the images of Native Americans in the press at several pivotal points in the twentieth century. It will look at the ways journalism's values, forms, and practices affected the selection of stories about Native Americans and the forms those stories took. It will look at newspaper and magazine coverage of Native Americans from the point of view of the audience—the readers whose views of Indians and Indian policy would have been affected by what they read in the press. This scrutiny of the way the press treated stories about Indians contributes to the history of coverage of minorities and to analyses of how the press has perceived and reacted to groups outside the ethnic mainstream.

THE HISTORICAL DIMENSION

Journalists, by nature, are people of the here and now. The past is old news, nothing that will help them make today's deadline. But the images and events they encounter today, and the practices by which journalists turn them into news, all have roots in the past.

Current patterns, attitudes, ways of thinking about Native Americans were not invented yesterday or last week. The images of Indians date back to the earliest contacts between Europeans and natives of the western hemisphere. Similarly, the news values and definitions of what is newsworthy and what is not have histories, as does the press' treatment of those outside the mainstream. It is important to know where both the images and the press practices came from, how they have evolved. While the past does not repeat itself, knowledge of what has gone before certainly can help inform today's discussions.

Stories in the news media are, by their nature, fleeting in their timeliness. They are reports of events that are usually written without time or opportunity for reflection and refinement. Thus, news media portrayals of Native Americans give us clues to how society viewed Indians at a given time. Images in the press are not created in the writer's imagination as fictional accounts might be. Instead, because they are linked to events, they powerfully reflect popular thought.

SCOPE OF THE STUDY

This study deals with the twentieth century. Specifically, it deals with the decades from the 1920s to the 1990s. During this time, public policy affecting Native Americans changed frequently and radically. By the 1920s, white reformers were calling for fundamental changes in the ways whites regarded Native Americans. These advocates of "cultural pluralism" believed that there was value to native cultures and that they should be preserved. They rejected the conventional view of Indians as a "vanishing race" that would be killed off or assimilated. They opposed the official policy that called for "civilizing" Indians by breaking up tribal landholdings and obliterating native cultures. The challenge of the pluralists laid the groundwork for several shifts in public policy concerning Native Americans. John Collier, the 1920s reformer who helped put the issue of cultural pluralism on the national agenda, became commissioner of Indian affairs in the Roosevelt administration and tried, on a grand scale, to put his ideas into practice in the "Indian New Deal."

After World War II, images of Indian heroism in the war in conjunction with Cold War ideology and governmental cost-cutting brought calls for "termination" of federal services to Native Americans. This call to "free" Indians from government services amounted to an updated version of assimilation. The policies that followed deprived some groups of their lands and tribal status and drew many Native Americans from the reservations into the cities.

The bitter legacy of termination, combined with the heady atmosphere of the civil rights movement of the 1960s and other factors, led to cries of "red power" and some dramatic direct actions by Native American activists in the late 1960s and early 1970s. Among these were the takeover and occupation of Alcatraz Island, California, in 1969–71 and the occupation of Wounded Knee, South Dakota, in 1973. These confrontations plus a shift in the national mood led to policies allowing native people increased self-determination.[6]

Thus in the space of about seventy years, the official view of how Native Americans should be treated shifted from forced assimilation to cultural pluralism to termination to limited self-determination. At the same time these policy shifts were going on, the nation's press was undergoing changes of its own, though its fundamental values and practices remained essentially intact.

Two events in the early 1920s make that time a useful starting point. In November 1922 the activist John Collier and other white reformers launched a spectacularly successful publicity campaign to defeat legislation that would have deprived the Pueblo Indians of New Mexico of some of their lands.[7] In April 1923 the year-old American Society of Newspaper Editors (ASNE) met in Washington and adopted its first ethics code, the Canons of Journalism.[8]

For Indian-white relations, the protests of the 1920s marked the first widespread public challenge to the idea that forced assimilation into white culture was the inevitable and desirable end to the Indian "problem." For journalism, the adoption of a national ethics code by more than one hundred influential newspaper editors brought new weight to the press' self-examination of its role and performance, an examination that continues today. The Canons of Journalism, however, did not mention coverage of Indians, or of any racial, ethnic, or religious minority, for that matter. Indeed, press critics and journalism educators were virtually silent on that subject until after World War II. Because coverage of minorities was not expressed, one can only take at face value the press' public rhetoric that its ideal of fair and factual coverage extended to all groups.

THE ROLE OF THE PRESS

By the time the Canons of Journalism were adopted in 1923, the mainstream press had accepted certain roles and values linked to its unique First Amendment protection. The First Amendment to the Constitution buttressed the press against government interference when it said, "Congress shall make no law . . . abridging the freedom of speech, or of the press." The press saw itself as being a provider of facts necessary for citizens to vote intelligently and as being a watchdog on government. It also subscribed to the values of presenting information accurately, truthfully, and impartially.

The canons asserted the press' responsibility to the "public welfare" and its right to "discuss whatever is not explicitly forbidden by law." Newspapers were to stay free "from all obligations except that of fidelity to the public interest" and were "constrained to be truthful." News reports "should be free from opinion or bias of any kind."[9]

The role of the press as conduit for information vital to citizenship was expressed succinctly by the author of one of the first books on journalism ethics, Nelson Antrim Crawford. Voters, he wrote, need facts on which to base their decisions and the press is "the only potentially satisfactory agency" to provide them. "Successful popular government, being dependent on facts, is therefore dependent on the press."[10]

The role of the press as public informant was given further attention after World War II by the Commission on Freedom of the Press. The group, called the Hutchins Commission after its chairman, University of Chicago Chancellor Robert M. Hutchins, in its 1947 report asserted that the press had a social responsibility to inform citizens so that they could make wise decisions on government affairs.[11] Citizens, according to this view, should be able to look to the press to find accurate information, as well as entertaining fare and articles of opinion.

In his 1952 study of the development of the notion of freedom of the press in England, Fredrick S. Siebert wrote that as democracy superseded monarchy, press freedom expanded and the press "took on an extra-legal function, that of an informant and a watchdog of public affairs."[12] That function reached its apex in the 1970s with the flourishing of investigative reporting such as the *Washington Post*'s exposure of the Watergate scandal.

In addition, the press saw its mission as being fair and factual and free from outside influence.[13] The press was called on to be accurate and "objective" in news reports.

The Canons of Journalism took a broad view of both the scope of newspapers' coverage and their audiences. "The primary function of newspapers is to communicate to the human race what its members do, feel and think," the opening sentence read.[14] There was no mention of race, class, gender, or the like. Indeed, journalism was considered to serve everyone, according to Casper S. Yost, the first president of the American Society of Newspaper Editors.

"There is no influence in the world so ubiquitous, so persuasive, so persistent as the newspaper," Yost wrote. "No man is so poor or so remote that it does not touch him." Journalism, he continued, is "a profession that exists upon the events of the day, that mirrors all life and presents it to the view of every individual, thereby bringing all mankind to a closer unity and to a clearer conception of its kinship."[15]

By implication it would seem, then, that the injunction to accuracy and impartiality extended to coverage of Native Americans both as subjects of stories and as readers, though they, like other subdivisions of society, were not specifically addressed. Subsequent chapters will examine whether and how these roles and values applied to coverage of Native Americans.

RACIAL AND ETHNIC GROUPS AND THE PRESS

Before World War II, general statements of journalistic values and principles addressed an undifferentiated, generic audience and gave the newspapers' scope of coverage an all-encompassing definition. There apparently was little attention to coverage of minority racial or ethnic groups. College-level journalism textbooks, for example, virtually ignored the topic. Textbooks, as Professor Linda Steiner wrote, "emphasize rather than challenge prevailing definitions; they dramatize, not undermine, conventional practices and relations of power." Journalism texts, she continued, "are likely to reflect standard newsroom conventions, demographics and dynamics."[16]

For much of the century, journalism texts paid scant consideration to the ways the press covered—or failed to cover—racial and ethnic minorities. According to Steiner, "[N]o pre-1970s textbook addressed [race and ethnicity] beyond stylebook rules on how to refer to the minority status of subjects."[17] A study of twenty-four journalism textbooks published between 1908 and 1988 found that early reporting texts confined their attention to minorities to discussions of the use of racial designations in crime stories and prohibitions against demeaning racial terms and dialect.[18] Indians were not specifically mentioned in the early texts.

The post–World War II era brought two important statements on press coverage of racial and ethnic minorities. In 1947 the prestigious Hutchins

Commission warned the press about its use of imagery in coverage of racial groups. The commission expressed concern with coverage of "groups which are partially insulated from one another and which need to be interpreted to one another." It said:

Factually correct but substantially untrue accounts of the behavior of members of one of these social islands can intensify the antagonisms of others toward them. A single incident will be accepted as a sample of group action unless the press has given a flow of information and interpretation concerning the relations between two racial groups such as to enable the reader to set a single event in its proper perspective.[19]

The Hutchins Commission went on to call on the press to present "a representative picture of the constituent groups in the society." It explained:

People make decisions in large part in terms of favorable or unfavorable images. They relate fact and opinion to stereotypes. Today the [mass media are] principal agents in creating and perpetuating these conventional conceptions. When the images they portray fail to present the social group truly, they tend to pervert judgment. . . . Responsible performance here simply means that the images repeated and emphasized be such as are in total representative of the social group as it is.[20]

This recommendation was one of five requirements for the press put forth by the commission in a controversial report that asserted that the press had a social responsibility to the public.[21] The press' reaction to this departure from the traditional libertarian theory of the press overshadowed the commission's recommendation concerning imagery and racial groups. The report was "read, reviewed, discussed, and quickly buried," though it did eventually provide a framework for future press criticism.[22]

A landmark indictment of the press' coverage of African Americans—and, by extension, other racial groups—came in the 1968 *Report of the National Advisory Commission on Civil Disorders*, popularly known as the Kerner Commission after its chairman, then-Illinois Gov. Otto Kerner.[23] The commission, which was set up by President Lyndon B. Johnson after the devastating 1967 urban riots in Newark, Detroit, and other cities, took a wide-ranging look at the causes of the unrest and some possible remedies. It devoted only a chapter to the news media. In that chapter it analyzed coverage of the 1967 riots, then laid down some pointed criticisms.[24]

The media report and write from the standpoint of a white man's world. The ills of the ghetto, the difficulties of life there, the Negro's burning sense of grievance, are seldom conveyed. . . . [The press] repeatedly, if unconsciously, reflects the biases, the paternalism, the indifference of white America. . . . It is the responsibility of the news media to tell the story of race relations in America, and with notable exceptions the media have not yet turned to the task with the wisdom, sensitivity, and expertise it demands.[25]

The Kerner Commission report became the benchmark against which coverage of all those outside the mainstream has been measured ever since. Even though it dealt expressly with coverage of African Americans, its admonitions could be applied to coverage of Native Americans. However, few studies specifically addressed the press' treatment of Native Americans.[26]

DEFINITIONS OF NEWS

The definitions the mainstream press used for what is news and what is newsworthy did not change radically during the years covered in this study. In his survey of news "from the drum to the satellite," Mitchell Stephens defined news as "new information about a subject of some public interest that is shared with some portion of the public," or, in short, "what is on a society's mind."[27] Definitions by twentieth-century journalists and journalism educators reflected substantial agreement on certain elements. Most stressed the unusual, proximity (both emotional and physical), consequence or importance, prominence or celebrity, timeliness, and human interest.

These elements, according to Curtis MacDougall, author of a popular journalism text, "have been tested by years of experience and, rightly or wrongly, are in vogue in all but a negligible number of news rooms."[28]

Writing in 1911 Will Irwin defined news as "a departure from the established order." But within that general category, Irwin wrote, people want to read about things that are familiar, that affect their "personal concerns," that involve important persons or activities.[29] A 1975 text defined news as "the timely report of facts or opinion that hold interest or importance, or both, for a considerable number of people."[30]

As will be seen in subsequent chapters, some of the ways news was defined, such as emphasis on the unusual (especially conflict), the consequential, and human interest, encouraged the perpetuation of inaccurate images of Native Americans. The journalistic choices made based on these definitions were done from a white perspective. Though this was not stated, the clear practice was to measure an event according to its importance to white, usually male, journalistic gatekeepers.[31] This practice, by definition, relegated news of Native Americans to the periphery unless the news values of conflict or uniqueness brought them onto the mainstream agenda. Since Native Americans *were* on the periphery because they lacked significant political or economic influence, they had little leverage to influence the news themselves.

CONSTRAINTS ON THE PRESS

Any critique of press coverage should take a realistic look at the constraints that keep newspapers and magazines from publishing ideal products. It is important to understand the day-to-day realities that influence what is covered and what is not, how well and how long a story is written, its placement in the publication, the size and kind of headlines and illustrations that accompany it, indeed, whether it appears at all. Consider some of the influences that affect the coverage of any "story":

- Someone must be available to get the information and write it. That is, a publication must have a reporter, staff member, or freelance writer who can gather the information and shape it into a story. Often, newspapers depend on the wire services to send stories from outside the local community.
- The reporter or writer must be able to get to the location of the story and find sources who will cooperate. Publicists and aggressive, publicity-hungry sources can powerfully influence reporting by pushing their messages on reporters who may not have time, initiative, or resources to get other information on their own.
- The publication must have room for the story. The size of the "news hole" or space for editorial copy in a newspaper depends on a number of factors, but a primary one is the amount of advertising sold. Editors often have little control over this, and reporters have none.
- Every story must compete with the rest of the day's news for the limited space available. Major events, such as a natural disaster, election, or war, drive out stories that might be featured prominently on a "slow news day," when less is happening.[32]
- Journalistic gatekeepers must be interested in the story. Beyond the calamitous events that are unarguably newsworthy, there is a great discretionary space. This is where reporters' and editors' "news judgment" comes into play. A story that falls into this discretionary area must pique the gatekeepers' interest, or it will be ignored.
- The audience must be interested in the story. Content of general circulation newspapers and magazines is a delicate balance of news editors believe their readers should have and news they believe readers want.[33]
- The story must meet the publication's deadline. Whether the deadline is "every minute," as in the case of the wire services; several times a day as for newspapers; weekly or monthly, as for magazines, the story must be written and edited by the deadline, or it will not appear.

Working journalists must balance all these forces and more on a daily, even hourly, basis. Though circumstances and technology were different, this was no less true in the 1920s than in the 1970s or, for that matter, today.

In addition to these constraints, stories about Native Americans often pose unique challenges for mainstream journalists. Frequently, particularly before World War II, the story was on a reservation in a remote, rural area. Also, particularly before World War II, many Indians did not speak English and were justifiably wary of outsiders coming around to ask questions. And, journalists, especially those who came from distant areas to do stories about Indians, frequently were ignorant of their cultures.

Any criticism of press performance that aspires to be taken seriously by those in the profession must take into account the constraints such as these that necessarily flaw an ideal journalistic product. All of these forces and more were at play when decisions were made on coverage of Native Americans.

IMAGES OF INDIANS

The idea of "the Indian" holds a special, some would say essential, place in the American psyche. Scholars have examined the history of the idea of the Indian for what it says about Europeans and, later, Americans—how they thought of themselves, the world they had inhabited, and the one they had newly come upon. The image of the Indian has roots in the European idea of the noble savage, but that philosophical and literary construct, which was an effective device for social criticism, collided with the real "savages" Europeans encountered in America. Then, Europeans tried to make sense of a group of people who had no place in their world view.

These images constructed by Europeans and Euro-Americans not only helped them make sense of themselves and the world, but they undergirded the policies by which whites dealt with Indians. Thus, however erroneous the images, they had profound impacts on real Native-American people. And, importantly, the images remain today. They are embodied not only in the names of sports teams and automobiles, but often in the formulation, writing, selection, and presentation of the news.

To colonists and, later, frontiersmen, the Indian was the means by which they could define themselves. What they saw as the Indian's savagery defined their civilization. In the Indian they could see the antithesis of their values and world view. Consequently, American "progress" and "civilization" inevitably spelled doom for Indians.

According to historian Robert F. Berkhofer, Jr., three fundamental themes have persisted as images have evolved:

- First, conceiving of the Indian in a generic way by generalizing the traits of one tribe to all Indians, thus denying the wide variety of cultural, linguistic, and other differences among the indigenous Americans.
- Second, describing Indians in terms of white society. Rather than describing Indians as they saw themselves, they were viewed according to how they did or did not measure up to white norms.
- Third, mixing examination of Indians and their institutions with moral judgments about them. As Berkhofer put it, "Whites overwhelmingly measured the Indian as a general category against those beliefs, values, or institutions they most cherished in themselves at the time."[34]

Though expressions changed over the years, the themes and images of the Indian changed far less. The images had been elaborated on over the centuries, but their basic substance was largely unchanged.

Good and Bad Indians

Basically, images of the Indian have embraced two contradictory conceptions: the good Indian (or noble savage) and the bad Indian. The two images—the noble redman and the bloodthirsty devil—have persisted in literature and popular culture from captivity narratives of the seventeenth century to made-for-television movies of the late twentieth century.

The image of the good Indian, according to Berkhofer, brought together a lengthy series of attributes, including friendliness, courtesy, handsomeness, dignity, tenderness toward family and children, independence, and a "wholesome enjoyment of nature's gifts," which in some ways summarized white romantic yearnings for an idealized state of nature.[35]

The noble savage was a European notion that dated, in one form or another, from the time of Columbus. It referred to a remote time and place where people once lived in a pure and uncorrupted natural state, as described, for example, in the writings of Jean-Jacques Rousseau. Such an abstraction was a useful vehicle for attacking the established order.[36] In the hands of American writers who had some acquaintance with real people who, in their view, were savages, noble savages were sometimes depicted romantically as doomed to be swept away by the advances of civilization. Also, they were seen as a "refined, purer version of the true American."[37]

The antithesis of the good Indian was the bad Indian, who, in the view of whites, exhibited all the uncivilized traits that embodied European fears of savagery. He was naked, lecherous, promiscuous, constantly at war. His habits and customs were seen by whites as brutal, loathsome, filthy, and cruel. He lived a life of indolence, improvidence, thievery, and treachery. In Berkhofer's words, "(T)his list substituted license for liberty, a harsh lot for simplicity, and dissimulation and deceit for innocence."[38]

To the seventeenth century Puritan colonists, for example, Indians were savage Satanic heathens, brutal and bestial, who were ordained by God to be civilized by conversion to Christianity, or exterminated.[39]

By the nineteenth century, as Indians were pushed west, noble/ignoble savage depictions were folded into what historian Brian W. Dippie called a "theory of vices and virtues." According to this view, Indians who mixed with whites absorbed their vices, such as alcohol abuse, but not their virtues. Thus, Indians who had not been contaminated by white contact were still noble savages, but those who had been touched by white civilization were degraded and, ultimately, doomed.[40] The "degraded" Indian, no longer a threat but an object of pity, was a variant of the bad Indian image.[41]

As the circumstances of both Indians and Euro-Americans changed, the images were modified and elaborated upon, but many of their central elements remained. Good or bad, there was a "curious timelessness" in the depiction of the Indian as a being frozen in the past.[42] Thus, even contemporary Indians were described with reference to a distant, earlier time.

To the images in poetry and prose in the seventeenth, eighteenth and nineteenth centuries was added a vividly visual element in the twentieth with the advent of motion pictures. If the medium changed, the depictions did not. In the movies, good Indians were noble but doomed children of nature who were victims of white progress, or loyal followers of paternalistic whites, such as the Lone Ranger's companion Tonto. Bad Indians were bloodthirsty savages who stood in the way of whites' westward expansion.[43] Others have labeled the good and bad Indians of the movies the "noble anachronism" and the "savage reactionary" and described a related good Indian image for Indian women, a Pocahontas figure who was "deeply affectionate, yet maidenly" and who sacrificed her life.[44]

By the 1970s when Native Americans sought to define themselves in the media, the good/bad Indian images were bitterly interpreted by some as a means to "reinforce the white man's concept of his own superiority and at the same time provide a phony folklore and a sense of identity and history to this rootless and grasping society which the sons of the invaders have created."[45] By the 1990s Native Americans' criticisms of their treatment in the news were reaching mainstream audiences.

NATIVE AMERICANS AND THE NEWS

If Indians were staples of popular fiction on the page or screen, they were also frequently in the news. Indians have been in the news ever since there were newspapers in the territory that became the United States. The paper considered by many to be the first newspaper in the English colonies of North America, *Publick Occurrences, Both Forreign and Domestick*, was filled with news of Indians, both as enemies in the French and Indian War and as allies. Later colonial newspapers also printed a significant amount of news about Native Americans, much of it recounting Indian attacks and atrocities.[46]

Through the eighteenth and nineteenth century, while the colonies and the young nation struggled to wrest the land from its native people, Indians got a lot of newspaper attention, most of it bad. Though some stories portrayed Native Americans as good Indians or noble savages, more carried negative images of Indians as brutish and degraded. If the news often was not good, it often was ignored, too. For obvious reasons, stories that were covered were those important to whites, and almost always they were told from the white point of view.[47]

IMAGERY AND JOURNALISM

Images of Indians such as those discussed earlier were expressed journalistically in a variety of ways related to the "framing" of articles. Todd Gitlin defined frames, in the context of the mass media, this way: "Media frames are persistent patterns of cognition, interpretation, and presentation, of selection, emphasis, and exclusion, by which symbol-handlers routinely organize discourse."[48] These frames are "composed of little tacit theories about what exists, what happens, and what matters."[49] In other words, frames impose order and make sense of the world, both for those who report on it and for their audiences. The following are some of the journalistic practices that can go into the framing of stories. In the coverage of Native Americans, each contributed in various ways to the images of Indians in the press:

- Tone and language. Whether it was casting stories in a bemused, slightly humorous tone that implied nothing concerning Indians was to be taken seriously, or using overtly stereotypical language, the words used contributed powerfully to the images of Native Americans. It was, for example, common usage until at least the 1960s to refer to native men as "haughty" or "stoic" "chiefs," "braves," or "bucks"; women as "shy" or "giggling" "squaws"; and children as "papooses" regardless of the publication, story, or circumstances. In addition, local newspapers routinely identified those mentioned in police stories as Indians or by tribal name, undoubtedly contributing to the "degraded" image of Native Americans as people who were frequently criminals or victims of crimes.
- Organization. The decisions writers made as to what pieces of information, quotations, sources, descriptive language, and so on to include and emphasize, what elements to put at the beginning, middle, and end can make two accounts of the same event markedly different.
- Form. Journalistic conventions of the 1920s and later usually dictated whether a story would be a "straight" news story or a feature. Through much of this time, the staple of journalistic writing was the straightforward, "objective," "hard news" story. This was, ideally, an unbiased account of an event, organized in inverted pyramid fashion that put the most significant facts first. Straight news "objective" stories emphasized the details of daily events but seldom dealt with their larger cultural context. Features were less rigid in structure and language. They were intended to convey the personal side of the news in a colorful way and emphasized the unusual and emotional. Such an emphasis left the feature form vulnerable to distorting and trivializing unfamiliar Indian cultures and dress for bizarre and dramatic effects.
- Selection. The conventional definitions of news discussed earlier usually influenced decisions as to which stories would be included and which would not. Beyond major events and policy stories that were indisputably news, what was reported seemed often to fit white definitions of what Indian stories ought to be. Thus news that reinforced images of Indians as exotic, warlike, childlike, or improvident often took precedence over stories of more intrinsic importance to Native Americans, such as land claims or government stock-reduction policies.

Widely accepted journalistic practices, such as emphasizing the eye-catching and unusual, reporting on events more than on trends or issues, writing with verve and color, can also stereotype, misrepresent, and trivialize. While individual stories seldom were grossly inaccurate, the cumulative effect has been one of reinforcing inaccurate images instead of dispelling them with facts. This study will examine how the very practice of journalism—the ways news is defined, written, and selected—contributed to perpetuating the images so prevalent in popular culture.

A NOTE ON ORGANIZATION, SOURCES, AND METHOD

Each of the subsequent chapters is centered around a public policy issue or event involving Native Americans:

- The 1920s controversies over the Bursum (Pueblo lands) bill and Indian ceremonial dances;
- The 1930s debates about the Indian Reorganization Act with emphasis on the Indian congresses of 1934;
- Native American participation in World War II;
- The termination and relocation policies of the 1950s, concentrating on the termination of the Menominee tribe of Wisconsin and the relocation of Native Americans of many tribes to cities;
- The direct actions of the 1960s and 1970s, exemplified by the takeover of Alcatraz Island in 1969–71 and the occupation of Wounded Knee, South Dakota, in 1973;
- Cultural concerns of the 1980s and 1990s, such as the sports team mascot issue.

Each chapter examines the background of the issue and the social-political-cultural climate of the time. It surveys issues confronting the press related to coverage of those outside the mainstream. Then it describes the imagery found in stories about Native Americans, and the journalistic use of those images. This is not a comprehensive review of twentieth-century Indian-white relations. Rather, certain time periods, incidents, and situations were selected and scrutinized. The objective was to look at portrayals in news coverage, rather than to examine the history of the period.

The terms "Indian" and "Native American" are used interchangeably though "Indian" was used almost exclusively in the mainstream press until the 1980s.

Examples were drawn from a wide variety of publications. Newspapers included the *New York Times* and local and regional newspapers close to where events took place. Magazines were also examined, because during much of the time period under discussion, they commanded national audiences that newspapers did not.[50] Thus, magazines were at times actually more important as image builders and opinion molders.

This variety of publications adds an important dimension. To local papers in Arizona, New Mexico, South Dakota, or Wisconsin, Indians were part of the community. They were a hometown story that had political, economic, and sometimes social dimensions different from those that would capture the attention of the national press. Local papers often detailed tribal factionalism and intertribal conflicts and rivalries ignored by the distant press. Frequently papers such as the *Santa Fe New Mexican* or the *Muskogee (Oklahoma) Daily Phoenix* printed news of Indians involved both in crimes and in community events such as school programs or fairs and celebrations. These papers thus revealed Native Americans as people with many-faceted lives not unlike their white neighbors.

This is not to say coverage in the local press was either equal to that afforded whites or always fair to Native Americans. Frequently, there were, in addition to the even-handed news stories and community notices, stories that evoked images of Indians as exotic tourist attractions who dressed in colorful costumes and engaged in picturesque ceremonies while boosting the local economies. Until fairly recent times, Native Americans involved in crimes were often gratuitously identified in the local press as Indians. In some papers tribal concerns were given short shrift.

Analysis of the local and national press suggests a relationship between stereotypical images of Indians and the distance of a publication from the story. A paper in New Mexico or South Dakota might cover an event involving Indians in a detailed, straightforward manner. But when a news magazine or newspaper from New York sought to describe the same event to its distant readers, inaccurate imagery grew. Examples appear in subsequent chapters.

The difference in portrayals points up the danger of generalizing from a few prominent examples to the press as a whole. Despite the homogenizing effects of technology and wire-service copy, papers in South Dakota or Arizona or Wisconsin did not cover the same stories in the same ways as papers in New York or Chicago or Washington. National magazines added even more dimensions to the coverage. Because most of the population and opinion leaders did not live in Indian Country and had little access to the detailed accounts of the Indian New Deal in Arizona or termination in Wisconsin, the portrayal of Indians in influential mainstream publications such as the *New York Times*, the news magazines, and the national consumer magazines was a powerful factor in creating and reinforcing the images most Americans had of Native Americans.

This work endeavors to take a humanistic approach to examining and interpreting press coverage of Native Americans. No claim is made to having looked at every story about Native Americans during the time period or in the publications under scrutiny. Careful scrutiny was done, however, of indexes of publications, where available, to select stories representing a range of coverage. Where publications were not indexed, attempts were made to pinpoint time periods when Native American issues were likely to be covered and look at stories that appeared then. These methods yielded thousands of stories. Those referred to directly in the text are footnoted. The reader should keep in mind, however, that they represent examples, selections of selections.

In America, "the Indian" is ubiquitous, but Native Americans are virtually invisible. That is, mass culture images of Indians, noble or degraded, strange or ancient, resonate widely. But real Native Americans, because of their small numbers and relative lack of political and economic influence, are often unseen and unheard. The author hopes that this examination of Native Americans and the news process will contribute to the understanding of the place of the press in creating and perpetuating the imagery by which this group is seen and, often, judged.

Another reason examining portrayals of Indians is important is that it adds to what we know about the history of coverage of racial and ethnic groups in the mainstream press, a press that commands not only large audiences but audiences that include influential decision makers.

NOTES

1. *Chicago Tribune,* July 30, 1933, part 1, p. 7.

2. *Chicago Sun-Times,* Nov. 7, 1989, 1.

3. See, for example, Robert F. Berkhofer, Jr., *The White Man's Indian* (New York: Vintage Books, 1978); Berkhofer, "White Conceptions of Indians," and Michael T. Marsden and Jack Nachbar, "The Indian in the Movies," in Wilcomb E. Washburn, ed., *History of Indian-White Relations,* vol. 4 of *Handbook of North American Indians,* ed. William C. Sturtevant (Washington: Smithsonian Institution, 1988), 522–547, 607–616; Raymond W. Stedman, *Shadows of the Indian* (Norman: University of Oklahoma Press, 1982); Roy Harvey Pearce, *Savagism and Civilization* (Baltimore: Johns Hopkins Press, 1953, 1965); Ralph E. Friar and Natasha A. Friar, *The Only Good Indian . . . The Hollywood Gospel* (New York: Drama Book Specialists, 1972); Michael Hilger, *The American Indian in Film* (Metuchen, N.J.: The Scarecrow Press, Inc., 1986).

4. Walter Lippmann, *Public Opinion* (New York: The Macmillan Company, 1922), 16, 355.

5. Here I am adopting the meanings of "image" and "stereotype" used by Robert F. Berkhofer, Jr. in which he calls image "the more literal, even pictorial, representation people had of the Indian in their minds" and stereotype "any image we today no longer find accurate in light of our knowledge." See Berkhofer, *White Man's Indian,* xvii.

6. A comprehensive history of Indian-white relations is Francis Paul Prucha, *The Great Father* (2 vols.) (Lincoln: University of Nebraska Press, 1984).

7. Lawrence C. Kelly, *The Assault on Assimilation: John Collier and the Origins of Indian Policy Reform* (Albuquerque: University of New Mexico Press, 1983), 237–238; Kenneth R. Philp, *John Collier's Crusade for Indian Reform* (Tucson: University of Arizona Press, 1977), 38–39.

8. *Problems of Journalism: Proceedings of the First Annual Meeting of the American Society of Newspaper Editors*, Washington, D.C., April 27–28, 1923, 124.

9. Quoted in Casper S. Yost, *The Principles of Journalism* (New York: D. Appleton and Company, 1924), 162–163.

10. Nelson Antrim Crawford, *The Ethics of Journalism* (New York: Alfred A. Knopf, 1924), 37.

11. Commission on Freedom of the Press, *A Free and Responsible Press* (Chicago: University of Chicago Press, 1947), 17–18.

12. Fredrick S. Siebert, *Freedom of the Press in England: 1476–1776* (Urbana: The University of Illinois Press, 1952), 10.

13. For a discussion, see Marion T. Marzolf, *Civilizing Voices: American Press Criticism, 1880–1950* (New York: Longman, 1991), 119–132.

14. Yost, 161.

15. Ibid., 7–8.

16. Linda Steiner, "Construction of Gender in Newsreporting Textbooks: 1890–1990," *Journalism Monographs* 135 (October 1992): 1.

17. Ibid., 3, note 13.

18. Gene Burd, "Minorities in Reporting Texts: Before and After the 1968 Kerner Report," *Mass Comm Review* 15, nos. 2 and 3 (1988): 45–60, 68.

19. Commission on Freedom of the Press, 23.

20. Ibid., 26.

21. Marzolf, 163–176.

22. Ibid., 169.

23. National Advisory Commission on Civil Disorders, *Report of the National Advisory Commission on Civil Disorders* (New York: Bantam Books, 1968).

24. Ibid., 362–389.

25. Ibid., 366, 384.

26. See, for example, James E. Murphy and Sharon M. Murphy, *Let My People Know: American Indian Journalism, 1828–1978* (Norman: University of Oklahoma Press, 1981), 7–12.

27. Mitchell Stephens, *A History of News from the Drum to the Satellite* (New York: Penguin Books, 1988), 9.

28. Curtis MacDougall, *Interpretative Reporting*, 6th ed. (New York: The Macmillan Company, 1972), 59.

29. Will Irwin, "The American Newspaper," *Colliers*, 1911, quoted in Thomas Goldstein, ed., *Killing the Messenger: 100 Years of Media Criticism* (New York: Columbia University Press, 1989), 126–130.

30. Mitchell V. Charnley, *Reporting*, 3d ed. (New York: Holt, Rinehart and Winston, 1975), 44.

31. Clint C. Wilson II and Félix Gutiérrez, *Minorities and Media* (Beverly Hills: Sage Publications, 1985), 141–142.

32. Yost, 30–31.

33. Ibid., 10–11.

34. Berkhofer, *White Man's Indian*, 25–27.

35. Ibid., 28.

36. Brian W. Dippie, *The Vanishing American* (Middletown, Conn.: Wesleyan University Press, 1982), 18–19. See also Pearce, 136.

37. Dippie, 20.

38. Berkhofer, *White Man's Indian*, 28.
39. Pearce, 19–35.
40. Dippie, 25.
41. Berkhofer, *White Man's Indian*, 30.
42. Ibid., 28, 30.
43. Hilger, 1–2.
44. Marsden and Nachbar, 609.
45. Gerald Wilkinson, "Colonialism Through the Media," *The Indian Historian* (Summer, 1974): 29.
46. David A. Copeland, " 'The Sculking Indian Enemy': Colonial Newspapers' Portrayal of Native Americans," paper presented to the History Division, Association for Education in Journalism and Mass Communications, Kansas City, Mo., 1993.
47. For a discussion of nineteenth century newspaper portrayals of Indians, see John M. Coward, "The Newspaper Indian: Native Americans and the Press in the 19th Century" (Ph.D. diss., University of Texas at Austin, 1989). For an overview of news media coverage of American Indians, see Murphy and Murphy, 3–15.
48. Todd Gitlin, *The Whole World Is Watching* (Berkeley: University of California Press, 1980), 7.
49. Ibid., 6.
50. A list of newspapers and magazines studied is at the end of the book.

2

The 1920s: Assimilation versus Cultural Pluralism

At the beginning of the twentieth century, American Indians, in both popular belief and public policy, were a "vanishing race"[1] that would sooner or later either succumb or be assimilated into Euro-American society. That is, the surviving remnants of the tribes that had been decimated by European diseases, defeated in military combat, and forcibly removed from their ancestral lands would be "civilized" by being taught "American" values. This was generally understood to mean that they would be persuaded or forced to become Christians who farmed individually-owned plots of land.[2] The eventual outcome was to be the elimination of native cultures and the assimilation of Indians into Euro-American society.

Military defeats and treaties had forced most Native Americans onto reservations by 1868, though in the West some resisted violently until the final deadly encounter, the massacre of a band of Sioux at Wounded Knee in 1890.[3] But perhaps the greatest blow to Native American autonomy came in 1887 with passage of the Dawes Severalty Act. The act put the muscle of federal law behind the ideology of assimilation by attempting to force Indians to become individual landowners and farmers. The Dawes Act provided that reservations would be divided up into individual tracts of land for each member of a tribe. All "surplus" land not allotted to tribal members was to be made available for purchase by whites. Indians could lease their allotments to whites and, after the twenty-five-year trust period expired or they were declared "competent" by the government, could sell them. The act, which was later extended to include the Five Tribes (Cherokee, Choctaw, Chickasaw, Creek, and Seminole) and Osage of Oklahoma, did not apply to Indians in Arizona and New Mexico.[4]

For many Native Americans, allotment was a disastrous policy. Indian land holdings declined from an estimated 113 million acres in 1887 to some 47 million acres in 1932. Many Indians, whose culture was communal and who came from hunting, not agricultural traditions, were unable or unwilling to become farmers of small individual land holdings.[5] Some allotted lands were unsuitable for farming; some Indians lacked agricultural implements or instruction.

The act made insufficient provision for the heirs of allottees. As a result, some plots were subdivided into tiny, unworkable parcels. When oil was discovered on some Indian lands, particularly in Oklahoma, the frauds by which Indians were swindled out of their lands reached scandalous proportions.[6]

Forced assimilation was also carried out in education policies that were designed to " 'kill the Indian' to save the man."[7] Indian children were sometimes forcibly taken from their families and sent to distant boarding schools where they were required to cut their hair, forbidden to speak their native languages, severely punished, poorly taught, and crowded into unhealthy conditions. By the early twentieth century, many government boarding schools had been phased out in favor of public or reservation-based day schools. But though there was disagreement as to whether Indians should receive a classical or practical education, all agreed on the ultimate goal: "civilization," that is, assimilation.[8] Reformers and missionaries promoted these policies as being in the "best interests" of Indians, who were generally regarded as uncivilized savages who could only be saved by adopting the white man's ways.

JOHN COLLIER AND CULTURAL PLURALISM

A few disagreed. Among them was John Collier. He wrote that the assimilationist policies, which were destroying tribal cultures, languages, and religious practices, were "all mantled over by the concept of racial inferiority and racial doom."[9] Collier, a man of "passionate dogmatism,"[10] was a former social worker and lifelong reformer who "discovered" American Indians after World War I and made their cause his "all-consuming passion."[11] In 1923 he helped organize and became general secretary of the American Indian Defense Association and from this platform bedeviled the Indian Bureau for its treatment of Indians. A decade later President Franklin D. Roosevelt named Collier commissioner of Indian affairs. He held the post until 1945, and his "Indian New Deal" was the most sweeping change in Indian policy since the Dawes act.[12]

By the early 1920s Collier and others were noisily challenging the official policy of forced assimilation. They advocated the philosophy of cultural pluralism, a radically different view of Indians and their place in society that asserted that Indian cultures were valuable and should be preserved.[13]

This view not only sought to protect Indian cultures and religions but also saw in the communal institutions, particularly of the Pueblo Indians, "a model for reforming society at large."[14] Collier wrote:

> Yet it might be that only the Indians, among the peoples of this hemisphere at least, were still the possessors and users of the fundamental secret of human life—the secret of building great personality through the instrumentality of social institutions. And it might be, as well, that the Indian life would not survive.[15]

This clash of philosophies, assimilation versus cultural pluralism, was played out in the press in the early 1920s because of two controversies. One involved the Bursum bill, a measure that, opponents argued, would have taken ancestral lands from the Pueblo Indians of New Mexico. The second involved government restrictions on Indian ceremonial dances. The reformers' protests against these government measures were the opening assaults in a crusade that culminated in the 1930s when a compromised version of cultural pluralism became law with the Indian New Deal.

Collier was a pivotal figure in the coverage of Indians in the 1920s because he was instrumental in catapulting the Pueblo Indians into the nation's consciousness in the Bursum bill controversy. The publicity blitz he spearheaded, with ample help from Stella Atwood, chair of the Indian Welfare Committee of the General Federation of Women's Clubs, and the expatriate artists and writers who had gathered in Taos and Santa Fe after World War I, was the opening wedge in the reformers' assault on the Indian Bureau's destructive policies.

The Indians could not have had a more effective press agent than Collier, a "gifted polemicist" who, as he traveled in the 1920s and 1930s, "always carried with him a portable typewriter. Whenever there was an idle moment, he dashed off a newspaper or a magazine article, a press release, or a newsletter. An incredible volume of words, which told only his side of the story, poured forth from the tiny machine."[16]

In addition, the presence of the well-connected white artists and writers in Taos and Santa Fe immeasurably aided the Pueblos. The writers and intellectuals had access to influential Eastern editors who sympathized with their cause.[17] During the Bursum bill controversy, the names of such luminaries as Mary Austin, Zane Grey, D. H. Lawrence, Elsie Clews Parsons, Carl Sandburg, Maxfield Parrish, Edwin Markham, Edgar Lee Masters, Vachel Lindsay, and William Allen White appeared on appeals calling for defeat of the measure.[18]

It was primarily Collier and his allies who put the mistreatment of Indians and the notion of cultural pluralism before the public in what one writer called "an orgy of muckraking."[19] This chapter will examine coverage of two controversies they brought to widespread attention. These were not the only Indian issues of the 1920s, but they were among the first to be reported in the press across the nation. An examination of the coverage of these issues shows how the press reflected and shaped images of Native Americans.

THE PRESS IN THE 1920s

The post–World War I era saw the "first generation" of press critics. Reacting to the increasing commercialization of the press, the rise of tabloid newspapers, and other factors, the critics called on the press to be factual, fair, and free from bias.[20] As seen earlier, the newly-minted American Society of Newspaper Editors code of ethics, the Canons of Journalism, exhorted the press to be truthful, accurate, and fair. Authors such as Upton Sinclair castigated the press for catering to the interests of big business, to the detriment of other elements of society.[21] In 1924 the president of the American Society of Newspaper Editors, Paul Bellamy, listed three main criticisms of the press: "business office control . . . overemphasis on sex, crime, and trivia; and . . . poor newswriting."[22]

Little if any of this criticism was directed at coverage of minorities in general or Indians in particular. For example, a 1925 case book on journalism ethics mentioned racial issues briefly only twice. Both cases involved treatment of African Americans by newspapers in the South. No mention was found of Indians. The book did advise against unwarranted use of race, nationality, or religion.[23] Of the twenty-two codes of ethics for journalism printed in the book's appendix, only two, those of the Brooklyn *Eagle* and Sacramento *Bee*, specifically mentioned race, nationality, or religion. Both warned against writing anything offensive to members of such groups.[24] Journalism texts of the time did not mention coverage of minorities.[25]

Nevertheless, Native Americans were in the news, sometimes prominently. During the two controversies described here, numerous articles appeared in a variety of newspapers and magazines. Newspaper articles examined for this chapter came from the *New York Times*; the *Chicago Tribune*; the *Chicago Daily News*; *Magee's Independent* (renamed the *New Mexico State Tribune*), a weekly Democratic newspaper in Albuquerque edited by Carl Magee, an implacable foe of Republican officeholders such as Interior Secretary Albert B. Fall; and the *Santa Fe New Mexican*, edited by E. Dana Johnson, a close friend of Collier's who supported the Indians and their white allies.[26] The *New Mexican* reprinted many of the articles from Eastern newspapers and magazines about the two controversies.

Magazine articles came from a variety of national magazines including *The Ladies' Home Journal*, *Current Opinion*, *The Literary Digest*, *The Outlook*, *The Nation*, and *The New Republic*. Those involved in the controversy sought to "place," and indeed sometimes wrote, articles supporting their views in magazines.

THE BURSUM BILL CONTROVERSY

In July 1922 Sen. Holm Olaf Bursum, Republican of New Mexico, acting on behalf of his political ally, Interior Secretary Albert B. Fall, introduced a bill in the Senate designed to settle disputed land claims by white Spanish-American settlers on Pueblo Indian lands. The bill would have legalized almost all non-Indian claims. Indian claims to the land stemmed from thirty-five Spanish land grants to the tribes that were confirmed by Congress when the lands came under American rule after the Mexican War of 1848, though Indian ability to sell the land to non-Indians was thrown into question after New Mexico became a state. Some of the white settlers were descendants of those who had purchased land from the Indians in good faith; others were squatters.

While the land claims represented only about 10 percent of the Indians' lands, they were a much larger portion of the irrigated acreage. For example, one pueblo, San Juan, had lost the use of 3,500 of its 4,000 irrigated acres to the whites. In dry New Mexico, water was the key to survival.[27] One effect of this measure, supporters of the Indians pointed out, would have been to deprive Indians of large portions of the land that was essential to their survival. The bill would also have destroyed the Pueblos' self-government by assigning internal disputes to the jurisdiction of federal courts, they contended.[28]

White supporters of the Pueblo Indians mounted an intensive campaign to prevent enactment of the Bursum bill and to publicize the destruction of the tribes they were certain would follow if it became law. Spearheading the campaign were Stella Atwood, Collier, and others. Eventually, several of the artists and writers who had gathered in Santa Fe and Taos after World War I added their voices.[29] Once Pueblo leaders became aware of the implications of the bill, they called an all-Pueblo council in November of 1922 to devise ways to stop it. This was the first such council since the Pueblos united in 1680 to drive out the Spaniards.[30] Though the Senate originally passed the Bursum bill without debate as an "administrative measure," it was recalled after the storm of controversy blew up. Both houses of Congress then had hearings on alternative ways to settle the Pueblo land dispute, effectively stopping passage of the Bursum measure. Eventually, in 1924, a compromise bill was passed.[31]

The controversy over the Bursum bill was widely reported in the press, largely through the efforts of the Indians' supporters.[32] It was so widely reported, in fact, that one newspaper writer commented that "the Pueblos have received more attention in the press than any other Indian tribe in the past fifty years."[33] The *Santa Fe New Mexican*, which covered the controversy in detail, mentioned or quoted from stories in at least forty-nine newspapers, magazines, wire services, and syndicates about the matter between November 1922 and February 1923.

Pueblos as Good Indians

The newspaper and magazine coverage of the Bursum bill controversy overwhelmingly used good Indian imagery to portray the Pueblos. Such imagery was part of the "romantic idealization" of Pueblo culture by whites that began in the late nineteenth century, spurred by the arrival of the railroad, which opened New Mexico to white tourists and settlers. By the 1920s this romance was in full flower, and Pueblos were thought to be "the most interesting of the American Indian tribes. Their positive qualities had grown larger than life."[34] Collier, the Indians' *ad hoc* publicist, was one of the most energetic promoters of this idealistic view.

Variations on the good Indian theme abounded in coverage of the Bursum controversy. The Pueblos were variously depicted as noble savages, innocent children of nature, and possessors of secrets of tranquillity that had been lost by individualistic, materialistic whites. Without disputing the laudable qualities of Pueblo life, it is interesting to see how certain of those qualities were depicted by non-Indians for a non-Indian audience.

For example, the image of the noble savage was vividly brought forth in a *New York Times* editorial calling for defeat of the Bursum bill that said such an outcome "should not require the picturesque presence in Washington of these solemn aborigines, or their laconic protest."[35]

Some stories about the Pueblos clearly reflected romanticized white images of the good Indian, describing them positively from a white viewpoint. Attributes similar to or prized by white culture were described approvingly:

> They are brave and splendid fighters but their wars . . . always have been on the defensive. They are peacefully inclined. . . . The Pueblos have always been farmers. . . . They are monogamists. . . . [N]owhere on earth is there to be found a finer family life than that of the average Pueblo Indian.
>
> The Pueblo's wife is the mistress of her home in every sense of that word. Reverence for their women is almost a religion with them. . . . [N]o white parents are more tender in the care of their children than the Pueblos. The discipline of these children is almost perfect, but they are never punished.
>
> . . . [T]he Pueblo . . . never has wavered in his loyalty to or his confidence in the National government at Washington. . . . Hospitality is a law of the Pueblos. . . . They are wonderful dancers."[36]

Arthur Brisbane, writing in the *New York Evening Journal*, constructed a similar list of admirable qualities: "Pueblos . . . are hard-working, good Indians. They don't fight and never wanted to. . . . The Pueblos have very beautiful poetic dances. . . . Their children are beautiful. Their women are good mothers. . . . They are self-supporting. . . . They are very religious, practically all of them good Catholics."[37]

What was not said but was implied in these articles was that Pueblos were more worthy of public support because they had white-like qualities, in contrast to other, "bad" Indians. The distinction between the "good" Pueblos and the "bad" others, particularly the once-nomadic Plains Indians, was made clearly in an article in the *Ladies' Home Journal*: "[N]o adequate distinction . . . has been made by American officials . . . between the wandering and formerly warring tribes and these agricultural and pastoral village dwellers of the Southwest."[38]

Unlike many popular culture depictions of Indians, this and other articles about the Pueblos drew clear distinctions between the Pueblos and other Indian tribes. The distinctions invariably showed the Pueblos to be more acceptable in white eyes than other tribes.

Part of the good Indian imagery was the romantic notion that in some aspects of life the Pueblos were innately superior to whites. This notion was seen frequently in the Bursum bill stories. For example, the Pueblos were depicted as having an internal capacity for humor not available to whites: "White men's eyes have no special shine, even when they laugh. But these brown eyes, flashing out of the thick haze of cornhusk cigarettes, seemed to come to a brilliant point of liquid light at the iris and in every point now was a glint of humor."[39]

The good Pueblo Indian was depicted as superior to whites in certain spiritual and psychic realms. Often writers drew distinctions between the perceived serenity of the Pueblos and the hectic pace of modern life, making it clear that the Indians' ways were preferred.

> No Pueblo housewife ever had nervous prostration. What American women . . . are frantically groping for in their present pursuit of one strange cult after another is . . . peace of mind. The Indian woman has that as a matter of course. It is the sure part of her spiritual inheritance through many centuries. . . . [Pueblos] are inferior no doubt in mechanical industry and in money getting. In things of the spirit they are equal to the best of us and superior to most of us.[40]

Author Mary Austin cited superior Pueblo abilities at public administration and economic organization: "Four or five thousand years before we thought of it, the Pueblo Indians had achieved a competent form of representative, republican government in which there were no rich and no poor, no unprotected widow, no institutionalized orphans, no prisons and no prostitutes."[41]

Pueblos also had superior artistic gifts, according to the romantic image: "They are artists in ceremonial dances, in music, in poetry, in pottery, in weaving, in silver-work; and in the art of pure design alone . . . their continuing and developing achievement is superb . . . far surpassing the most ambitious achievements of American artists in this direction."[42]

Collier, writing in the *San Francisco Chronicle*, also depicted the Pueblos as superior to whites artistically:

Every one born in the Pueblo becomes a dancer, a singer, an actor and a producer of drama. There are times of the year when [virtually] the whole Pueblo population . . . is an actor in marvelous pageant-dramas, religious in character, which probably have no rivals on earth for complexity and rhythmic, dramatic power.

In addition, the Pueblos are masters of pottery arts, of costuming, and of pure design.[43]

But if Pueblos were superior spiritually and artistically, whites seemed to doubt their intellectual acuity. One story, for example, marveled that they could comprehend the intricacies of the white man's politics. When a Pueblo delegation appeared at a Senate hearing on the Bursum bill, a *New York Times* story said, "The room was filled with picturesque Pueblos wearing their bright colored blankets. . . . In spite of their primitive appearance, the majority of the Pueblos were perfectly able to understand the proceedings."[44]

Bad Indians—A Minority View

Though by far the dominant press image was of Pueblos as good Indians, some New Mexicans who took the side of the white settlers depicted Pueblos as bad, or at least degraded, Indians who were exploiting both the government and their white friends; who were lazy and far from poverty stricken. This was the view of a witness at the Congressional hearings in Washington, reported in the *Santa Fe New Mexican*. The witness, A. H. Renehan of Santa Fe, said the Pueblos were "deteriorating on account of their laziness and disinclination to work," that they had been "petted too much" and "were paid too much by artists to pose and made much money out of pottery." The newspaper's attitude toward this characterization was made clear at the end of the news story, which carried no byline. It said, "Renehan's testimony was much weakened by extreme exaggeration."[45]

Another New Mexico paper was more sympathetic to the settlers' viewpoint. According to the *Albuquerque Evening Herald*, "The Pueblo Indian of today has more rights, more comfort, more peace, income and general happiness than he has ever had. . . . He lives off the fat of the richest lands, an easy and protected, a carefree and tax-free existence."[46]

This characterization of the Pueblos as rich beneficiaries of government handouts did not resonate beyond New Mexico. Stories in the national press did not use this image. Even when the bill's supporters attacked what they viewed as the propaganda campaign against the measure, they made the fight a political one. As will be seen, they did not attack the image of Pueblos as good Indians.

Indians as Exotic and Ancient

Basic to the whole notion of the Indian was the Indian as "other," a different, exotic, being whose ways were the antithesis of those of whites.[47]

Indians were also thought of as timeless and unchanged from the time of European contact, despite abundant evidence to the contrary.[48] A version of this imagery persisted in the coverage of the Pueblo Indians' fight against the Bursum bill. In nearly all stories, they were described physically: by their physiognomy, clothing, and jewelry. For example, a *New York Times Magazine* feature story about the all-Pueblo council that united the twenty Pueblo tribes to fight the Bursum bill said of the men there, "Most of them wore bright colored blankets, turquoise earrings and chains, and long hair bobbed under a bright band about the forehead."[49]

When a Pueblo delegation journeyed to Washington via Chicago and New York to rally supporters against the Bursum bill, virtually every story found included prominent and detailed descriptions of the men. The *New York Times* said "the Indians appeared in full regalia, feathered head-dress, blue and red blankets and beaded moccasins."[50] *The Outlook* said they were "wrapped in blankets and wearing feathered head-dresses."[51]

In Chicago a photo of the Indians in blankets and feathered headdresses in the *Chicago Tribune* was accompanied by an article that played up the incongruity of the blanket- and moccasin-clad Indians from the desert being feted by the cream of Chicago society. "Waving war plumes and sipping a demi-tasse; jingling with ancestral wrought silver bangles and smart with modern 'tie clips'; wrapped in ancient tribal blankets and talking learnedly of legislation, . . . twelve Pueblo Indians yesterday invaded the Chicago Women's Club," the article began.[52]

The imagery in the lead paragraph of this story not only showed Indians as exotic strangers, but also as relics of the past, seemingly misplaced in the modern world, by describing their jewelry and garments as "ancestral" and "ancient" and striking a contrast between their attire and their "talking learnedly."

The afternoon *Chicago Daily News* story, also heavy on description, brought forth the image of the Indians as ancient and exotic strangers out of place in the modern world. It said, "The moccasins, the wampum belts, the bead and deer-tooth necklaces, the Navajo blankets and ceremonial drums . . . made an incongruous picture as the delegation dismounted from a Santa Fe train and walked through the dark areaways to waiting cabs."[53]

Pueblos were depicted as exotic relics when their delegation came to New York to raise public interest and funds for their fight against the Bursum bill. The *Times* story described their "sacred ceremonial of songs and dances" as a "weird and colorful program." It also mentioned speeches "made by two young Pueblos, who, arrayed in their gaudy robes and feathers, gained the sympathy of the large assembly with their simple but impassioned talk."[54]

The content of the Indians' talks, or, for that matter, of the bill they opposed, was not mentioned. The image the reader was likely to get from articles such as this was of Pueblos as colorful, exotic people who were somehow being wronged by the government. But readers would know more about their unusual dress and dance than about the issue that brought them to New York.

Some of the descriptions of the Pueblos may also have been inaccurate. "Pow wow,"[55] for example, a term of Algonquian origin, is more often associated with Plains or Woodlands tribes. Wampum,[56] originally made from shells of the quahog clam and other mollusks found on Long Island, was used primarily by Iroquois and Algonquian tribes of the Northeast.[57] While it was not impossible that a Pueblo would possess a wampum belt in the 1920s, it was not likely. And it is doubtful that the Pueblo culture was related to that of the Aztecs and Mayas,[58] though in the 1920s this might have been thought to be the case. These erroneous descriptions, while certainly less egregious than the generic Indian images often depicted in Western movies and fiction, still indicated that in the press, as in popular culture, Indian traits were sometimes generalized and little distinction made from one aboriginal culture to another.

Exotic descriptions were not confined to the Pueblo people. A story about an Osage delegation in Washington said the delegation included "squaws in vari-colored tribal blankets, and . . . several Osage 'flappers' in the more modern styles of Broadway, bobbed hair and all."[59] While such descriptions undoubtedly served the journalistic purpose of making the articles more colorful and interesting, they also conveyed images of the Indians as unusual, distant, and separate. It is quite possible that the Indians, mindful of whites' curiosity, intentionally dressed in traditional clothing to attract attention.

The images of the Indians as remnants of ancient civilizations called forth imagery of the "vanishing race" and at times seemed to depict them as museum exhibits, rather than members of contemporary human communities. Writing in the *San Francisco Chronicle*, Collier quoted former President Theodore Roosevelt that "[The Pueblos] are one of America's most precious possessions. Let us cherish them tenderly and proudly!"[60] *The Nation* described Pueblo culture as "a precious heritage and asset to the country at large," then called on readers to help save it: "Opposition to the [Bursum] bill should be nation-wide and party-free unless America wishes to see the Pueblo civilization die within the next ten years."[61] The *New York Times*, in an editorial arguing for defeat of the Bursum bill in order to rescue the Pueblos, mixed anthropological and humanitarian concerns:

> In losing these picturesque people . . . we should be losing a great national asset of beauty and strangeness, as expressed in their sacred observances. Still another [reason for saving the Pueblos] is their value as an archaeological asset. But the chief reason, after all, is that it would be neither decent nor civilized to let these people die.[62]

Imagery and Cultural Pluralism

Several articles covering the Bursum controversy endorsed the notion of cultural pluralism by their approving descriptions of Pueblo resistance to assimilation:

[T]he Pueblo is not convinced that the white man's secret, his prescription of life, is as good as the Pueblo's prescription. Government officials, teachers, Protestant missionaries have told him that it is better, have tried to make him ashamed of his blanket, his bright head band, his long hair and his turquoise, his 'pagan' ceremonials; have sought to stir him to revolt against his system of government. . . . Yet, deaf to our propaganda and example, the Pueblo goes his own way.[63]

Some writers depicted cultural pluralism in terms of an Indian struggle against the corrupting forces of the dominant society:

Culturally [Pueblos] are being hard pressed. They dare to differ. They dare to ignore our mechanical standards; they dare to maintain customs and privacies we do not understand; they dare to be simple, to be natural, to be sincere, to be religious; they dare, in New Mexico, to find happiness under a communal system of land ownership.[64]

D. H. Lawrence, whose pen had been pressed into service of the Pueblos' cause shortly after he arrived at Taos, also dealt with cultural pluralism. Suggesting it was the Indians, not the whites, who were "at the core of American life," he called on his readers to appreciate another's viewpoint:

Let us try to adjust ourselves to the Indian outlook, to take up an old dark thread from their vision, and see again as they see, without forgetting we are ourselves.

For it is a new era we have now got to cross into. And our own electric light won't show us over the gulf. We have to feel our way by the dark thread of the old vision. Before it lapses, let us take it up.[65]

Perhaps the clearest statement of the cultural pluralist view that Indian—or at least Pueblo—cultures not only had value in themselves but also held lessons for white society came in an article in the *Ladies' Home Journal* castigating the government's assimilationist policies:

There never has been in the Government any sympathetic understanding of the past traditions of these people, . . . no realization of the fact that there are in the still surviving portions of that culture lessons and examples worth while for ourselves in art, community government, devotion to religion and, above all, in the matter of serene and harmonious adjustment to environment and circumstance.[66]

THE CEREMONIAL DANCES CONTROVERSY

The conflicting views of assimilationists and cultural pluralists were also brought into sharp relief in the controversy over Indian ceremonial dances that overlapped the Bursum affair. The dances controversy's roots dated to a series of reports made in 1913–16 that denounced certain ceremonies of the Hopi and other Pueblo Indians of Arizona and New Mexico. The Hopi snake dance was one of those singled out. It was said to be accompanied by the "utter abandon of moral and legal restraints imposed by marital obligations" and by the "most depraved and immoral practices." The reports also were said to document "obscenities connected with the religious rites of the more backward pueblos and their barbaric cruelties when inflicting punishment."[67]

(The Snake Dance, one of many ceremonies in the Hopi spiritual calendar, doubtless attracted the attention of non-Indians because of its climactic ritual. On the ninth day of the ceremony, which is for rain and crop fertility, members of the Snake Society hold live snakes in their mouths while dancing. Later the dancers deposit the reptiles at sacred sites outside the village. This and other ceremonies at Hopi and other pueblos, containing as some did ritual floggings and frank—though symbolic—representations of copulation and sexual activity, may well have offended the sensibilities of whites.[68])

The reports on Indian dances, sent to Commissioner of Indian Affairs Charles H. Burke, apparently were accepted at face value and led him to issue a series of directives between 1921 and 1923 in which he called on Indians to limit dances voluntarily, hinting darkly that punitive measures would be taken if they did not comply. The directives seemed to be aimed at Pueblo ceremonies, at the Sun Dance of the Plains Indians, and at the use of peyote, a hallucinogen, in the Native American Church.

(The Sun Dance, which is based on the concept of sacrifice, links the participants through prayer to all the universe. It often involves participants perforating their chest muscles with skewers and tying the skewers to a central pole, "physically manifesting the linking of the heart to the cosmic axis. Dancers would dance, linked thus, until the skewers pulled free from their chests."[69] Both the Sun Dance and use of peyote may have shocked whites, particularly if descriptions of them were taken out of their larger religious context.)

Burke's April 1921 Circular No. 1665 ordered restrictions on the Sun Dance and also "dances involving 'self-torture, immoral relations between the sexes, the sacrificial destruction of clothing or other useful articles of protection, the reckless giving away of property, the use of injurious drugs or intoxicants' . . . and any dance that lasted for prolonged periods of time, thereby causing neglect of 'crops, livestock, and home interests.' "[70]

In February 1923 Burke issued a supplement to the earlier recommendations that was designed to limit Indian dances to only one a month, lasting no more than a day with none at all during planting and harvesting seasons. Only those over age 50 could attend. Impetus for the recommendations came from missionaries and other assimilationists who attacked the ceremonies as "obscene," "superstitious," "immoral," and "degrading."[71]

The tone and content of the February 1923 order showed vividly the gulf in perceptions between white assimilationist bureaucrats and their Indian wards. It addressed Indians in the same tone a parent would use on a misbehaving child and indicated no awareness that the offending dances were sacred religious ceremonies. Burke's directive, addressed "TO ALL INDIANS" and written in first person, said in part:

> Now, what I want you to think about very seriously is that you must first of all try to make your own living, which you cannot do unless you work faithfully and take care of what comes from your labor and go to dances or other meetings only when your home work will not suffer by it. I do not want to deprive you of decent amusements or occasional feast days, but you should not do evil or foolish things or take so much time for these occasions. No good comes from your "giveaway" custom at dances and it should be stopped. It is not right to torture your bodies or to handle poisonous snakes in your ceremonies. All such extreme things are wrong and should be put aside and forgotten.[72]

Burke ended the message with a thinly-veiled threat:

> I could issue an order against those useless and harmful performances, but I would much rather have you give them up of your own free will. . . . If at the end of one year the reports which I receive show that you are doing as requested, I shall be very glad for I will know that you are making progress . . . but if the reports show that you reject this plea, then some other course will have to be taken.[73]

The directive brought a storm of protest from the Indians' defenders, who condemned Burke for "subservience to the missionaries."[74] The defenders, who included Collier and some of the Taos artists and writers, again took their protests to the press. According to the *Literary Digest*, nearly all the newspapers that commented on the matter were "in favor of the Indian and against the Commissioner."[75]

In response to the protests, Interior Secretary Hubert Work issued a statement intended to clarify which Indian dances the government did and did not disapprove of. "There are certain practices," the statement said, "which are against the law of nature or moral laws, and all who wish to perpetuate the integrity of their race must refrain from them."[76]

Though defenders of the dances did so on grounds of religious freedom, for some there was an economic motive, too. In Arizona and New Mexico, Indian ceremonies were drawing thousands of tourists. Limiting dances could cut into tourist revenues. The *Santa Fe New Mexican* cited both rationales in an editorial:

> Beside the real danger of seeking to impose on these Indians an order subversive of their religious liberty and suppressive of their racial life, its execution will be a

serious blow to the prosperity of . . . Central New Mexico. . . . [T]he foolish order of the Indian commissioner . . . would take away one of the greatest business assets of the Southwest.[77]

The Santa Fe Kiwanis Club poked fun at the potentially damaging order by staging a parody of a Pueblo ceremony, which it called the "Bull Dance," at a luncheon meeting and announcing a telegram, ostensibly from the Indian commissioner, "ordering the dance stopped, as the commissioner did not desire the Pueblos to associate with Kiwanians, in view of the efforts being made to protect their morals," the *Santa Fe New Mexican* reported.[78]

Eventually both sides in the controversy used the constitutional guarantee of religious freedom to back their positions. The All Pueblo Council, made up of representatives from many of the Rio Grande pueblos and backed by Collier and the newly-formed American Indian Defense Association, urged easing of the dance restrictions and recognition of the religious value of the ceremonies. It also endorsed the practice of removing a few Pueblo boys from government boarding schools for long periods to undergo religious instruction. This, it was argued, was necessary to keep the tribes' religious traditions alive.[79]

Collier wrote that limiting the dances amounted to unconstitutional infringement of Indians' religious rights: "Religious persecution—ruthless, unapologetic, designed to assassinate a religion by force—has been reinstituted in America, and the immediate victim is the American Indian, our nation's child and ward."[80]

Among those opposing Collier and the cultural pluralists was a newly-formed group of Christianized Pueblos, the Council of Progressive Christian Indians. They demanded government protection for their right to practice their Christian beliefs and to refuse to participate in "pagan" ceremonies.[81] They also endorsed the government's move to restrict traditional dances, declaring that they had been discriminated against because of their refusal to take part in the "secret and unchristian dances."[82] Both sides—assimilationist and cultural pluralist—tried to use the controversy to improve their public positions.

Images of Indians in the Controversy

D. H. Lawrence, writing in the *New York Times Magazine*, neatly summarized Americans' contradictory attitudes toward Native Americans:

It is almost impossible for the white people to approach the Indian without either sentimentality or dislike. . . . Why? Both the reactions are due to the same feeling in the white man. The Indian is not in line with us. He is not coming our way. His whole being is going a different way from ours. And the minute you set eyes on him you know it.

And then, there's only two things you can do. You can detest the insidious devil for having an utterly different way from our own great way. Or you can perform the mental trick and fool yourself and others into believing that the befeathered and bedaubed darling is nearer to the true ideal gods than we are.[83]

The feelings Lawrence described so vividly informed and inspired the opposing assimilationist and cultural pluralism notions of how Indians should be treated. They were at the root of the disparate images that appeared in literature, popular culture, and the press.

Articles containing the assimilationist point of view often portrayed Indians as childlike and vulnerable to being victimized by the complexities of the modern world. This was amply illustrated by an article in the *Saturday Evening Post* under the byline of Interior Secretary Hubert Work, which stated, "The Indian is instinctively trusting and confiding. . . . His childlike faith is racial, but his confidence has been constantly abused."[84] The article, a lengthy exposition of assimilationist philosophy, often mixed description with judgment and presented Indians in terms of their deficiencies from the white point of view. For example, subheadings included, "Prey for the Unscrupulous," "Crippled by Ignorance," and "Fat Pickings for Lawyers."[85]

Only if Indians were taught the white man's way would they be able to survive and succeed, the article suggested. "The Indian office . . . for many years has been directing its efforts toward the absorption of this primitive, nomadic people without industrial, social or political entity into the complex organization of society which exists today," it said.[86]

This exemplified the assimilationist view that the solution to the Indian "problem" was to make them "civilized" like whites, ignoring the positive aspects of Indian cultures. It also represented an inaccurate generalizing of the traits of some Indian groups to all. Not all Indians, for example, were nomads.

The assimilationist view of Indians as uncivilized unless they became like whites also was stated clearly in a long *New York Times* article that quoted a Bureau of Indian Affairs official, "Thousands of these people are still in a state of quasi barbarism, although strongly influenced by contact with whites, and thousands are as civilized as their white neighbors."[87]

Living on reservations, the same article said, "has resulted in no small measure in keeping many of the Indians in the state of existence fostered by their forefathers. Civilization has barely breathed on many of them."[88] The clear implication was that native cultures were by definition uncivilized; the only road to improvement lay through emulation of white society. This and similar articles put forth the then-prevailing view of the inherent deficiency of Indian ways.

In the assimilationist view, Indian religious and ceremonial practices, including the dances that were an integral part of the sacred rites of many tribes, were primitive, barbaric, pagan, and generally a force that held back Indian development and "civilization." As one *Times* article said, "Many an Indian living in a house with all improvements that progress has discovered and devised, nevertheless will revert to ancient and often demoralizing forms of worship."[89]

In the *Saturday Evening Post* article cited earlier, the secretary of the interior all but endorsed making Indians into Christians:

> The government is not attempting to supplant Indian religion with other forms of worship, but approves of efforts to modify its ordinances into harmony with the forms of the Christian religion which civilization has approved, from which our rules of life are drafted and upon which our government is founded.[90]

Indian dances in particular were criticized by assimilationists as being unchristian, as taking Indians away from their farming duties, and as vaguely immoral and unnatural, all descriptions, obviously, in terms of perceived deficiencies of Native American culture *vis-à-vis* white culture.

While protesting that the Indian Bureau was not trying to prohibit Indian dances, Work wrote in the *Saturday Evening Post* that the government "hopes through rising intelligence and a fuller education that the Indian may be reasoned away from practices attached to some of [the dances] . . . which tend to destroy the higher instincts that should be safeguarded in any people."[91] In only slightly more direct language, the article referred disapprovingly to "tribal dances which are sexually suggestive and unworthy."[92]

Articles advancing the cultural pluralist view also often depicted Indians as childlike and innocent. But the pluralists used this imagery to draw the opposite conclusion from the assimilationists; the cultural pluralists concluded that these children of nature should be allowed to keep their ways and traditions.

For example, an article in the *New York Times Magazine* about Navajo ceremonies clearly evoked the image of Navajos as naive, confused by the government's intrusion on their religious practices.

> There is mourning on the Navajo Reservation. . . . [T]here is worry and childlike confusion and a vague fear. Navajo nomads gather around campfires in the lonely canyons . . . and they talk about it in their strange tongue, shaking their heads in solemn amaze. What sort of a Great White Father is it that will put the taboo on a fellow's religion?[93]

Here the imagery of Indians as innocent children of nature who should be left alone to follow their traditional ways was used in an article written from the cultural pluralist point of view that argued for religious liberty for the Navajos.

Articles advocating cultural pluralism in the dances controversy, as in the earlier Bursum affair, often relied heavily on good Indian imagery, bestowing upon Indians—particularly Pueblos—laudable qualities that, the articles said or implied, were lacking in whites. For example, Collier, writing in *Sunset* magazine, argued forcefully that restricting Pueblo dances amounted to religious persecution that would destroy an exemplary way of life.

> [T]he following traits are known by all observers to be the outstanding characters of Pueblo life: Kindness to children, to women and to the old; mutual aid in all things; public service to the community rendered without pay; faithfulness to family life; truth-telling and honest dealing; tolerance and freedom from hate; freedom from fear and worry; and complete absence of sexual indecency.[94]

The article went on to say that "white persons can hardly understand the completeness with which Pueblo morals, Pueblo human relations, loyalties and the very mode of existence of the Pueblos . . . are entwined with the religion and dependent on it."[95]

Writing in the *New Republic*, Elizabeth Shepley Sergeant described Pueblo ceremonies in lyrical terms and argued that whites who observed them gained "more than an ethnological or artistic interest; their great gift is a breath, a transfusion of the radiant freshness of man's first deep religious experience."[96] The image was one of Pueblos as somehow more basic and elemental in their spirituality than whites.

Articles dealing with Indians' dances often made the point that the dances were valid expressions of Indians' religious feelings. Indians, the reasoning went, had an equal right to religious freedom with other Americans. One quoted an expert on Indians of the Southwest:

> The Pueblo instruction of boys who are to become the spiritual leaders of their people is more complicated than any degree of Masonry and just as high-minded. It is as careful and as noble as any training for the Christian priesthoods. . . . An attempt is being made to deprive the Pueblo Indians of their constitutional rights of freedom of religious worship.[97]

The image conveyed here was of Indians as mature religious beings whose beliefs, though different from mainstream white Protestantism, were nevertheless legitimate and worthy of equal protection. Another example of this was a *New York Times* article that described in restrained and fairly unsentimental language the place of ceremonial dances in the lives of Pueblos.

> Although the Pueblos were converted to Catholicism by the Spanish padres, the inherited religion of the Indian is a pantheistic one, both complicated and beautiful, in which every force of nature is sentient and the succession of seasons, from seed planting to harvest, is observed and helped along with appropriate ceremonies . . .

Therefore the forces which controlled his life were beseeched in elaborate rituals. . . . The important events of the Indians' existence were dramatized in highly symbolic ceremonies which are an expression of all their great natural gifts of music, poetry, drama and decoration.[98]

Though the article, which contained detailed descriptions of several Pueblo ceremonies, did not freely mix moralizing messages with its descriptions, the explicit as well as implicit effect was to render the Pueblos as good Indians who had "great natural gifts of music, poetry, drama and decoration" and whose only character flaws were those introduced by whites. The article concluded with a brief reference to puberty rites where "the young are instructed in the mysteries of creation. But if any element less than reverence enters into what takes place there it is likely enough a taint brought in from the outside and not one conceived by the mind of the Indian."[99]

While the *New York Times* article rendered the Pueblos as artistic and reverent, another tribe was portrayed far less generously in the same issue of the same newspaper. A story about the Paiute tribe[100] of Utah described their struggles against encroaching white cattlemen. In the *New York Times* story, the Paiutes were depicted as not only uncivilized but resisting civilization to the end: "They are not picturesque, these poor cousins of the Utes. They are poverty stricken, dirty, diseased, sometimes drunken. . . . But they are persistent, they are unwavering in their decision to stay on the land they feel they own," it said.[101]

Here the article employed imagery of the degraded Indian who, "neither noble nor wildly savage" was described by Berkhofer as being portrayed as exhibiting "the worse qualities of Indian character with none of its redeeming features."[102]

While newspaper and magazine articles depicting Pueblo and Navajo dances were generally sympathetic and sensitive to the religious nature of the ceremonies, articles about the dances of other tribes often evoked images of paganism and barbarism, describing the rites unfavorably through white eyes. For example, an article about the revival of the Sun Dance among members of the Shoshone and Bannock tribes of Idaho called it "a three-day marathon about a weird totem pole" and a "barbaric rite."[103] (The dance had been banned under Commissioner Burke's earlier recommendations because it involved self-mutilation.)

Similarly, a story on the Yaqui Indians Pasqua ceremony in Arizona called forth abundant imagery of Indians as savages whose observances were curious tourist attractions. The story described a "picturesque mingling of pagan and Christian rites" in which "weird-looking Yaqui tribesmen" danced to "mystic chanting and the rhythmic beat of rattles and tom-toms" and "the strains of semi-barbaric music."[104]

Anthropologist Edward Spicer may have had this very article in mind when he wrote, many years later, of the unfortunate influence of such press accounts:

> Anglo-Americans began to come out at Easter time with their cameras. They called what they were seeing "the Yaqui Easter Dances," a label which . . . emphasized the cultural gap which separated Yaquis and their neighbors. It was the aboriginal elements . . . which struck Anglos as the most interesting—and the most mysterious. It was these, associated in newspaper stories with "tom-toms" and "half-pagan rites," which by as early as the 1920s had become an important tourist attraction in Southern Arizona. What was to Yaquis an integral whole with historical, ritual, and religious meanings became for their neighbors a spectacular cultural survival, less a bridge than a barrier to understanding of Yaquis.[105]

The newspaper articles on the Sun Dance and the Pascua ceremonies were short news accounts rather than long feature stories. This brevity led to emphasis on the unusual rituals themselves, giving short shrift to their cultural or religious context. The stories lacked the elaborate, sympathetic description of the ceremonies or explanation of their place in tribal life that was seen in articles on Pueblo and Navajo dances.

The *New York Times* and Cultural Pluralism

The editorial stance of the *New York Times* at this juncture seemed to be, "The only good Indian is a Pueblo Indian." Editorials endorsed the idea of cultural pluralism and religious freedom for the Pueblos, but took a more assimilationist stance when referring to other tribes. In fact, at one point when editorially urging the collection of Native American ethnographic material before the cultures died out, it called Pueblo culture "more advanced than that of other native tribes."[106]

The paper's editorials in favor of Indian religious freedom for Pueblo dances adopted the same good Indian imagery that appeared in several articles. For example, in refuting the contention that Indian dances were obscene or indecent, the *Times* editorialized that the Pueblos were "peculiarly free from those forms of depravity to which the white men so justly object."[107]

The same editorial called for religious freedom for Indians as for other Americans:

> The religious dances play an even more important part in the religious and social life of the Indians than does the Church among most Christian peoples. . . . [D]epriving them of the right to freedom of worship . . . violates a fundamental American principle.[108]

In this case the *Times* editorially came down on the side of cultural pluralism—for Pueblos, at least.

This view was repeated in a later editorial, also opposing restrictions on Pueblo dances, which criticized the policy of the missionaries and government, calling it "intolerance which in spiritual matters damns, ipso facto, all that may be classed as pagan, and in social and civic affairs condemns anything that departs from our own standards. It has preferred to kill the Indians by 'civilizing' them, rather than have them develop peacefully their own culture."[109]

Editorializing on another Indian issue that arose at the same time, the uprising of Paiutes in Utah against whites, the *Times* made only negative allusions to Paiute lifestyles. It described them as "a poor tribe of Indians, looked down upon by their Navajo neighbors as idlers, given to thievery, and scorned because they lived on a fare which the Navajos considered contemptible."[110] Neither in news articles nor in editorials about the Paiute situation was there the rich description or cultural sensitivity seen in articles about the Pueblos. The image employed to depict the Paiutes was that of degraded Indians who must inevitably yield to the onslaught of white civilization. In contrast to the notion of cultural pluralism used in articles and editorials about the Pueblos, the Paiutes seemed doomed to the assimilationist view of Indians as a "vanishing race."

JOURNALISTIC USES OF IMAGES

Newspaper and magazine articles about the Bursum bill and Indian ceremonial dances controversies used the journalistic practices of the time to select and frame events into stories. These practices were critical in emphasizing some images of Indians and obliterating others.

In the Bursum bill controversy, the press accommodated Collier and his allies who exploited their contacts at Eastern publications to produce a torrent of articles portraying the Pueblos as good Indians—a noble people as well as a cultural treasure—who were being terribly wronged by the government. Backers of the bill, whether by instinct or design, generally declined to take on the Pueblos and their reformer-allies on their own terms. Instead of disputing the good Indian images, they used a political framework to attack the propaganda campaign and to argue for the bill in unemotional, bureaucratic terms.

The journalistic forms stories took also influenced images. If the story was a newspaper or magazine feature, as was often the case in reformer-inspired articles, Indians were likely to be depicted colorfully, if sometimes erroneously. If the matter was framed as a news story or political analysis, as was often the case with stories giving the bill's backers' position, Indians might be present only by oblique reference.

In the ceremonial dances controversy, both sides used vivid images of Indians. At various times, both the cultural pluralists, who saw restrictions on the dances as a threat to Indian religious liberty, and the assimilationists, who saw the dances as a deterrent to Indians' "civilization," used similar images that were variations on the "noble savage" theme. They both depicted Native Americans as innocent, ingenuous, and childlike to argue their positions. Stories about ceremonies of other tribes contained different representations. Some Indians, such as the Yaquis and the Plains tribes, were depicted as degraded pagans who practiced weird rites that were not shown as especially culturally rich or worthy religious practices.

In coverage of both matters, the voices of Indians often went unheard. Sometimes they were rendered in dialect, a practice that made it difficult for a reader to take their points seriously. When Indians did speak for themselves as concerned adults, it was more likely to be in the local press than in national publications or those far from the Southwest.

FRAMING OF STORIES

The articles about the Bursum bill controversy were framed in three general ways by the 1920s press.

Politics as Usual

Many stories, especially in daily and weekly newspapers, framed the issue as a political story. An example is the coverage of *Magee's Independent*, a weekly newspaper in Albuquerque, New Mexico, that carried a good deal of political commentary. Its editor, Carl Magee, was an implacable political enemy of Interior Secretary Fall, and his views clearly colored the paper's coverage.[111] Early stories on the Bursum bill in November 1922 focused almost exclusively on its recall after being passed by the Senate. Its provisions were mentioned mainly in the context of New Mexico politics; the efforts of the New Mexico artists and writers to help the Pueblos were mentioned only at the end of one article.[112] While the commentary in a later story made clear the writer's sympathy with the Pueblos' cause, the emotional language and strong imagery was reserved for Senator Bursum and the bill itself, which was described as "one of the worst pieces of legislation ever attempted in Congress."

> The fact is that the New Mexico bunch were caught stealing jam and had it smeared all over their faces. . . . When Senator Bursum faces the people of this state for re-election next year he will be forced to defend his conduct in this matter. He can never do it successfully.[113]

While the reformers who were seeking to defeat the bill usually framed their stories in emotional, human terms (see next section), the stories containing Senator Bursum and Interior Secretary Fall's defense were usually framed in political terms. For example, a story in which Fall defended the bill was written in terms of Fall denouncing the reformers' stories as "propaganda" and saying their motives were aimed at eliminating the federal Indian bureau.[114]

Thus the matter was framed as a bureaucratic squabble, a story of political infighting. These stories did not evoke Indian imagery of any sort. Indeed, the Pueblos might as well have been wheat growers or railroad workers. A short interpretative piece in the Sunday *New York Times* cited Fall and Bursum's arguments that the bill would settle an unclear situation of land titles. While not refuting in detail the reformers' charges that the measure would destroy the Indians, the article stated in restrained language that "in the opinion of some government officials the picture that has been presented to the public is . . . one-sided to a degree that approaches unfairness."[115]

Save the Pueblos

Here vivid description and emotional evocations of good Indian imagery framed the story in human, emotional terms as a David-and-Goliath contest of a small group of Indians fighting against extermination at the hands of powerful government forces. Many of these articles, often in magazines or newspaper feature sections, were written by the reformers themselves as part of their publicity campaign to arouse opposition to the Bursum bill.[116] Though often compelling, they presented a one-sided picture of the controversy and often of the Indians themselves, as a writer in *The Outlook* noted:

> There is some danger lest those who plead on their behalf should injure these Indians' cause by representing them as idyllic people, superior in every way to whites. . . . [P]robably as much harm has been done to the Indians . . . by doing too much for them as by doing too little. What is demanded . . . is not . . . generosity or sentimentality, but a simple square deal.[117]

This realistic and unsentimental view, however, was rare. Stories full of flowery and romantic descriptions of the Pueblos were far more numerous.

Human Interest

Another framing technique was the human interest feature. These features were often daily newspaper stories that focused on the dress and activities of the Pueblos, particularly when a delegation went to Washington, via Chicago and New York, to build opposition to the Bursum bill. Typically, these stories were centered on descriptions of the odd and unusual, as when the *New York Times* asked the visiting Pueblos their impressions of the city.[118] The stories emphasized colorful, if sometimes inaccurate, descriptions of the Indians' clothes but paid little attention to nuances that would have put the Indians' "regalia" in cultural context.

The degree of sentimental good Indian imagery and the descriptions of the Pueblos as strange and exotic increased as publications' distance from New Mexico lengthened. In interpreting a people largely unknown to their readers, writers fell back on the familiar imagery of the good Indian and exotic stranger. Those who were not New Mexicans, such as reporters in Chicago and New York writing about the Pueblos' visits to their cities, were clearly unfamiliar with Pueblo culture. In the case of Collier and the Taos expatriates, it appeared that their view of the Pueblos, albeit gleaned from first-hand contact, was an essentially romantic one that lent itself to the sentimental, emotional writing already noted.

UNSEEN SETTLERS

One element that was largely left out of the Bursum bill articles was the story from the white settlers' point of view. No stories outside of the New Mexico press quoted settlers directly or described their concerns. No national magazine or newspaper feature articles described in detail the white settlers who were the other parties to the controversy.

For example, an editorial in the *Albuquerque Evening Herald* pointed out that many of the settlers had lived for generations on the disputed land and that they, unlike the Indians, were potentially taxpayers. "This state, surely, has as much interest and concern for the rights of productive, tax-paying citizens as it has for the retention by the Indians of all the land to which they lay claim," it said.[119] This view, however, did not resonate beyond the borders of the state. Those defending the bill in the national press referred to its aim of settling long-standing land claims but never portrayed the claimants in the human terms the reformers used for the Pueblos.

NATIVE VOICES NEAR AND FAR

When Native Americans were quoted or used as sources in the national press, they often were portrayed in stereotypical, cartoon-like fashion. If they spoke at all, it was often in broken English. A Paiute named Mancos Jim, who was described as "a shrewd old fellow, cautious and peaceable" was quoted in stereotypical dialect: "We no want t'raise row. . . . We not last long an' while we do las' all we want is chance to hunt little, fish little, rest a lot . . ."[120] Of course, it is not known whether Mancos Jim's language was recorded correctly. What is important is the image it conveyed—of Indians being lazy and unable to speak proper English.

Another article quoted Chee Dodge, the Navajo leader, on the subject of restricting his tribe's songs and dances. His direct quotes were well reasoned, grammatically correct, and used sophisticated vocabulary. However, he was described in the article as an exceptional Indian: ". . . an able man, revered by the tribe . . . he has gained through his business experience the ability to go straight to the point of a matter and speak his mind clearly. He uses the best of English."[121] Other Navajos quoted in the story used simple words and short sentences, though they were not rendered in dialect.

This image of Indians as laconic (understandable because many did not know English well) was repeated in a story in the *Christian Science Monitor* that described the reactions of a delegation of Pueblos who were visiting Manhattan. "Too much noise and hurry,' declared one of the visitors; 'too shut in!' There was no need to multiply words in order to convey the meaning intended. No one could fail to get the sense of the abbreviated summing up."[122]

Native voices were clearer in the local press. For example, when the Pueblo delegation met in Santa Fe before traveling to Washington to lobby against the Bursum bill, the *Santa Fe New Mexican* reported that "a feature [of the meeting] was a speech by Frank Paitano [of Laguna Pueblo] who urged the importance of concerted appeal and team work in making the Indians' grievance known to the senators at Washington."

The article went on to quote another Indian, Antonio Romero of Taos Pueblo, who had previously met with Presidents Roosevelt and Taft, on the inhospitable Eastern climate. "[W]e have all we can do to bear it. The odor of countless motor cars is itself stifling to nostrils accustomed to the oxygen of the Rocky Mountains. And the dampness and cloudy weather endanger one's health."[123] Thus, in their hometown paper the Pueblos were portrayed as intelligent, sophisticated people setting out on an important mission.

DISCUSSION

During the 1920s controversies over the Bursum bill and Indian ceremonial dances, the press carried a wide variety of articles from varying viewpoints. While stories generated by the publicity campaign of the reformers succeeded in stopping the Bursum bill, raised the issue of religious freedom, and publicly articulated the philosophy of cultural pluralism, the imagery employed and the framing of the stories worked against presenting a nuanced and complete picture of the Pueblos or other tribes.

In virtually all articles examined, Indian people themselves were treated in stereotypical ways. The images varied according to the type and viewpoint of the article, but few of them could be labeled accurate.

The Pueblos' portrayal in the press largely conformed to the prevailing imagery of Indians, showing them as quintessential good Indians. This picture was far from realistic or balanced. The complimentary descriptions of Pueblo lifestyles often idealized them unrealistically, and the colorful stories emphasizing their exotic dress depicted them as cartoon-like characters. Both types of portrayals worked to obscure the complexities of their lives and cultures.

Stories that argued for cultural pluralism—at least for Pueblo culture—in moving terms were frequently written from an ethnocentric white viewpoint that mixed moral judgments with description. The discussion of cultural pluralism as a philosophy in opposition to forced assimilation frequently depicted the Pueblos as latter-day versions of the romanticized noble savage who held the secrets of a simpler civilization, superior to the individualistic and materialistic civilization of whites. In short, the articles adapted the established Indian imagery to the ideology of cultural pluralism.

The portrayals of Indians examined here seemed to be influenced greatly by the attractiveness to whites of the Indians' material culture and a tribe's accessibility to the majority culture. Pueblos, popular with tourists as well as the artist expatriates of Taos, were romanticized as good Indians who possessed artistic talents, spiritual gifts, and community institutions enviable by whites. Navajos, enjoying similar popularity, also were portrayed sympathetically. Stories about other tribes, such as the Paiutes or the Plains tribes that revived the Sun Dance, had little or none of the rich description of the articles on the Pueblos or Navajos.

Press coverage of the controversies by some of the nation's premier newspapers and magazines as well as the local press did not, for the most part, measure up to the press' stated aspirations to factuality, fairness, and independence. Prestigious publications such as the *New York Times* and *The New Republic* became virtually uncritical mouthpieces for the white reformers such as John Collier. There was little evidence found of skeptical, independent reporting that examined all sides of the issue, including the viewpoints of the white settlers. When stories were put in a political frame, they emphasized the dynamics of political power and process rather than the people it served or victimized. Articles framed as human interest stories played up unusual or colorful details without putting them into cultural context.

Whether they were trusting, easily-exploited children of the "Great White Father" who had to be civilized by erasing their heritage, as in the assimilationist view, or noble, spiritual, and artistic children of nature, as the cultural pluralists held, Indians in the 1920s press were portrayed according to whites' views of them.

NOTES

1. Though the term was used earlier, one of its most compelling evocations came from photographer Edward S. Curtis who gave the title "The Vanishing Race" to a photo of Navajos that he used as the first plate in the supplementary series to his collection *The North American Indian* (1907). He explained, "The thought which this picture is meant to convey is that the Indians as a race, already shorn of their tribal strength and stripped of their primitive dress, are passing into the darkness of an unknown future." See Florence Curtis Graybill and Victor

Boesen, *Edward Sheriff Curtis: Visions of a Vanishing Race* (New York: American Legacy Press, 1976), 18.

2. Lawrence C. Kelly, *The Assault on Assimilation* (Albuquerque: University of New Mexico Press, 1983), 148–151.

3. Kelly, *Assault on Assimilation*, 146–147; Francis Paul Prucha, *The Great Father*, vol. 2 (Lincoln: University of Nebraska Press, 1984), 726–729.

4. Kelly, *Assault on Assimilation*, 148–151.

5. Ibid., 150.

6. For a detailed account of the plunder of Oklahoma Indians' lands, see Angie Debo, *And Still the Waters Run* (Princeton: Princeton University Press, 1940).

7. Christine Bolt, *American Indian Policy and American Reform* (London: Allen and Unwin, 1987), 222.

8. Brian W. Dippie, *The Vanishing American* (Middletown, Conn.: Wesleyan University Press, 1982), 185–188; Bolt, 216–234.

9. John Collier, *From Every Zenith* (Denver: Sage Books, 1963), 131.

10. Kelly, *Assault on Assimilation*, 100.

11. Dippie, 276.

12. For an account of Collier's early life and work, see Kelly, *Assault on Assimilation*; a detailed account of Collier's career and later life is in Kenneth R. Philp, *John Collier's Crusade for Indian Reform* (Tucson: University of Arizona Press, 1977); see also Randolph C. Downes, "A Crusade for Indian Reform, 1922–1934," *Mississippi Valley Historical Review* 32, no. 3 (December 1945): 331–354.

13. See Lawrence C. Kelly, "United States Indian Policies, 1900–1980," in Wilcomb E. Washburn, ed., *History of Indian-White Relations*, vol. 4 of *Handbook of North American Indians*, ed. William C. Sturtevant (Washington: Smithsonian Institution, 1988), 66–80 for an overview.

14. Philp, xi.

15. Collier, *Zenith*, 126.

16. Kelly, *Assault on Assimilation*, 100.

17. Philp, 34.

18. *Santa Fe New Mexican*, Nov. 18, 1922, 5; Jan. 13, 1923, 6.

19. Downes, 337.

20. Marion Marzolf, *Civilizing Voices: American Press Criticism, 1880–1950* (New York: Longman Publishing Group, 1991), 76–105. For contemporary views of the function and ethics of the press, see, among others, Willard Grosvenor Bleyer, *Newspaper Writing and Editing* (Boston: Houghton Mifflin Co., 1913, 1923), 331–359, and Nelson A. Crawford, *The Ethics of Journalism* (New York: Alfred A. Knopf, 1924).

21. Upton Sinclair, *The Brass Check: A Study of American Journalism* (Pasadena: published by the author, 1920).

22. Marzolf, 94.

23. Leon Nelson Flint, *The Conscience of the Newspaper* (New York: D. Appleton and Company, 1925), 18, 93.

24. Ibid., 448, 456.

25. Linda Steiner, "Construction of Gender in Newsreporting Textbooks, 1890–1990," *Journalism Monographs* 135 (October 1992): 3, note 13.

26. Philp, 34–35; Donald L. Parman, *The Navajos and the New Deal* (New Haven and London: Yale University Press, 1976), 155.

27. Philp, 28–30.

28. Ibid., 32.

29. Ibid., 34.

30. *Santa Fe New Mexican*, Nov. 4, 1922, 8; Nov. 6, 1922, 1, 6; Philp, 35–36; Kelly, *Assault on Assimilation*, 218–220.

31. Dippie, 274–279.

32. Kelly, *Assault on Assimilation*, 220–221.

33. Harvey Fergusson in the *Baltimore Evening Sun*, quoted in "The Pueblos' Plea for Justice," *The Literary Digest*, Feb. 17, 1923, 17.

34. Richard H. Frost, "The Romantic Inflation of Pueblo Culture," *The American West*, Jan./Feb., 1980, 5–9, 56–60.

35. *New York Times*, Jan. 4, 1923, 18.

36. *New York Times*, Jan. 21, 1923, sec. VIII, p. 4.

37. Reprinted in *Santa Fe New Mexican*, Jan. 29, 1923, 4.

38. Charles A. Selden, "Women Saved the Pueblos," *The Ladies' Home Journal*, July 1923, 19, 128.

39. Elizabeth Shepley Sergeant, "Big Pow wow of Pueblos," *New York Times Magazine*, Nov. 26, 1922, sec. IV, p. 6

40. Selden, 128.

41. Quoted in *Santa Fe New Mexican*, Jan. 30, 1923, 2.

42. "Are the Pueblo Indians to Be Robbed of Their Heritage?" *Current Opinion*, Feb., 1923, 213–214. See also Alice Corbin Henderson, "The Death of the Pueblos," *The New Republic*, Nov. 29, 1922, 11–13.

43. Quoted in "The Pueblos' Plea for Justice," *Literary Digest*, Feb. 17, 1923, 17.

44. *New York Times*, Jan. 17, 1923, 17.

45. *Santa Fe New Mexican*, Feb. 15, 1923, 1.

46. Reprinted in *Santa Fe New Mexican*, Nov. 9, 1922, 4.

47. Robert Berkhofer, Jr., *The White Man's Indian*, (New York: Vintage Books, 1978), xv.

48. Ibid., 28–29.

49. Sergeant, "Big Pow wow of Pueblos," sec. IV, p. 6.

50. *New York Times*, Jan. 15, 1923, 28.

51. "A Square Deal for the Pueblos," *The Outlook*, Feb. 7, 1923, 249.

52. *Chicago Tribune*, Jan. 13, 1923, 13.

53. *Chicago Daily News*, Jan. 12, 1923, 3.

54. *New York Times*, Feb. 9, 1924, 14.

55. Sergeant, "Big Pow wow of Pueblos," sec. IV, p. 6.

56. *Chicago Daily News*, Jan. 12, 1923, 3.

57. James A. Maxwell, ed., *America's Fascinating Indian Heritage* (Pleasantville, N.Y.: The Reader's Digest Association, Inc., 1978), 397, 130–131.

58. Philip Kopper, *The Smithsonian Book of North American Indians* (Washington, D.C.: Smithsonian Books, 1986), 245, 260.

59. *New York Times*, Jan. 11, 1923, 35.

60. Quoted in "The Pueblos' Plea for Justice," 17.

61. "The Last First Americans," *Nation*, Nov. 29, 1922, 570.

62. *New York Times*, Jan. 25, 1923, 16.

63. Elizabeth Shepley Sergeant, "The Principales Speak," *New Republic*, Feb. 7, 1923, 273–275.

64. Witter Bynner, "New Mexico Aflame Against Two Bills: II 'From Him That Hath Not,' " *The Outlook*, Jan. 17, 1923, 124–127.

65. D. H. Lawrence, "Certain Americans and an Englishman," *New York Times Magazine*, Dec. 24, 1922, sec. IV, p. 3.

66. Selden, 19, 128.

67. Quoted in Kelly, *Assault on Assimilation*, 302.

68. For descriptions of Hopi and Pueblo ceremonies and culture see, among others, John James Collins, *Native American Religions: A Geographical Survey* (Lewiston, New York: The Edwin Mellen Press, 1991), 17–19, 22–24; Fred Eggan, "Pueblos: Introduction," and Arlette Frigout, "Hopi Ceremonial Organization," in Alfonso Ortiz, ed., *Southwest*, vol. 9 of *Handbook of North American Indians*, ed. William C. Sturtevant (Washington: Smithsonian Institution, 1978–1990), 224–235, 564–576.

69. Arthur Versluis, *The Elements of Native American Traditions* (Shaftsbury, Dorset, Great Britain: Element, 1993), 46–48.

70. Kelly, *Assault on Assimilation*, 303–304.

71. Dippie, 280.

72. *Santa Fe New Mexican*, March 7, 1923, 1.

73. Ibid.

74. Kelly, *Assault on Assimilation*, 308.

75. "Taking the Indianism Out of the Indian," *Literary Digest*, April 28, 1923, 28.

76. Quoted in *New York Times*, Feb. 24, 1924, 7.

77. *Santa Fe New Mexican*, Mar. 9, 1923, 4.

78. *Santa Fe New Mexican*, Mar. 15, 1923, 3.

79. Kelly, *Assault on Assimilation*, 310. See also John Collier, "Persecuting the Pueblos," *Sunset Magazine*, July, 1924, 50.

80. Collier, "Persecuting the Pueblos," 50.

81. Kelly, *Assault on Assimilation*, 311–312.

82. *New York Times*, June 19, 1924, 10.

83. D. H. Lawrence, "Indians and Entertainment," *New York Times Magazine*, Oct. 26, 1924, sec. IV, p. 3.

84. Hubert Work, "Our American Indians," *Saturday Evening Post*, May 31, 1924, 27, 92.

85. Ibid.

86. Ibid., 92.

87. *New York Times*, March 16, 1924, Sec. IX, p. 3.

88. Ibid.

89. Ibid.

90. Work, 92.

91. Ibid.

92. Ibid.

93. Carl Moon, "Navajo's Plea for His Dances," *New York Times Magazine*, Nov. 18, 1923, sec. III, p. 7.

94. Collier, "Persecuting the Pueblos," 93.

95. Ibid.

96. Elizabeth Shepley Sergeant, "Death to the Golden Age," *New Republic*, Aug. 22, 1923, 355.

97. *New York Times*, July 13, 1924, sec. VIII, p. 12.

98. Alida Sims Malkus, "Those Doomed Indian Dances," *New York Times Magazine*, April 8, 1923, sec. IV, p. 1.

99. Ibid., 2.

100. In the newspaper stories the tribe's name was spelled "Piute." Here it has been rendered into its current preferred spelling.

101. *New York Times*, April 8, 1923, sec. IX, p. 2.

102. Berkhofer, *White Man's Indian*, 30.

103. *New York Times*, July 18, 1926, 9.

104. *New York Times*, April 11, 1925, 28.

105. Muriel Thayer Painter, Edward H. Spicer, and Wilma Kaemlein, eds., *With Good Heart: Yaqui Beliefs and Ceremonies in Pascua Village*. (Tucson: The University of Arizona Press, 1986), xi–xv.

106. *New York Times*, May 27, 1923, sec. II, p. 4.

107. *New York Times*, May 8, 1923, 16.

108. Ibid.

109. *New York Times*, Aug. 19, 1923, sec. II, p. 4.

110. *New York Times*, Apr. 26, 1923, 18.

111. For an account of some of the political battles of Magee and his paper, see *Problems of Journalism* 5 (1927): 133–147.

112. *Magee's Independent*, Nov. 23, 1922, 1, 2, 8; Nov. 30, 1922, 1.

113. *Magee's Independent*, Mar. 9, 1923, 1.

114. *New York Times*, Jan. 26, 1923, 9; see also *New York Times*, Feb. 16, 1923, 4.

115. *New York Times*, Jan. 28, 1923, sec. VII, p. 12.

116. See, for example, Sergeant, "Big Pow wow of Pueblos," sec. IV, p. 6; Henderson, "The Death of the Pueblos," 11–13; Sergeant, "The Principales Speak," 273–275; Bynner, 124–127; Lawrence, "Certain Americans and an Englishman," sec. IV, p. 3.

117. "A Square Deal for the Pueblos," *The Outlook*, Feb. 7, 1923, 249.

118. *New York Times*, Jan. 15, 1923, 28.

119. *Albuquerque Evening Herald*, quoted in *Santa Fe New Mexican*, Nov. 9, 1922, 4.

120. *New York Times*, Apr. 8, 1923, sec. IX, p. 2

121. Moon, "Navajo's Plea for His Dances," 7, 13.

122. *Christian Science Monitor*, reprinted in *Santa Fe New Mexican*, Feb. 1, 1923, 2.

123. *Santa Fe New Mexican*, Jan. 11, 1923, 3.

3

The 1930s: In New Deal Legislation, Reform Meets Reality

On April 20, 1933, John Collier was confirmed as commissioner of Indian affairs under Secretary of the Interior Harold L. Ickes. The appointment of one of the Indian Bureau's most severe and persistent critics—the "grim, dynamic fighter" who had been a "battling, indomitable crusader" for Indians for fifteen years[1]—sent a powerful message that New Deal reforms would reach Indians, too, and that assimilationist ideology was now in official disfavor. No longer would government policies seek to "civilize" Indians by stamping out their traditional ways.

Collier, variously described in the press as "a little grey man, smoking a corn cob pipe,"[2] "effervescent," and "visionary,"[3] immediately tackled the problems of Indian administration with zest, imagination, and energy. Aided by an enthusiastic staff and supported by Ickes and Roosevelt, he set about putting his views of cultural pluralism into practice.

The eventual result of his efforts was the Indian Reorganization Act (IRA)—landmark legislation intended to end allotment and the shrinkage of the tribal land base and to allow Indian tribes an unprecedented degree of self-government. Its passage was a watershed in Indian-white relations because of its assumptions about Indians and their place in society. Rather than forcing Indians to become like whites, the new policy encouraged them to realize their Indian-ness. The education section of the original version of the bill specifically repudiated assimilation when it said that "It is hereby declared to be the purpose and policy of Congress to promote the study of Indian civilization and preserve and develop the special cultural contributions and achievements of such civilization, including Indian arts, crafts, skills and traditions."[4] That language was cut from the final bill, but the principle guided Collier's administration.

Although the philosophy behind Collier's policy was cultural pluralism, the interpretation of this notion was very much Collier's particular view of what Indians needed. According to historian Francis Paul Prucha, "It was a paternalistic program for the Indians, who were expected to accept it willy-nilly."[5] The policy imposed another set of Euro-American views on Indians, who had been subjected to a bewildering variety of policies, all of which were ultimately detrimental to them. Collier's views, at least, were more cognizant of traditional cultures than those of his predecessors in policy-making positions.

Collier had made his views of cultural pluralism well known in the previous decade as he noisily denounced what he and other reformers saw as Indian Bureau outrages in treatment of their "wards."[6] Now, with the Roosevelt administration in office, Collier, the most outspoken of the reformers, had the perilous opportunity to put his often-expressed ideas into practice. First, though, he had to deal with the Congress, the bureaucracy, Indians who themselves were greatly divided, missionaries, and others who had economic or social interests in the conduct of Native American affairs.

Collier's cause was aided by the climate of the time. The Depression had dumped unprecedented numbers of Americans into economic limbo or worse. Those dislocations led to more widespread sympathy for the poor, the dispossessed, and members of minority groups. People were more willing than before to think in new ways about Indians and their place in the national scheme of things. What were perceived as Indian communal institutions and reverence for the land now seemed more relevant and sensible in the light of the failures of individualism and industrialism in the Depression. Collier's once-iconoclastic views of cultural pluralism seemed now to fit the national mood.[7]

IMPLEMENTING CULTURAL PLURALISM

The ever-energetic Collier lost no time in implementing his pluralistic philosophy, first by administrative order and later by legislation.[8] In August 1933 he issued an order stopping the allotment and sale of Indian lands until further notice.[9] He also implemented an Indian version of the Civilian Conservation Corps, giving Native Americans federally-paid work on conservation projects determined by the tribes.[10] He aroused controversy with another administrative action, an order calling for "the fullest constitutional liberty, in all matters affecting religion, conscience, and culture" for Indians. The order also said, "No interference with Indian religious life or ceremonial expression will hereafter be tolerated." This aroused a storm of protest among missionaries and Christianized Indians, who denounced Collier for promoting paganism.[11]

The legislation was a forty-eight-page bill introduced in February of 1934 by Sen. Burton K. Wheeler of Montana and Rep. Edgar Howard of Nebraska. It embodied the fundamental changes in policy and philosophy Collier sought from Congress. The philosophy behind the original version of the bill was revolutionary and complex. It was rooted in Collier's beliefs that tribal cultures should be preserved, not assimilated out of existence. Its goal was to allow Indians to develop within their own cultures, preparing themselves for full participation in American life. As Frank Ernest Hill wrote in the *New York Times Magazine*, this goal came from the "growing conviction . . . that Indian life had latent strength and important cultural values and that the Indian if given the right opportunities could do what the government had failed to do: he could arrange a place for himself and his customs in this modern America."[12] As Collier himself put it, "Our design is to plow up the Indian soul, to make the Indian again the master of his own mind. If this fails, everything fails; if it succeeds, we believe the Indian will do the rest."[13]

To critics this sounded like sending Indians "back to the blanket," to be segregated on backward reservations. "Nonsense," Collier scoffed. "But if he happens to be a blanket Indian, we think he should not be ashamed of it." Collier proposed that the government's policy should "recognize and respect the Indian as he is. We think he must be so accepted before he can be assisted to become something else, if that is desirable."[14]

"Instead of a policy designed to educate the Indian to be a good white man, a vigorous campaign will be undertaken to restore him to his status as a good Indian," wrote Maria L. Rogers and Edward J. Fitzgerald in *Nation*.[15]

The most important provision of the Wheeler-Howard bill, in Collier's view, was ending allotment and seeking to consolidate scattered Indian lands into workable tracts. Also, in the original version of the bill, Indians were to be able to organize "for self-government and economic enterprise." Essentially, after a sufficient number of tribal members ratified its charter, a tribe would have many of the same powers as local governments. Federal control would be phased out, though the secretary of the interior would retain veto power over many aspects, such as protecting the rights of minorities and conserving a community's resources. Another title of the bill dealt with revamping the Indian education system by getting rid of Indian Bureau boarding schools in favor of day schools, which were intended to respect native cultures and to serve as community centers. Other provisions of the bill were aimed at establishing a revolving loan fund to make credit available to Indians, opening Indian Bureau jobs to Indians, and setting up a court of Indian affairs.[16]

To inform Indians of the measure and gain their backing, Collier held a series of ten "congresses" in March and April of 1934 throughout the West. Tribal members and others gathered to learn the bill's provisions and to voice their concerns. Collier's energetic salesmanship generated widespread approval for the measure.

OPPOSITION TO WHEELER-HOWARD

But there was strong opposition, too, from many quarters. The bill's aims of ending the allotment system and preserving Indian collective institutions aroused fear in some Indians and tribes. Those Indians who had taken to heart the government's and missionaries' assimilationist exhortations felt threatened that they would be segregated on reservations away from the mainstream of American life. Those who had worked their allotments worried that the land would be taken from them.[17]

Also, not all tribes had the centralized cultural institutions of the Southwest tribes that provided Collier's model. It would be hard if not impossible for some to recapture practices and traditions that had been virtually assimilated out of existence. The Five Tribes of Oklahoma, for example, had no reservations and for decades their lands and lives had been intertwined with those of whites. An editorial in the *Muskogee Daily Phoenix* bitterly took Collier to task for his failure to recognize this:

> The language of the Wheeler-Howard bill does not fit the Oklahoma Indian. For over 100 years he has lived with his white brother, hopelessly "checkerboarded" [i.e., with Indian and white lands interspersed] . . . but content to know that the white man was his friend and that he was the white man's brother. Now comes his new "great white father" with a proposal that he shall . . . throw off the mantle of civilization he has assumed, and . . . revert to the supervised barbarian.[18]

In the end the Oklahoma Indians were excluded from many of the provisions of Wheeler-Howard, and separate legislation was passed for them in 1936.[19]

Finally, Collier's bill sought to induce tribes that accepted the Indian New Deal to form corporations and adopt representative-style constitutions under the Indian Bureau. In the view of some tribes, these government forms were as alien to their cultures as were the earlier religions of the missionaries. Traditionalists feared that adopting such institutions would undermine the authority of hereditary tribal leaders.[20]

Non-Indians also criticized the legislation. Missionaries believed its guarantees of religious freedom were anti-Christian and encouraged paganism.[21] Western landholders feared loss of influence and land.[22] Conservatives saw in its promotion of tribal institutions a collectivism that was communistic and un-American. Bureaucrats in the Indian Bureau feared loss of influence as more positions were opened to Indians. All these forces sought, with varying degrees of success, to modify the bill and, after it became law, to delay, dilute, and sabotage its implementation.[23]

The Indian Reorganization Act, a much shorter (six pages) compromise bill that eventually passed, was signed by Roosevelt on June 18, 1934. It kept many of the provisions ending allotments and remnants of the self-government scheme, but much else was changed or eliminated, including the court of Indian affairs and the language endorsing Indian civilizations and cultures.[24] Tribes were, however, empowered to form corporations that would be operated by tribal councils that had written constitutions and bylaws. While this significantly increased Native Americans' self-government powers, the form of government was dictated by the Interior Department. And, the department retained final authority over the tribes, effectively limiting true autonomy.

Any tribe could vote to be excluded from the act. In fact, there was a fair amount of Indian opposition to the act, whether because of misunderstanding, as Collier claimed, or because of sincere disagreement with its aims. In any case, 78 of the 252 bands or tribes that could vote rejected coming under the act. Included among the rejecters was the Navajo tribe, one of the largest in the nation.[25]

The Indian Reorganization Act and Collier's administration probably caused greater changes in Native American life than anything since allotment began in the 1880s. Still, Collier accomplished far less than he had hoped or intended. Refusal of some tribes to come under the act and of others to write constitutions; stinginess of Congress in funding some of its provisions; and, finally, the outbreak of World War II all diminished its effectiveness.

CHALLENGES FOR THE PRESS

Reporting this immense change in Indian policy presented the New Deal–era press with a considerable challenge at the same time it was facing several challenges of its own. The way the press dealt with these journalistic challenges indirectly influenced portrayals of Native Americans, though Indians were seldom—if ever—mentioned in the discussions of journalistic practices and ethics. One challenge that preoccupied the press was the intense feelings the Roosevelt administration aroused in publishers and journalists. Newspaper publishers hotly debated whether press freedom was compromised by the inclusion of newspapers in the National Industrial Recovery Act (NIRA). The act dealt with wages, hours of work, and other business practices, including union organizing.[26] The debate over the NIRA brought into sharp focus the "dual character of the newspaper," which, as Willard Grosvenor Bleyer of the University of Wisconsin put it, "is both a private enterprise and a quasi-public institution."[27] Press criticism of the time centered mainly on two themes related to this duality. Publishers and their allies feared that the legislative initiatives and political power of the Roosevelt administration would infringe on freedom of the press. Critics on the left charged that the press was dominated by commercial and business interests that detrimentally affected the fairness of the news report.

A related accusation was that the press, or at least some elements of it such as Col. Robert R. McCormick's *Chicago Tribune* and William Randolph Hearst's newspaper chain, not only opposed Roosevelt editorially but were biased in their news coverage of the New Deal.[28] While these concerns did not relate directly to the coverage of news about Native Americans, there were indirect links. If elements of the press were not only hostile to Roosevelt editorially but also biased against the New Deal, then coverage of the Indian legislation was likely to suffer from the same bias.

OBJECTIVE AND INTERPRETATIVE REPORTING

There was a closer relationship to the portrayal of Native Americans in a second challenge confronting the 1930s press—the discussion of "objective" and "interpretative" reporting. Though origins of the notion of "objective" news reporting are unclear, it was the "accepted national standard" by the 1930s.[29] Objective reporting was defined as conveying demonstrable facts in an unbiased way. Critics of the unvarnished recitation of observable facts that characterized objective "straight news" reporting were concerned that the press was not meeting its responsibility to fully and fairly inform the public about the fundamental social change sweeping the country.

"[P]eople have come to depend upon [the newspaper] for the news of the day, for instruction and entertainment, for interpretation of local, state, national, and world affairs," wrote Kenneth E. Olson, then of the University of Minnesota, in 1935. But he warned that audiences were growing dissatisfied with a social institution that provided "comic strips, serial stories, movie gossip and advice to the love-lorn while they are desperately groping for the answers to bewildering new social questions," one that "should be providing its readers with a dependable and understandable picture of this changing world in which they are living."[30]

Olson worried that the press "may lag too far behind in recognizing the social changes that have taken place."[31] Moreover, he was concerned about the form of the news report. "Spot news," he said, did not help the reader understand the relationship of events to one another. "The newspaper must do more than present the mere surface of the stream of life. It must dig deeper and present a story of this changing world which the reader can understand. . . . Reporting public affairs can no longer be merely factual—it must be more and more interpretive."[32]

An early advocate of "interpretative reporting" was Curtis D. MacDougall of Northwestern University's Medill School of Journalism. He first used the term in his 1932 book *Reporting for Beginners*, which he revised in 1938 and retitled *Interpretative Reporting*. In an introductory note, MacDougall wrote of his belief "that changing social conditions . . . are causing news gathering and disseminating agencies to change their methods of reporting and interpreting the news. The trend is unmistakably in the direction of combining the function of interpreter with that of reporter."[33]

Elaborating, he wrote:

> Because the contemporary world is so complex and because the average man has neither the time nor the facilities to apply the proper tests to determine the significance of current events, mere reporting of the "what" by newspapers is insufficient. . . . In addition, the "why" must be explained in terms of factual background and general principles which make the immediate understandable in terms of the general.[34]

While critics of interpretation did not oppose making the news understandable, they worried that interpretation was often opinion in thin disguise. Roosevelt, in addition, objected to interpretation because he felt it interfered with the flow of information from government to the people.[35]

MacDougall's textbook noted that reporters who hoped to interpret the news must be widely read in history, economics, sociology, political science, and other disciplines and must have an unbiased outlook. "The interpretative reporter . . . cannot succeed if he is hampered by prejudices and stereotyped attitudes which would bias his perception of human affairs."[36]

While *Interpretative Reporting* made no direct reference to treatment of specific groups such as Native Americans, it did warn against the use of clichéd figures of speech, "bromides," "journalese," and "shopworn personifications." But it did not mention the use of racial or ethnic stereotypes.[37] Though the book did not list race or ethnicity as one of the elements reporters should use to identify persons in news stories, some of its examples gratuitously identified African Americans by their race.[38]

The lack of instructions on how the press should cover outside-the-mainstream groups such as Native Americans was not surprising. Such concerns were simply not on the minds of journalists and journalism educators in the 1930s. A study of twenty-four journalism textbooks published between 1908 and 1988 noted that few of those first published during the 1930s devoted much attention to coverage of minorities. Those that did generally focused on African Americans and issues such as use of dialect, and racial identification in crime stories.[39]

COVERING INDIANS NEAR AND FAR

In the 1930s when the country was only beginning to be served by radio news and had not yet felt the homogenizing effects of television news, local newspapers were a potent source of information. Because of this, the local press could play a powerful role in originating, perpetuating, and modifying images of Indians in the minds of its audience.

Comparing coverage of national publications with that of local newspapers in areas with significant Indian populations demonstrates how both types of publications treated news about Native Americans. There was a direct correlation between the vividness of the imagery and the distance of a publication from the Indians it wrote about. The more distant a native person or group, the more likely was the story to engage in sweeping generalizations that amounted to stereotyping.

An example is the coverage of the 1934 Indian congresses called by Collier to explain and build support for the Wheeler-Howard bill. Each congress was covered fairly extensively by papers in its area. But only the first one, in Rapid City, South Dakota, on March 2–5, 1934, drew much notice in the national press. Comparing stories about the meeting in *Time* magazine, the *Literary Digest*, and the *Rapid City Daily Journal* shows how Indians in the same event were portrayed in the local and national press.

The Rapid City paper treated the meeting as an important local event. Coverage was detailed and even-handed, with a touch of hometown boosterism. The *Journal* ran stories on the meeting every day it published from the first to the seventh of March. In addition, it ran an editorial favorable to Collier's proposals on the ninth of March and another detailing missionaries' objections to the bill the following day.

The first story framed the congress as a major civic happening. It dwelt on numbers (of people, beds, blankets) and other logistical details. It did not describe or characterize the Native Americans attending except to name their tribes. The gathering could have easily been one of Rotarians.[40] As the meetings went on, stories became more vivid in their characterizations:

> Where once they and their ancestors hunted buffalo and pitched their tepees, an area now in the midst of civilization, close to 300 leaders of many tribes gathered here today for a council with the Great White Father, John Collier . . . Minus war paint and pinto ponies, the warriors and descendants of warriors came in last night and this morning from five states.[41]

Other stories listed virtually everyone connected with the meeting and added historical sidelights that explained how traditional rivalries between tribes had been set aside for this event and how Indians might be justifiably suspicious of yet another "helpful" government plan.[42] Stories about the congress itself quoted Indian delegates by name and gave ample space to their views, as well as those of the press-savvy Collier. Indians were represented as intelligent adults who had worthwhile viewpoints. For example: "Max Big Man of Crow Reservation in Montana, said today he believed the delegates, although still unsettled, were leaning toward approval of the Collier plan."[43]

When national publications distilled news of the three-day meeting into a single story for a distant audience, the images of Indians changed significantly. In *Time* magazine, for example, the delegates became relics of the past who "shuffled" into Rapid City, made camp "not in clay-painted buffalo hide wikiups, but in closed government school buildings" and met "not crouched around council fires but seated in armchairs in an oak-paneled room."[44]

The article declared that "Three hundred years of suspicion stared from his copper-skinned listeners' eyes" as Collier urged the Indians to support the New Deal. Collier was quoted at length, but Indians were not.[45] Thus the only image readers got of the delegates was of "shuffling" "copper-skinned" beings who were seemingly more at home in "clay-painted buffalo hide wikiups" than in contemporary government buildings.

The *Literary Digest* story centered on Collier presenting his "new deal" to a listening audience of "young bucks, old men with sculptured faces, a few squaws and a few papooses too young to be left behind." It related some highly stereotypical history of Indian-white relations ("They were a kindly, cultured people when the white man set foot on Jamestown Island and Plymouth Rock. . . . They were a moral people, with a firm belief in God, and their family life was a lesson to the invader."), and summarized provisions of the bill. But nowhere in the article were contemporary Indians given voice. The image conveyed, thus, was of passive victims who were about to be uplifted by a white benefactor.[46]

Audiences far from an event, reading about it in a national publication, were more likely to get an account colored by distorted, stereotypical images. This was particularly unfortunate because these audiences were also less likely to have first-hand knowledge of the real people who had been edited out of the national stories.

Even when Indians were not a major story, they appeared in the local press. They often figured in stories of community activities that were the mainstay of such papers. Stories about Indian school choir performances, yearbook publications, women learning home nursing, and the like were regular fare in papers such as the *(Phoenix) Arizona Republic*, *Rapid City Daily Journal*, and the *Muskogee Daily Phoenix*. One effect of such stories was to portray Indians as real people who were part of the community fabric. Another staple of the local press, however, cast Indians in a negative light. This was the practice of gratuitously identifying them as Indians or by tribal name in police stories.

Local papers in such areas as South Dakota, Arizona, Oklahoma, and New Mexico coped with many of the same criticisms of the press and the New Deal as did large metropolitan dailies. But for them, there were additional concerns. The Indian New Deal was a big local story. As tribes wrestled with acceptance and, later, implementation of the IRA; as Collier and his aides came to town to push their views; as politicians, missionaries, and stockmen met to oppose them, there were plenty of events to cover. These papers, especially, were challenged to go beyond the events to interpret for their readers the meaning behind the proposed legislation. At the same time, local papers were generally thinner in resources—they had fewer reporters and editors, a smaller "news hole" in which to print stories—than were the big dailies. This made coverage of spot news uneven and interpretation difficult.

MAGAZINES

While newspapers reached citizens with fresh information every day, none had truly national audiences. However, a wide variety of magazines reached citizens nationwide. They ranged from the news weeklies, relative newcomers to the journalistic scene, to established publications such as the *Literary Digest*, to consumer magazines such as *Collier's* and journals of opinion such as the *Nation*.

Critics of newspapers' overreliance on objectivity at the expense of interpretation often cited the news magazines such as *Time* and *Newsweek*[47] as examples of the successful use of interpretation. *Time*, the first of the modern news magazine genre, was begun in 1923 by Henry Luce and Briton Hadden. Its aim was to organize the week's news into "departments," tell "what the news means," and to describe the personalities of the people who made news. The format was highly successful by the 1930s, and parts of it were imitated by newcomers such as *Newsweek* and *United States News*, both founded in 1933.[48] A key ingredient was *Time*'s distinctive writing style, described as an "air of brassy omniscience" fed by the use of jargon, inverted sentences, and "slick epithets."[49] But, while news magazines may have at times presented background information to make their stories about Native Americans more understandable, their peculiar style of writing encouraged superficial generalizations and terms that were stereotypical at best. News magazines' interpretation, and the style of writing that accompanied it, did not serve well the unbiased understanding of Native American issues.

The punchy, succinct, upbeat writing lent itself to stereotypes, often in stories that were otherwise factually accurate and well balanced. For example, *Time*, in an otherwise balanced story on the signing of the first tribal constitution under the Indian Reorganization Act by the Flathead tribe of Montana, observed that Ickes and Collier were "solemn as the Indians." Later the magazine used the pervasive terminology of the time when it said Collier "had to hold many a powwow to persuade braves and squaws that his plan is good."[50]

Likewise *Newsweek* turned a story about a court of claims settlement with the Blackfeet and Gros Ventre into a piece that contained sentences such as this: "Said the governmental reckoners in their Washingtonian wigwam, we have paid out heap big money to the Blackfeet for their uplift. We have sent them plenty wampum for their Christian Civilization."[51]

There were two problems with this description. First, the overall imagery portrayed Indians' legitimate claims on the government as somehow humorous or objects of ridicule. Also, since Western tribes such as the Blackfeet and Gros Ventre did not traditionally live in wigwams or use wampum, the inaccurate terminology reinforced the simplistic notion that any term associated with any Indian group was accurate for all.

In addition to the news magazines, the large circulation consumer magazines such as *Reader's Digest*, *Collier's*, and *Saturday Evening Post* ran long, descriptive articles about Native Americans, usually with a clear ideological point of view. The journals of opinion, such as *Nation* and *New Republic* and religious publications such as *Christian Century* often provided a forum for partisans in the ideological battles of cultural pluralism versus assimilation.

THE PORTRAYALS

Stories in national and local publications during the 1930s contained some familiar images of Indians as well as some new ones. Just as the legislation that was to mark a new deal for the Indians was complex, so too was the press coverage, both in the imagery used to portray Indians and the journalistic forms that used or relied on these images.

In the 1930s press, the positive image of the good Indian or noble savage was used both to promote and to oppose the ideology of cultural pluralism. The negative image of the bad or degraded Indian likewise was present, but in the 1930s, this type was also often an object of ridicule, someone to be trivialized and made light of. Because Indians no longer represented a military threat, they were belittled by humor. A third image that persisted in the 1930s from earlier times was of Indians as exotic relics of the past who were more museum exhibits than human beings.

As new government policies involved Indians in decision making, they became news sources. A new image seldom seen in previous decades, the "involved Indian citizen," appeared. The involved Indian citizen was merely a source in a news story, a conduit for information who was not further described or characterized. Since most white news sources were treated this way, stripping the involved Indian citizen of the baggage of descriptive adjectives gave him an image of equality with white sources such as bureaucrats, politicians, missionaries, and stockmen. He (virtually all those portrayed were men) was a player in the event being reported. He spoke for himself without the mediation of a white "friend" or interpreter.

These images—good Indian, bad Indian, exotic relic of the past, involved Indian citizen—appeared in the press in several ways. Most obvious was language and tone of the stories. Journalistic conventions also contributed to the imagery. The use of such terms as "chiefs," "braves," or "bucks" for men; "squaws" or occasionally "princesses" for women, and "papooses" for children was widespread in all publications and types of stories. Such terms implicitly connoted social separation and inferiority.

A second way images were incorporated in journalistic forms was through the selection of stories. Using white definitions of news, of what was unusual and of consequence, for example, helped to perpetuate inaccurate imagery.

Finally, the forms stories took—how an event was shaped or framed into something that would be known as a "story"—also played into the perpetuation of the images noted. Whether a story was a straight news story, an interpretative article, a human interest feature, a long, descriptive magazine piece, or a highly stylized news magazine article contributed in varying degrees to the portrayal and, thus, perception of Native Americans.

Good Indian/Noble Savage Images

Journalistic interpreters of the philosophy of cultural pluralism that informed the Indian Bureau's policies in the 1930s often used idealized imagery of Native Americans as possessing characteristics superior to those of whites. In arguing that Indians should be allowed to develop their traditional cultures and to retain what was left of their land base rather than being forced to assimilate into the white world, articles sometimes employed an image of native people as noble savages.

For example, Mary Heaton Vorse, in an article in *Scholastic* magazine explaining the benefits of the Indian Reorganization Act, asserted that the public was beginning to realize that "The Indian . . . had a way of life which possessed an extraordinary wholeness, possessed satisfactions forgotten by people living in our distracted machine of civilization."[52]

Cash Asher wrote in the *New York Times* that "The Indian never tries to change the face of nature and create artificial surroundings as does the white man. He is a very part of nature and in his native habitat is in direct contact with her for his livelihood . . . He loves every meadow and mountain of his native clime with patriotic fervor."[53] In addition to inaccurately generalizing these traits to a nonexistent "Indian," both articles showed how presumed cultural traits were idealized by pro–New Deal writers.

Opponents of the Indian New Deal sometimes used similar imagery to argue the opposite side of the issue. Writing in the *Saturday Evening Post*, Flora Warren Seymour, a Chicago attorney who had been a member of the Federal Board of Indian Commissioners, a body eliminated by Collier, energetically attacked New Deal policies toward the Navajos. The Navajo, she wrote, "has remained among the most primitive and the most independent of Indians. Until these late years he has gone his own way—a simple way of hardships and privations, it is true, but a way that has much to satisfy his spirit." The traditional life of these Indians, the article contended, was being trampled by misguided ideologues and romantics.[54] Interestingly, the article employed imagery similar to that often used by

Collier partisans in arguing *for* the Indian New Deal. Here, however, Seymour was saying that the rhetoric of cultural pluralism was deceptive and that a regimented, government-imposed way of life, not freedom, was being forced upon the Navajos.

The image of Indians—particularly Pueblos—as noble and innocent and in some ways superior to whites that appeared frequently in the 1920s survived into the 1930s, as in this breathless article from *Good Housekeeping* magazine. The author, Alice Booth, who confessed that "in all my life I had never seen a real, live North American Indian outside of a circus," told of encountering Indians on a train trip West and correcting some misimpressions: "An Indian village. Somehow I had expected wigwams, but here were tiny cottages of adobe, pink, or blue, or ivory, or orange." And, after watching dancers: "I have seen the dancers of a dozen countries; here was the equal of them all. And for all my life I had gone about thinking that Indian dances were merely a matter of hobbling around yipping to the senseless beat of an absent-minded drum."[55]

The main thrust of the article, however, was to make the Pueblos out to be superior to whites in parenting and family life. "There is no scolding in an Indian home; father and mother set an example of quiet and serene living which cannot fail to influence the babies they love so well," a photo caption said. In the body of the article, Booth related how a small boy accidentally dropped and broke a bowl and how his mother, unlike whites, comforted but did not punish him. "We call ourselves civilized. . . . but is it possible that the Indians can teach us lessons in gentleness and consideration and poise?"[56]

Degraded/Bad Indian Images

Indians had not been a significant military threat to whites for several decades, so the bad Indian image of savage predators was hardly applicable to 1930s news journalism. However, an equally negative corollary image evolved of the Indian as "degraded," either through his own innate improvidence and laziness or through the corrupting influences of white culture. The degraded Indian image had a number of facets. Indians might be seen as lazy, dumb, uncivilized, or extravagant. By the 1930s this image was so well worn in the press that reporters and headline writers often simply referred to such Indians as "Poor Lo,"[57] a journalistic shorthand reference to the phrase "Lo, the poor Indian," from Alexander Pope's *An Essay on Man*, written in 1774.

> Lo, the poor Indian whose untutor'd mind
> Sees God in clouds, or hears him in the wind;
> His soul proud Science never taught to stray
> Far as the solar walk or milky way;[58]

Sometimes the degraded Indian image was applied collectively to a group, as in stories about the Osage tribe of Oklahoma whose members acquired sudden oil wealth in the early part of the century, only to see much of it squandered or stolen. In the press the whole tribe was characterized as profligate spenders who could not handle their money. Stories were studded with examples of Osages buying expensive cars, homes, and clothing, only to go broke when oil revenues dried up in the Depression. In 1933, when the tribe's oil revenues were scant, a story in the *Literary Digest* quoting the *New York Herald Tribune* characterized the Osages as not only extravagant ("Being broke is hard on Lo.") but uncomprehending: "[T]he big (oil) producers . . . put deep holes in the earth, and by some magic Lo never understood, sucked from the ground a thick black liquid that resulted in millions for the Osage tribe."[59]

A 1935 *New York Times* story stated flatly that "the Indians are free with their money. They don't keep it long." The article told of how the oil income of tribe members, once "the richest people in the world," had plummeted in the Depression and was now on the rebound. "It means the Indians are buying again," the article said.[60]

Seminoles of Florida, without the dubious benefit of oil money, were collectively described as "a disconsolate, defeated and uneducated people" who "occupy their present jungle area only because white men have found it too difficult to penetrate."[61] Hill Indians of Montana were described as "Homeless, destitute and lacking tribal ties."[62] In both stories the degraded characterizations were followed by proposals for assistance from the Indian Bureau.

The degraded Indian imagery was carried out on a grand scale in two articles in *Collier's* by Owen P. White in which he bitterly described how white policies and institutions had "denatured" Indians by seeking to "civilize" them: "[T]he red man . . . has been denatured. Once wild, he is now mild; once a menace, he is now a mendicant." Efforts at civilization, "in return for having taught a man to wear breeches and shoes in place of a breech-clout and moccasins, has taken the life out of him, robbed him of his initiative, deprived him of his right to do as he please with that which is his."[63]

At other times, the degraded Indian image was conveyed through the newsroom practice of labeling those named in crime stories. Thus if an Indian was arrested or victimized by crime, his tribe or the generic label "Indian" was a routine part of his identification. It was not unusual, thus, to see headlines in Indian Country newspapers that said: "Indian Sentenced For Grocery Theft";[64] "Navajo Held Under Guard";[65] "Indian Youth Held, Murder."[66] This practice, which was also true for African Americans, quite likely conditioned readers to think of Native Americans mainly as violent, drunken, or dishonest people involved in crimes.

A more subtle but equally damaging practice was the journalistic habit of rendering stories about Indians in a bemused tone, liberally laced with clichés, stereotypical terms such as "fire water," "redskin," and "paleface"; and incorrect usage of terms such as "wampum," "wigwam," and "peace pipe." The effect of such articles was to trivialize Native Americans, to render even their legitimate concerns as subjects for humor and ridicule.

For example, in 1934 when the Creek tribe of Oklahoma held its first election since 1899, the outcome was treated matter-of-factly by the *(Oklahoma City) Daily Oklahoman*: "Roly E. Canard of Wetumka has been elected principal chief of the Creek Indians. It is the first time since 1899 that the Creeks have been permitted to elect their own chief."[67]

In *Newsweek*, however, the story attempted to strike a humorous contrast between what it characterized as traditional tribal practices and the modern activity of voting. The aboriginal Creeks, the article indicated, "killed their scalped enemies by slow torture, hunted big game . . . and held pow-wows in mud-chinked huts." Modern tribe members picking candidates for chief "meet in a church, sit on chairs, talk English, and follow parliamentary procedure." The Creeks cast their ballots "in ballot boxes, without a feather or a war-whoop to give an Indian flavor to the Anglo-Saxon procedure."[68]

The images of the Creeks in the two stories contrasted starkly. In the *Daily Oklahoman* they were responsible citizens exercising their tribal franchise after being denied it for a generation. In *Newsweek* they were recently-primitive and picturesque. Their exercise in democracy was made to seem laughable.

Stories making Native Americans the objects of humor also cropped up in newspaper travel, entertainment, and feature sections. An article in the *New York Times* described Indians who answered a casting call for a film version of *The Last of the Mohicans*:

> There were coppery ones and pale ones; some were attired in buckskinned, face-painted regalia of the warpath, and others in the latest thing from the reservations surrounding England's Bond Street.[69]

The article expressed disappointment in Indian aspirants who didn't measure up to the Hollywood image, such as "a dumpy, whitish and unprepossessing man," though he was said to be a descendant of Uncas, the hero of the novel, and approval for those who did, such as "the classic, fourteen-carat, gorgeous Indian brave to life" who had an "aquiline profile that would make a nickel turn tail in shame."[70]

A short item poking fun at an Indian could find its way onto the front page, even if the information was neither local nor newsworthy. An Associated Press dispatch from Denver that appeared on the front page of the *Arizona Republic* described in belittling and humorous terms an Indian man who pleaded guilty to intoxication and was given castor oil as a punishment. "White man's firewater—O.K. White man's medicine—ugh! Plenty nasty!" the article began.[71] Items such as this not only reinforced the image of Indians as drunken and degraded but also made their situation somehow humorous. According to the article, the judge gave the same penalty to all, yet assigning the penalty to an Indian apparently allowed the writer of the item to use stereotypical terms—"firewater," "ugh"—and made the story newsworthy enough to be used by the wire service and chosen for a brief in the Arizona newspaper.

Even the esteemed Meyer Berger,[72] writing a long article about the Navajos in the *New York Times Magazine*, struck a needlessly humorous tone in describing some of the tribe's traditional lifeways. This, for example, is how the article treated the Navajo matrilineal family organization and mother-in-law taboo:

> Giggling squaws, who wear the pants and control the pursestrings in all well-regulated Navajo families, came to the powwow [a reference to a meeting of the Navajo Constitutional Assembly] too. They have no voice in tribal affairs; must remain mute at council meetings. . . .
>
> Many's the harried white man who might envy certain of the Indian marital customs. It is considered almost sure death, for example, for a married man to look upon his mother-in-law, or for a mother-in-law to see her daughter's husband. They have a belief that if sight of one another doesn't kill them, it will at least strike them blind.
>
> Yet the ascendancy of the male is a myth as far as the fierce Navajo is concerned. When he marries he takes his wife's family name. She controls the family funds, has complete and final say as to how the children shall be trained, if at all, and is more or less head of the house. At the Constitutional Assembly meeting the squaws giggled every time one of the Navajo wisecrackers said something funny about one of the palefaces.[73]

While the information was superficially accurate, the lighthearted tone belittled the Navajos. It interpreted their lifestyle from a white point of view, the nonchalant treatment implying that anything different from the Euro-American tradition was somehow less worthy. An unquestioned tenet of journalistic writing, then and now, was to make information interesting and relevant to the reader. One can speculate that this was Berger's intent. However, the effect, whether intentional or not, was also to make light of a people's long-standing traditions.

Indians who conformed to white norms of language and dress were also subjects of ridicule. A brief *Arizona Republic* story, which ran under the headline, "Perfect English Used By Indian," reported facetiously, on "a rounded and polished sentence from the lips of a copper-skinned Indian" as a newsworthy item.[74]

Occasionally the journalistic image of Indians as lazy was graphic and explicit as when the *Chicago Tribune* ran a front page editorial cartoon slamming what, in its view, was the laziness of lawmakers. It showed an Indian in feathered headdress sitting and smoking in front of a tepee. In the background was a capitol dome surrounded by the phrases, "Shorter hours of work," "5 hour day," "30 hour week!" The Indian was saying, "Hump! Paleface steal 'em my stuff!"[75] The Indian, collectively and generically, was a metaphor for indolence, in the *Chicago Tribune*.

Indians as Exotic Relics of the Past

Articles depicting Indians as relics of the past certainly were not new in the 1930s. Yet the persistence of the imagery was at a time when the same tribes depicted as virtual museum pieces were struggling in the present with complex legislation conferring greater self-government powers.

For example, in 1933 *Parents Magazine* ran a long article advising parents on the value of "playing Indian" with their children that portrayed Indians as exotic role models pulled from prehistory. The article first sought to remove what it called "the mass of falsehood . . . in which the Indian has been presented as a treacherous and bloodthirsty animal, with not a spark of true humanhood in him." The article then replaced the negative stereotype with a long list of positive ones, such as: "Outstanding virtues of the red people were courage, honesty and hospitality." "Indian children began while very young to learn how to be useful and efficient." "Perfect utility combined with beauty and grace was the Indian craftsman's ideal." All references to Indians in the article were in the past tense with little indication that these people still existed. And many, though not all, referred to "the Indian" as a generic whole, giving short shrift to the wide differences in native cultures.[76]

Similarly, an article in *Scientific American* lamented that "the Indian is now a creature of the past, who can be studied mostly in books and museums."[77] In 1938 an article in the *Reader's Digest* about the Inter-Tribal Indian Ceremonial at Gallup, New Mexico, described the tribes represented there in detail and in terms of their traditional appearance and attributes but made no reference to them as contemporary people.[78] While this is understandable in that it was the exotic dress and dance that helped draw tourists to Gallup, the effect was again to render Native Americans as people outside the present.

Such a notion was explicitly stated in an *Arizona Republic* article on an Indian pow wow in Flagstaff that said, "Like ghosts from the pages of the past, Indian dance teams in full regalia, picturesque riders from a score of tribes, gaily decorated wagons, Indians in holiday dress and native entertainers bedecked with strands of turquoise and silver jewelry, all will march forth in a brilliant panorama."[79]

At the same time papers in the Southwest were reporting on deliberations of Navajo or Pueblo tribes on government programs that would profoundly affect their futures, the papers also ran stories portraying the same Indians as almost other-worldly performers who put on spectacles for the entertainment of white tourists. An *Arizona Republic* article promoting an upcoming gathering noted:

> Teddy Neze's yabechi dancers and the sacred medicine and buffalo ceremonial troupe will follow [earlier acts]. . . . A carnival spirit will prevail under the direction of the white man.[80]

An article that seemingly made a stab at coming to grips with the dichotomy of Indians' practicing ancient cultures in the twentieth century ran in the *Chicago Tribune* in connection with the Indian villages at the Chicago World's Fair of 1933. The writer of the first-person article, James O'Donnell Bennett, through a series of questions sought to reconcile his stereotype of Indians with the people he was seeing at the fair. "Are these men who move with such beautiful poise really majestic or only stolid—or both? Are they truly laconic or only verbally dull? . . . Are they tractable? . . . Are they truthful? . . . Do they crave liquor? . . . Are they lazy? . . . Do Indians live longer than we do?" he asked.[81]

Clearly, in the 1930s many Indians were living in two worlds. But few articles successfully represented this tension. Most contained a single image or, when attempting to evoke Indians' traditional ways, rendered them as crude contrasts, rather than trying to evoke the tensions that must have been present for many Indians.

Images in "Briefs" or "Fillers"

Contributing to the portrayal of Indians as ancient and exotic was newspapers' selection of short "filler" stories. These one- to four-paragraph stories, usually carrying a one-column headline in eighteen- or twenty-four-point type, probably had the journalistic purpose of breaking up the large story elements in making up a page, and of introducing a change of pace both in tone and subject matter. But another effect was to reinforce the myth of Indians as relics of a distant time and place. Headlines from the *New York Times* included, "Indians in Full Regalia/Dance at White House"[82] and "Indian Tom-Toms Hail/Large Wild-Rice Crop."[83]

A filler in the *Muskogee (Oklahoma) Daily Phoenix* reported on movie star Mae West looking for a virtual reincarnation of the past. The story said West was seeking for her next film an Indian who was a "direct descendant of the Indian whose profile adorned the old pennies."[84]

Another manifestation of the exotic/ancient imagery appeared during the dry summers of the 1930s when pages of the Eastern press were sprinkled with stories of Indian rain dances. For the most part these were short stories taken from the Associated Press wire service. Often, longer, more detailed versions ran in Arizona or New Mexico papers. The most frequent subject was the Snake Dance of the Hopis of Arizona, quite possibly because of the sensational image of Indians dancing with live snakes in their mouths and also because of the popularity of tribes of the Southwest with Eastern tourists. In any case, some of the stories, while generally accurate, seemed to reinforce the exotic image by using language such as "weird appeals" and "chanting red men."[85] Others used less loaded terms. But even straightforward description reinforced the exotic image:

> [The snakes were] fondled fearlessly by the priests who chant and fashion beautiful, intricate sand paintings in honor of their unwilling visitors. . . . [S]hake priests and their aides, the grotesquely masked antelope men, dance with the squirming reptiles in their mouths and on their arms.[86]

Other stories reported on the Sun Dance of the Plains tribes, including a seeming rivalry between Arapahos and Cheyennes over whose rainmaking powers were more potent.[87] To a newspaper reader in New York, all of this might well have seemed outlandish at the least, and certainly foreign to mainstream Christian or Jewish religious traditions. Through the selection of details that played up the exotic aspects of the rituals and the brevity of the stories that left no room to explain the rites' larger significance, Indians' religious expressions were rendered as circus-like stunts.

Images of the Involved Indian Citizen

An image of Indians who spoke effectively for themselves, who could and did operate in the political arena, appeared in the 1930s. At least partly because of the New Deal's public emphasis on Indian participation, Indian voices, less mediated by white "friends," were heard more often in the press. This involved Indian was a source rather than a symbol. He might be a tribal leader or spokesman for an insurgent faction. Often, he had been educated in white schools or government schools for Indians, such as the Carlisle school in Pennsylvania. He spoke English, and this fact was often noted in stories. But the essential thing that set this image apart from others was that the involved Indian was not described or characterized. He was treated as a conduit for information, in the same way a white source—politician, missionary, or stockman—would be treated.

Examples of this could be seen in the *Muskogee Daily Phoenix*'s coverage of Collier's meeting there with representatives of the Five Tribes and others. For days before the meeting, which took place on March 22, 1934, the paper carried stories of tribal groups declaring opposition to the Wheeler-Howard bill, which the paper also editorially opposed. Those lining up against the bill were treated as mature and intelligent, and their views were presented respectfully, albeit with loaded words that revealed the paper's bias. (The measure was variously termed "Collier's segregation proposal"[88] and a bill for the "communization of Indian lands."[89]) Dozens of Indians on various "reception" and "interrogation" committees to meet with Collier were named and quoted.

An example, citing one of the few Indian women referred to in any paper's coverage, was the paper's mention of "Mrs. S. R. Lewis of Okmulgee" who "announced that the Indian Women's Club had drafted resolutions opposed to the bill which they intended to present the commissioner."[90]

Another was a story speculating on a possible successor to the acting chief of the Choctaw tribe, who was to be elected instead of appointed for the first time since 1900. In the manner of any piece of political speculation, the story noted that "It is understood that the scholarly . . . Stanford and Columbia [university] graduate [acting chief Ben Dwight] will be a candidate for reelection, though there are reports that several prominent Choctaws also seek the office."[91] Here Indians were treated as politicians in the same manner as other citizens. They were not burdened with further imagery.

Other papers, too, portrayed Indians as thoughtful and involved in determining their own fates. When Collier met with Osages in Oklahoma in October 1934, the *(Oklahoma City) Daily Oklahoman* pointed out the tribe's sophisticated approach to proposed legislation:

> Other tribes said they would not accept the bill until it is amended to remove (objectionable) features. The Osages said they would accept the bill with the agreement that those amendments were made.
>
> Where other tribes regarded the act and Collier with suspicion . . . , the Osages approached it with an attitude of confidence in Collier.[92]

The *Santa Fe New Mexican* portrayed Pueblo Indians as more knowledgeable than white lawmakers:

> The Pueblo Indians were chuckling today because the federal government asked them to do something that has been their custom for centuries. It was the self-rule provision of the Wheeler-Howard bill. . . . The Pueblos have been electing their governors for so long a time there is no memory of a different method.[93]

By portraying Indians as participants in events, the stories showed them as political beings with some power to affect their lives. Stories that reported on Indians' views of aspects of the IRA presented Indians as thoughtful individuals with varying interests and points of view. By framing such events as the Indian congresses and tribal councils as significant news stories and, often, playing them prominently on the front page, newspapers contributed to the image that Indians and their affairs were important and newsworthy.

Portrayals of Indians as involved citizens were not always consistent, however. For example, the *Muskogee Daily Phoenix* treated Indians who agreed with its editorial position opposing Collier's plans as mature and intelligent, but it treated those who supported Collier quite differently. The first major endorsement of the Wheeler-Howard bill in Oklahoma came from the Nighthawk Kee-too-wah society of the Cherokees, some six thousand fullblood traditionalists. When they expressed interest in setting up a cooperative community under the bill's provisions, the Muskogee paper ran a long feature characterizing the Nighthawks as people whose "natural indolence" led to the failure of a previous "communized existence." The feature ran under the headline, "Early Indian Communism Attempt in Hills Is Recalled as Failure." The only person quoted in the story was a member of a rival Cherokee group. No one from the Kee-too-wah Nighthawks was quoted.[94]

Overall the piece portrayed the Nighthawks as lazy and churlish, people who withdrew from the society of whites to practice an ersatz religion. The story described them as people who "lolled in the shade, shunned labor" and "were more interested in their rituals, in their worship of fire, than in making a success of a community project." The article went on to say:

> Once a proud landholding clan, they have been brought to want, and now call upon the government to finance another communistic attempt. . . . Kee-too-wahs contend that the white man's civilization has ruined the fullblood Cherokee Indian. Commissioner Collier has promised that with the adoption of the Wheeler-Howard bill the Nighthawks may revert to the segregated community out of whose wreckage they have only recently climbed.[95]

The article not only discredited the first Oklahoma Cherokee group to support Collier's legislation, but it did so by portraying them as degraded Indians whose efforts to practice traditional ways led to their ruin. The article suggested that it was not white civilization that hurt them, but their rejection of white values of hard work and individual ownership of property. Their religion, described by a source from a rival group, was portrayed as inauthentic, without value, and a force holding them back from a comfortable life. Thus in the *Muskogee Daily Phoenix*, Indians who agreed with its politics were portrayed as mature and responsible, while those who did not were characterized as backward and incompetent.

JOURNALISTIC USES OF IMAGES

Clearly, a great deal of newspaper and magazine writing in the 1930s picked up, perpetuated, and embellished images of Indians that had appeared in other times and other media. There were several ways journalistic forms and conventions perpetuated inaccurate imagery.

Language and Tone of Stories

Both the national and local publications routinely followed the conventions of the day by inaccurately calling Indians "chiefs," "braves," "squaws," or "papooses" without regard to tribe or circumstance. In addition to descriptions of clothing and lifestyles that portrayed Indians as exotic relics of the past, many stories bestowed upon Indians personality traits or physical abilities that reinforced the prevailing imagery. Thus the *Arizona Republic* described those at a pow wow as "tall, lithe young Navajo braves," "solemn bucks on horseback," and "squaws."[96] At a tribal council meeting, Navajo headmen "gravely greeted the representatives of the white man's law and convened solemnly the Navajo council."[97] Describing an upcoming Pueblo buffalo feast the *Santa Fe New Mexican* declared, "The Indian is never happier than when supplied with buffalo plunder."[98]

Newspapers sometimes demeaned Indian men by referring to them by their first name on second reference. Thus the famous Sac and Fox athlete Jim Thorpe was called "Jim" throughout a *New York Times* feature story about his political activities while his former coach, Glenn (Pop) Warner, was referred to by his surname: "With Warner's help, Jim was to become an all-American."[99] Such references to adults by their first names made them seem childlike and undignified.

When the press superimposed inaccurate imagery on authentic news events, the result was to trivialize the people and the proceedings. For example, when Collier met with representatives of Arizona tribes on March 16, 1934, in Phoenix, the *Arizona Republic*'s lead story depicted the Indian delegates in a patronizing manner.

> Faces of the listening Indians offered an unusual character study. Almost all were serious. Some wore expressions solely of curiosity. Others were quizzical. A keen sense of humor was displayed. Most of the braves were paunchy, and out of the conference room wore big hats, styled to the Southwest.[100]

Story Organization

The press painted images of Native Americans in ways more subtle than the language and tone of stories; portrayals of Indians were also affected by the ways stories were organized.

During the drought of 1936, Navajos of the Southwest invoked some seldom-used rituals to beseech their gods for rain. The story was reported by the Associated Press. Analyzing the same AP dispatch in three newspapers provides some insights into how the reporter, the wire service, and the newspaper editors who chose and edited the story viewed the same event. A twelve-paragraph story on the unusual Navajo rain ritual appeared in the *Santa Fe New Mexican*, an afternoon paper, on June 27, 1936. The story described the "mystic rites" of an "ancient tribal ritual" designed to bring rain to the parched lands. Near the end of the story, in the eleventh paragraph, the writer mentioned that a white man, trader Roman Hubbell, would take part in the "impressive ceremony."[101]

A different, ten-paragraph version carrying the AP logo but no byline and containing much of the same information appeared the next day, a Sunday, in the morning *(Phoenix) Arizona Republic*. The same story, pared to six paragraphs, ran the same day in the *New York Times*. In the Phoenix and New York papers, however, the participation of the white trader had been moved to the lead paragraph. The headline in the *Republic* reflected the changed emphasis: "Navajo Choose White Trader as Ritualistic Water-Bearer." The lead, similar in both the New York and Arizona papers, read, "A veteran white trader, trusted as a brother in secret councils of the Navajos, joined today in the renewal of the ancient Indian ceremony of supplication for rain."[102]

While the language of all three stories treated the Navajo religious ritual respectfully, moving the reference to the white trader to the beginning of the story shifted its emphasis and conveyed a vastly different impression. Readers of the Sunday stories could easily infer that white intervention was necessary for the ritual to succeed, or that the drought situation was so disastrous that the Navajos took the unusual step of admitting a white man to add power to their ceremony. The *Arizona Republic* story called Hubbell's inclusion "an almost unprecedented honor for a paleface."[103] Emphasizing a white man's participation in a Navajo ceremony was also subtly patronizing. Because of the efforts of white missionaries to convert Indians, a Navajo attending church would not rate a story in the mainstream press. But a white man participating in Navajo ceremonies was newsworthy.

One can only speculate on why the reference to Hubbell was moved up. The Hubbell family of traders was well known in the Southwest, so it is possible the "names make news" adage controlled. Also, the notion that the unusual should be played up in news stories might have led the AP's rewrite person to move up the Hubbell reference. Quite likely it shows the orientation of the press toward presenting stories from a white point of view: The most important aspect of the story was seen as a white's participation in the ritual.

Selection of Stories

In the 1930s some stories about Indians were indisputably news and were duly covered, such as events surrounding the Wheeler-Howard bill. But beyond the must-use news lay a broad discretionary area. Here, as will be seen, the stories about Indians considered newsworthy for mostly white audiences were those that fit white definitions of what stories about Indians ought to be: Indians were in the news when they conformed to the imagery already present in white consciousness.

Meeting in March and April of 1934, the Navajo Tribal Council wrestled with a difficult and painful decision. Government officials including Collier himself said the Navajos must reduce their livestock because land on the reservation was seriously overgrazed. Officials pointed out how overgrazing was eroding the fragile land. Soon, they warned, it would be unable to support the sheep, goats, and other livestock that underpinned the tribe's economy and culture.

Other matters, momentous and trivial, were on the council's agenda, too. At the March meeting Collier was there in person to describe the pending Wheeler-Howard bill and answer questions about it. Tribesmen asked and later received Collier's approval to institute a mounted police force to go after crime and vice on the reservation. The council also approved a resolution eliminating honorary tribal memberships that had been bestowed on politicians, movie stars, and other celebrities over the years.[104]

The issue of stock reduction was an immensely important one to the Navajos whose wealth, prestige, and, sometimes, survival were tied to their herds of sheep and goats. Sheep provided meat for food and wool to be sold or woven into blankets. Goats were a Navajo's last refuge against destitution. It was said they used "everything but the smell."[105]

The second issue, discussion of the proposed Wheeler-Howard legislation, was politically important to Collier, who sought to line up support of the nation's largest tribe for the measure then making its way through Congress. The third issue, the Navajo mounted police, was important because of the increase in bootlegging, prostitution, and gambling on and near the reservation. This was linked to the increase in wage earnings by Navajos in federal conservation programs. The last issue, the resolution revoking tribal membership for celebrities, was so trivial that it was not mentioned in the major histories of the time.

Story selection—and the consequent images—varied among papers. Newspapers close to the event—in Phoenix and Santa Fe—carried wire service stories about all four issues. But only the inauguration of the mounted police and the inconsequential story of honorary members being ousted from the tribe resonated beyond the Southwest. Thus the *New York Times* carried three stories on the mounted police and one on the ouster of the celebrities. Only in the last paragraph of one story was livestock reduction mentioned.

The *New York Times* story, an Associated Press dispatch carrying a Gallup, New Mexico, dateline, began, "The pale-face Indians—such notables as Douglas Fairbanks, Mary Pickford and Jimmy Walker—were read out of the Navajo Tribe today. The Navajo Council, composed of twelve real copper-skinned braves, [abolished] all honorary memberships in the tribe."[106]

The *Times* story did not carry the explanation, which appeared in the *Santa Fe New Mexican*, that "racial pride or prejudice did not figure in" the decision. Nor did the New York paper carry the quote from Navajo tribal chairman Tom Dodge that "It was merely an effort to be truthful and avoid making the Navajo tribes ridiculous by falling for every celebrity that comes along."[107] It was possible that the explanatory material was not carried in the AP story that reached New York. Nevertheless, the fact that the Eastern paper chose to use stories portraying Navajos as petty and silly conformed to the practice of making Indians subjects for humor.

In the *Chicago Daily News* the wire-service story was used as a take-off point to add a local angle and to spin the story into the realm of inaccuracy. The *Daily News* used the Navajo action to question memberships in other tribes, such as the Sioux, bestowed on celebrities at the Century of Progress world's fair in Chicago, then reassured readers that other tribes were not following the Navajos' lead.

> Heap Chief Flying Eagle, who is Gen. Italo Balbo to you, need not look to his laurels nor fear losing a single feather in his turkey-plume cap.
>
> Honors conferred by Indian tribes at [the 1933 world's fair] will "stick." . . . "Once a Sioux, always a Sioux."[108]

Quite likely the writer of the *Daily News* article was following the time-honored journalistic injunction to localize wire-service stories. This was a prime example of how apparent ignorance of the differences among tribes plus scanty information contributed to an inaccurate story that could only reinforce readers' stereotypes of Indians as something akin to circus acts or museum pieces, rather than real, contemporary people.

The story of the mounted Navajo tribal police, carrying an image of Indians on horseback that harked back to dime novels and Saturday afternoon movies, had a remarkably long life beyond the Navajo reservation. It was first mentioned in the *New York Times* on March 15, 1934. Another short story appeared on April 22, 1934. On December 16, 1934, a third short story ran stating that the mounted police "are establishing an enviable record" and asserting that "unexcelled bravery and the ability to follow any kind of a trail anywhere make the Indians particularly valuable."[109] The *Literary Digest* also ran a story on July 14, 1934, citing *Indians at Work*, the Office of Indian Affairs publication.[110]

Thus, at a time when Navajos were wrestling with issues such as livestock reduction and far-reaching federal legislation, their images in two major mainstream publications were of noble savages, this time on horseback, or of silly and petty people who banished celebrities from their ranks. These lopsided portrayals were accomplished not only through the tone and language of the stories but, perhaps more significantly, by the selection of stories. To today's reader, such close examination of what were, after all, inconsequential stories, may seem trivial. But the examination makes an important point. Widely accepted journalistic practices can have the effect of reinforcing inaccurate images instead of dispelling them with facts.

NEWSWORTHY "WHITE" WAYS

If Indians were often portrayed as exotic, strange, and separate from white society, their display of "white" ways would be unusual and, therefore, newsworthy. This seemed to be the journalistic reasoning behind the selection of many brief newspaper stories.

For example, short articles in the *New York Times* reported that a Cherokee woman paid a $13.95 bill that was fifteen years old[111] and that "Emulating their white sisters, Ute squaws . . . are taking an interest in their personal appearance" by using "marcelles and permanent waves . . . along with manicures and plucked eyebrows."[112] A story with a Lac du Flambeau, Wisconsin, dateline reported that "Thoughtful redmen of the Chippewa Indian tribe here have decided to try the white man's magic [to attract] tourists" by setting up an advertising fund.[113]

When a Sioux group, frustrated over lack of federal action on its land claims, threatened to sell the Black Hills to Canada, the action was termed a "walkout" in a *New York Times* article. The article ended with the observation that the Sioux were "showing an aptitude for publicizing their cases in the same forceful manner now being used by other groups in other sections of the country."[114] When members of the Navajo Tribal Council decided to abolish twenty-nine Indian service jobs, they were described in the *Arizona Republic* as "wielding the economy ax with the skill and precision of their white brothers."[115]

When an Indian tribe was reported to have turned down government money, the story, conveying the image of Indians not only emulating white values of self-sufficiency but going further in acting on these values than many whites did, resonated widely. The story—of Menominees in Wisconsin refusing to accept $30,000 in public works funds for road construction—was reported in a number of distant papers from Springfield, Massachusetts, to Phoenix, Arizona. At least three wrote approving editorials. Typical was the *Springfield Republican*, which noted that the tribe was "setting an example to their white civilizers that is really embarrassing."[116]

If news is, by definition, what is unusual, then Indians using white techniques of self-beautification, advertising, publicity-generating walkouts, and economizing were newsworthy because they were not expected to behave in the same ways as the dominant culture. Native Americans who adopted the attitudes or accouterments of white culture were shown to be praiseworthy—and newsworthy.

STORY FORMS

In the 1930s, to a greater extent than today, the staple of journalistic writing was the straightforward, objective, hard news story. This was, ideally, an unbiased account of an event, organized in inverted pyramid fashion, that put the latest, most significant facts first. Because electronic journalism was in its infancy, it is safe to say most Americans learned first of events outside their immediate experience through the print press. A great deal of the news coverage of Native Americans in the 1930s was in the form of such straightforward news stories—accounts of the hearings in Washington as the Indian Reorganization Act made its way through Congress, reports of the Indian congresses and tribal councils, speeches and testimony by Collier and his opponents. Like much of the New Deal legislation gushing from Washington, what became the Indian Reorganization Act was revolutionary and complex. It had to compete for the attention of a press corps already struggling to cover the extraordinary outpouring of New Deal measures in the early years of the Roosevelt administration.

A great many articles about the Indian New Deal were straightforward news stories that reported details of legislation or charges and countercharges by politicians. These articles, both in the national and regional press, were hard news stories that merely related the unfolding of an event. Often, however, these news stories lacked any cultural context that would explain the effect of the measures on native peoples.

For example, the *New York Times* story on Senate passage of the Wheeler-Howard bill began, "A 'new deal' for more than 200,000 Indians, designed, according to President Roosevelt, to save the race from 'impending extinction,' was voted by the Senate today in the form of a bill to establish a $10 million revolving fund to make loans to Indian tribes." The story was heavy on measurable, provable facts such as the amount of money set aside for land and water rights and scholarships, rules for allowing Indians to enter the Indian service, and the like. It quoted Roosevelt that the bill was "a measure of justice that is long overdue."[117]

Missing, however, was any explanation of why Indians were on the verge of "extinction," how, exactly, the allotment system worked to their detriment, or what injustices they had suffered. The root revolutionary concept of the Wheeler-Howard bill, cultural pluralism, was not related. Nor was there any explanation of why previous policies of forced assimilation had been abandoned. For that matter, the considerable changes in the measure passed by the Senate from the original bill, which had been largely written by Collier, were not mentioned.[118]

Several weeks earlier, when the bill was in trouble in Congress, Roosevelt stepped in with a forceful letter to its sponsors calling for prompt passage.[119] The story that appeared in the *New York Times* quoted Roosevelt's letter and Senator Wheeler's response. But again, there was no background, no explanation of why the bill's passage was imperiled. Nor were Roosevelt's arguments for its passage explained.[120]

Newspapers, of course, are neither history books nor legal tomes. Even the nation's paper of record, the *New York Times*, has deadline and space considerations that work against including the kind of background material that would put these stories into their cultural context. More to the point, most news stories, particularly in papers such as the *New York Times* that prided themselves on their objectivity, were not supposed to get into fuzzy areas of interpretation that could lay them open to charges of injecting opinion into the news columns. So, stories about the Wheeler-Howard bill summarized the immediate events—the bill's passage, Roosevelt's letter—and left interpretation for other days and other parts of the paper, if it appeared at all. But the lack of explanation and context left readers of the news stories ignorant of why Indians needed a "new deal" anyway.

Similarly, a 1936 story listed the number of Indians and tribes that had voted to accept or reject the IRA but gave no explanation of the complex forces that led Indians to vote one way or another. The elections could just as well have been for suburban school boards for all the explanation provided in the story.[121]

At times, lack of explanation made stories nearly incomprehensible. A three-paragraph story in the *New York Times*, for example, about the Blackfeet tribe of Montana mentioned tribal membership requirements, self-government, land disputes, and conditions for accepting Collier's New Deal plans—all in 118 words.[122] The story, as it appeared, was almost nonsense.

The point here is not that some news stories were incomplete, but that the prevailing *form* of the straight news story virtually precluded the kind of explanation and background that would make stories about the Indian New Deal understandable. Not only that, but the imagery—or lack thereof—rendered Indians as interchangeable pawns in the New Deal political game. Their uniqueness and difference from other groups claiming the administration's attention, such as farmers or unemployed workers, was obliterated. This kind of factual fragmentation on the far-reaching social issues being addressed by the Roosevelt administration led to the call for more interpretative reporting. But as will be seen, interpretation, when applied to Native American stories, had its own perils.

The *New York Times* was not alone. Straightforward news stories in the local press were frequently short on cultural context also. Some articles on the Wheeler-Howard bill included a paragraph of description, though many did not, and others simply referred to it as the "Indian self-government act," an Indian "new deal," a "bill of rights" for Indians, or some similar journalistic shorthand. Few touched even remotely on the history and culture that would explain why a tribe or faction took the position it did.

POLITICAL BIAS IN NEWS STORIES

While the ideal of such straight news writing was to be objective and free from bias, in some publications anti-Roosevelt sentiment spilled off the editorial page into news columns, sometimes influencing coverage of Indians. An example was the *Muskogee Daily Phoenix*'s coverage of the Five Tribes' reaction to John Collier's legislative proposals, described earlier. Others came from the fiercely anti–New Deal *Chicago Tribune*, which put a decidedly negative spin on news stories describing Collier and his policies. Under the headline "3 NY Lawyers Direct Indian New Deal/Their Qualifications for Job Questioned," one story's lead began:

> Responsibility for shaping the Happy Hunting Ground policy of the New Deal, a term applied by critics to legislation which seeks to restore the tribal life of the American Indian, is in the hands of three New York lawyers who are not Indians. They are Nathan Margold, solicitor for the department of the Interior, and his assistants Felix Cohen and Melvin H. Siegel.[123]

The story, attributing much of its information to Flora Warren Seymour, the Chicago attorney who had been a member of the Board of Indian Commissioners, which Collier abolished, went on to describe how "one of this coterie of 'brain trusters' " did not know what alfalfa was used for nor the difference between range and dairy cattle. It described Collier as "a former publicist" without mentioning his work in Indian affairs. Finally, it quoted criticisms of the Wheeler-Howard bill by two Native Americans who "show an unwillingness to accept a sentimental return to the past."[124]

By framing the story as part of the ideological struggle over the New Deal, the *Tribune* story pushed Indians to a peripheral role, bringing instead to center stage Collier and his critics. If Indians had any image at all in the article, it was as victims of misguided government policies and ill-informed personnel.

INTERPRETATIVE STORIES

Despite the push for more interpretation, unadorned straight news writing was the journalistic norm of the time. News stories were not expected to stray into the descriptive feature realm, nor were they to interpret events in such a way as to lay the reporter open to criticism of presenting an opinion in the guise of news. However, as has been seen, press critics and journalism educators were increasingly calling on the press not only to report what was happening but to interpret its meaning and significance. Such interpretation would have been particularly important in coverage of the Indian New Deal because it involved such controversial and revolutionary notions. In fact a good many interpretative articles appeared, both in the national and local press. Some were balanced and gave sensitive explanations of Native American issues. But more were written from the point of view of—and often by—partisans on either side of the issue who employed a variety of images to get their points across.

The interest groups on both sides—with the important exception of the Indians themselves—had fairly good access to the press and sought to use it to lobby for their positions. Collier, a forceful and prolific writer, had a talent for publicity. He and his allies wrote numerous articles that appeared in the *New York Times* and national magazines promoting his policies.[125]

Virtually every attack by an opponent was answered by a pungently-worded reply over Collier's name. Collier also started a biweekly magazine for the Indian Bureau, *Indians at Work*, edited by Mary Heaton Vorse, a liberal writer.[126] It carried many favorable articles about Indians that were picked up by general circulation newspapers and magazines. Commonly the portrayals of Indians in these articles were in line with Collier's own romantic notions: Indians were often depicted in the noble savage mold as possessors of cultural and racial strengths that, once they were allowed to use them, would enable native people to thrive. Alternately, Indians were portrayed as degraded, robbed of their lands, religions, and cultures because of the forced assimilationist policies of the past.

The opponents of Collier's legislation—assimilationists, missionaries, and others who felt threatened by the bill's provisions—also were heard in general circulation publications as well as in the religious press.[127] In these articles the image of Indians was of simple, primitive folk whose "progress" toward "civilization" was being disrupted by social experimenters who wanted to send them back to the primeval existence from which they had recently emerged.

Indians' voices were heard in interpretative stories in quotes that illustrated writers' points, but it was whites who dominated the arguments on both sides.

Interpretative, balanced, truly explanatory articles were scarce. More plentiful were opinion articles, signed or unsigned, that appeared on both news and opinion pages. This suggests that, in the local papers scrutinized at least, the call by journalism educators for interpretation had not been heard, or at least was not reflected in the reporting of Indian stories.

DISCUSSION

Portrayals of Native Americans in the 1930s press reflected the political realities and legislation of the New Deal. Yet to a surprising extent, they reproduced the familiar imagery of the past, using nostalgia, sentimentality, romance, and humor, more than solid analysis or meaningful description. Indians began to be heard on their own terms as intelligent and informed spokespersons for their own causes, involved participants in events. But this image emerged unevenly and more in the local than the national press. Still, they were frequently spoken *for* or *about* by the articulate John Collier or some other "friend of the Indian."

Collier's revolutionary policies were fairly faithfully recounted in terse hard news stories. But these stories were frequently fragmented and so lacking in cultural context as to be meaningless by themselves. The push for interpretative articles in newspapers and the interpretation already appearing in the newly popular news magazines in the end served accurate portrayals of Indians no better than earlier journalistic forms. Other stories, short and inconsequential, fulfilled the journalistic need for variety and a change of pace, but frequently built and reinforced inaccurate images of Indians as lazy, drunken, exotic, naive, and ignorant. Native religious practices, particularly, suffered in the press, often being rendered as bizarre entertainment, somewhere between a circus act and a museum exhibit.

In the 1930s the public and government were being asked to think of Indians in new ways by respecting their traditional cultures. Non-Indians were required to deal with Indian groups on a new basis, as at least partially self-governing entities. Yet the imagery, the mythology surrounding Indians, remained surprisingly unchanged from earlier times. Thus, however much Indians' lives changed, their image, as depicted in the press, changed far less.

NOTES

1. Vera Connolly, "The End of a Long, Long Trail," *Good Housekeeping*, Apr. 1, 1934, 50–1.

2. *Daily Oklahoman*, Mar. 18, 1934, 4D.

3. *Muskogee (Oklahoma) Daily Phoenix*, Oct. 3, 1934, 12.

4. Quoted in Robert F. Berkhofer, Jr., *The White Man's Indian* (New York: Vintage Books, 1978), 183.

5. Francis Paul Prucha, *The Great Father* vol. 2 (Lincoln: University of Nebraska Press, 1984), 945.

6. Even before the New Deal, the failures of government Indian policies were becoming clear. In February 1928 the so-called Meriam Report amply documented the failures of allotment, education, and health policies. Its recommendations, among other things, called for allowing Indians the option of assimilating or remaining separate within their traditional cultures, a modest though notable departure from the orthodoxy of forced assimilation. Later Congressional hearings further documented the shortcomings of government administration. Though President Herbert Hoover sought to overhaul the Indian Bureau when he took office in 1929, there was little fundamental change. Institute for Government Research, Lewis Meriam, technical director, *The Problem of Indian Administration* (Baltimore: Johns Hopkins Press, 1928); Prucha, 790–813.

7. Brian W. Dippie, *The Vanishing American* (Middletown, Conn.: Wesleyan University Press, 1982), 305–306; Prucha, 917–918; Richard Weiss, "Ethnicity and Reform: Minorities and the Ambience of the Depression Years," *Journal of American History* 66, no. 3 (December 1979): 566–585.

8. For more detailed accounts of Collier and the Indian New Deal see Kenneth R. Philp, *John Collier's Crusade for Indian Reform* (Tucson: University of Arizona Press, 1977); Graham D. Taylor, *The New Deal and American Indian Tribalism* (Lincoln: University of Nebraska Press, 1980); Donald L. Parman, *The Navajos and the New Deal* (New Haven and London: Yale University Press, 1976); Dippie, 304–318; Prucha, 917–919, 940–1005, 1009–1012; Vine Deloria, Jr., and Clifford M. Lytle, *The Nations Within* (New York: Pantheon Books, 1984). What follows is intended as a summary rather than an exhaustive treatment.

9. Philp, 127.

10. Dippie, 309; Prucha, 945–948; Philp, 120–122.

11. Quoted in Prucha, 951–952; see also Philp, 131–133.

12. Frank Ernest Hill, "A New Pattern of Life for the Indian," *New York Times Magazine*, July 14, 1935, 10.

13. Ibid.

14. Ibid.

15. Maria L. Rogers and Edward J. Fitzgerald, "New Medicine for the Sick Indian," *Nation*, Mar. 21, 1934, 326.

16. Dippie, 310–311; Prucha, 957–958; Philp, 140–144; Rogers and Fitzgerald, 326–327; John Collier, "A Lift for the Forgotten Red Man, Too," *New York Times Magazine*, May 6, 1934, 10–11.

17. Philp, 145–149.

18. *Muskogee Daily Phoenix*, Mar. 25, 1934, 12B.

19. Philp, 176–183.

20. These and other criticisms of the original bill are detailed in Larry W. Burt, *Tribalism in Crisis: Federal Indian Policy, 1953–1961* (Albuquerque: University of New Mexico Press, 1982), 3, and Dippie, 311–313.

21. See, for example, Elaine Goodale Eastman, "Does Uncle Sam Foster Paganism?" *Christian Century*, Aug. 8, 1934, 1016–1018, and John Collier, "A Reply to Mrs. Eastman," *Christian Century*, Aug. 8, 1934, 1018–1020.

22. "Red Constitution," *Time*, Nov. 11, 1935, 11.

23. Early criticisms and concerns expressed at the Indian congresses are in Philp, 145–160, and Deloria and Lytle, 101–115.

24. Berkhofer, *White Man's Indian*, 184.

25. Dippie, 311–318; Philp, 158–163.

26. Willard Grosvenor Bleyer, "Journalism in the United States: 1933," *Journalism Quarterly*, X, no. 4 (December 1933): 296–301.

27. Ibid., 296.

28. Marion T. Marzolf, *Civilizing Voices: American Press Criticism, 1880–1950* (New York: Longman Publishing Group, 1991), 137–141.

29. Ibid., 122.

30. Kenneth E. Olson, "The Newspaper in Times of Social Change," *Journalism Quarterly* XII, no. 1 (March 1935): 10–11.

31. Ibid., 13.

32. Ibid., 17, 19.

33. Curtis D. MacDougall, *Interpretative Reporting* (New York: The Macmillan Company, 1938), v.

34. Ibid., 14.

35. Graham J. White, *FDR and the Press* (Chicago: University of Chicago Press, 1979), 129–131.

36. MacDougall, 52–53.

37. Ibid., 200–202.

38. Ibid., 231–241, 385–404.

39. Gene Burd, "Minorities in Reporting Texts: Before and After the 1968 Kerner Report," *Mass Comm Review* 15, nos. 2 and 3 (1988): 45–60, 68.

40. *Rapid City (South Dakota) Daily Journal*, Mar. 1, 1934, 1.

41. *Rapid City Daily Journal*, Mar. 2, 1934, 1.

42. *Rapid City Daily Journal*, Mar. 2, 1934, 1, 2; Mar. 3, 1934, 1.

43. *Rapid City Daily Journal, Mar. 3, 1934,* 1. See also *Rapid City Daily Journal,* Mar. 5, 1934, 1, 5.

44. "Pow Wow," *Time,* Mar. 12, 1934, 15.

45. Ibid.

46. "A New Deal for the American Indian," *Literary Digest,* Apr. 7, 1934, 21.

47. The magazine was titled *News-Week* until 1937, when its name was changed to *Newsweek.* Theodore Peterson, *Magazines in the Twentieth Century* (Urbana: University of Illinois Press, 1956), 302–303.

48. Ibid., 298–303.

49. James Playsted Wood, *Magazines in the United States, (Second Edition)* (New York: The Ronald Press Company, 1956), 205.

50. "Red Constitution," *Time,* Nov. 11, 1935, 11.

51. "Indians: Tribes Losing Ground, U.S. Kicks Their Claim Around," *News-Week,* Dec. 19, 1936, 16.

52. Mary Heaton Vorse, "Helping The Indians to Help Themselves," *Scholastic,* Oct. 24, 1936, 3–4, 16.

53. Cash Asher, "Our Indian Youths Have A New Deal," *New York Times,* Aug. 5, 1934, sec. VIII, p. 4.

54. Flora Warren Seymour, "Thunder Over the Southwest," *Saturday Evening Post,* Apr. 1, 1939, 23, 71–72, 74, 76.

55. Alice Booth, "I Discover Some Americans," *Good Housekeeping,* Nov., 1936, 48–49, 227–229.

56. Ibid.

57. For example, the *Literary Digest* of Aug. 12, 1933, 33, headlined a story about the Osage losing their oil wealth in the depression "Poor Lo Rich No Longer." The phrase was used to make a contrast in a *Newsweek* story headed "Lo, the Modern Indian" Aug. 29, 1938, 13.

58. An Essay on Man (1773–1774: Epistle I) quoted in Robert F. Berkhofer, Jr., "White Conceptions of Indians," in Wilcomb E. Washburn, ed., *History of Indian-White Relations,* vol. 4 of *Handbook of North American Indians,* ed. William C. Sturtevant (Washington: Smithsonian Institution, 1988), 528. Berkhofer writes that " 'Lo the poor Indian' is always in reference to Indians who are taken advantage of or pitiable in some way."

59. *Literary Digest,* Aug. 12, 1933, 33.

60. *New York Times,* Aug. 5, 1935, 13.

61. *New York Times,* Nov. 15, 1936, sec. XII, p. 10.

62. *New York Times,* July 15, 1934, sec. IV, p. 7.

63. Owen P. White, "Red Men and White, *Collier's,* Mar. 17, 1934, 10–11, 49–50. See also Owen P. White, "Scalping the Indian," *Collier's,* Mar. 3, 1934, 10–11, 32, 35.

64. *Arizona Republic,* Aug. 12, 1936, sec. 2, p. 1.

65. *Santa Fe New Mexican,* June 26, 1935, 1.

66. *Rapid City Daily Journal,* Mar. 5, 1934, 1.

67. *Daily Oklahoman,* Sept. 16, 1934, 6A.

68. *News-week,* Sept. 22, 1934, 13.

69. *New York Times,* Aug. 16, 1936, sec. X, p. 4.

70. Ibid.

71. *Arizona Republic,* Mar. 13, 1934, 1.

72. Berger was described as "the star of the staff" of the *Times*. See Gay Talese, *The Kingdom and the Power* (New York: World Publishing Company, 1969), 223.

73. Meyer Berger, "Unvanishing Americans: The Hardy Navajos," *New York Times Magazine*, June 6, 1937, 9, 28, 31.

74. *Arizona Republic*, Mar. 16, 1934, 2.

75. *Chicago Tribune*, Apr. 17, 1933, 1.

76. Constance Lindsay Skinner, "Our Children's Indian Heritage," *Parents Magazine*, Oct. 1933, 16–17, 54–55.

77. Marius Barbeau, "The Disappearance of the Red Man's Culture," *Scientific American*, Jan., 1933, 22–24.

78. Anna Nolan Clark, "Indians to Gallup," *Reader's Digest*," Aug., 1938, 110–112.

79. *Arizona Republic*, June 28, 1936, sec. 2, p. 2.

80. *Arizona Republic*, July 2, 1933, 1.

81. *Chicago Tribune*, July 30, 1933, part I, p. 7.

82. *New York Times*, May 15, 1936, 1.

83. *New York Times*, Sept. 12, 1936, 34.

84. *Muskogee Daily Phoenix*, Sept. 27, 1934, 1.

85. *New York Times*, Aug. 16, 1934, 2.

86. *New York Times*, Aug. 15, 1937, 2.

87. *New York Times*, Aug. 21, 1934, 2, and Aug. 24, 1934, 2.

88. *Muskogee Daily Phoenix*, Mar. 13, 1934, 5.

89. *Muskogee Daily Phoenix*, Mar. 18, 1934, 1.

90. *Muskogee Daily Phoenix*, Mar. 13, 1934, 5.

91. *Muskogee Daily Phoenix*, Mar. 22, 1934, 5.

92. *Daily Oklahoman*, Oct. 18, 1934, 9.

93. *Santa Fe New Mexican*, Mar. 16, 1934, 2.

94. *Muskogee Daily Phoenix*, Apr. 22, 1934, 1, 4.

95. Ibid.

96. *Arizona Republic*, July 4, 1933, 1.

97. *Arizona Republic*, Oct. 31, 1933, 4.

98. *Santa Fe New Mexican*, Jan. 15, 1934, 1.

99. *New York Times*, Dec. 26, 1937, sec. II, p. 2.

100. *Arizona Republic*, Mar. 16, 1934, 1.

101. *Santa Fe New Mexican*, June 27, 1936, 2.

102. *New York Times*, June 28, 1936, 3; *Arizona Republic*, June 28, 1936, sec. 2, p. 2.

103. *Arizona Republic*, June 28, 1936, sec. 2, p. 2.

104. Information on the tribal council meetings is in Philp, 150–151 and Parman, 52–58. For information about the resolution concerning honorary tribal members, see the *Santa Fe New Mexican*, Mar. 14, 1934, 8, and Mar. 15, 1934, 8; the *Arizona Republic*, Mar. 15, 1934, 1, 4; and the *New York Times*, Mar. 15, 1934, 2.

105. *Santa Fe New Mexican*, Mar. 13, 1934, 2.

106. *New York Times*, Mar. 15, 1934, 2.

107. *Santa Fe New Mexican*, Mar. 15, 1934, 8.

108. *Chicago Daily News*, Mar. 15, 1934, 4.

109. *New York Times*, Dec. 16, 1934, sec. IV, p. 6.

110. "The Navajo Mounted Police," *Literary Digest*, July 14, 1934, 32.

111. *New York Times*, Dec. 13, 1934, 23.

112. *New York Times*, Dec. 30, 1934, sec. IV, p. 7.

113. *New York Times*, Sept. 13, 1936, sec. IV, p. 7.

114. *New York Times*, Sept. 5, 1937, sec. IV, p. 10.

115. *Arizona Republic*, July 9, 1933, 1.

116. Quoted in *Literary Digest*, Aug. 26, 1933, 33. Other articles were in the *New York Times*, July 31, 1933, 2, and, two years later, the *Arizona Republic*, June 15, 1935, sec. 2, p. 8.

117. *New York Times*, June 13, 1934, 6. A short, four-paragraph version of the same story appeared in the *Chicago Tribune*. See *Chicago Tribune*, June 13, 1934, 9.

118. According to one historian, the bill signed by Roosevelt "bore little resemblance to Collier's original proposal." See Philp, 155–159.

119. Philp, 158.

120. *New York Times*, Apr. 29, 1934, 34.

121. *New York Times*, Mar. 15, 1936, sec. IV, p. 12.

122. *New York Times*, Mar. 18, 1934, sec. IV, p. 1.

123. *Chicago Tribune*, May 16, 1934, 15.

124. Ibid.

125. See, among others, John Collier, "A Lift for the Forgotten Red Man, Too," *New York Times Magazine*, May 6, 1934, 10–11; Walter V. Woehlke, "The Battle for Grass," *Saturday Evening Post*, Nov. 25, 1933, 10–11, 79–81, 84; Willard W. Beatty, "New Schools for Old," *Scholastic*, Oct. 24, 1936, 19–20, 28; Mary Heaton Vorse, "Helping The Indians to Help Themselves," *Scholastic*, Oct. 24, 1936, 3–4, 16. Woehlke, a confidant of Collier, was a field representative for the Indian Bureau; Beatty was director of education in the Office of Indian Affairs, and Vorse edited *Indians at Work*.

126. Philp, 122; *Scholastic*, Oct. 24, 1936, 4.

127. See, among others, Seymour, 23, 71–72, 74, 76; Eastman, 1016–1018.

4

World War II: Braves on the Warpath

When the United States entered World War II, Native Americans were for the first time eligible for the draft. Though some ten thousand had served in World War I, most were not citizens and almost all were volunteers.[1] Indeed, Congress granted Indians citizenship in 1924 largely as a result of the wartime service of those men.[2] Even as citizens, though, Indians' legal status was anomalous because they were also wards of the federal government. In at least three states they could not vote in 1942.[3] Nevertheless, thousands of Indians entered military service, either as draftees or volunteers. Though a precise figure was hard to come by, one author estimated that by the end of the war about twenty-five thousand Native American men had served in the military. In addition, "several hundred" women served as nurses or in the women's auxiliary services—the Wacs and the Waves.[4]

Though there had been calls for creating all-Indian units, War Department officials discouraged the practice. So, unlike African Americans, most Native Americans were integrated into all areas of the military.[5] (An exception was the all-Indian training platoons for Navajos established so that those who failed English literacy tests could serve anyway. After learning some English, they were integrated with whites.[6]) Additional thousands of Indians left their reservations to work in war-related occupations as nurses or defense plant workers. For many, this was the first time they had left the reservation or had extensive contact with the white world.

The wartime service of Native Americans had far-reaching implications. For one thing, news coverage of the exploits of a few Indians brought them to the forefront of American consciousness. Among them:

- Major General Clarence L. Tinker, an Osage who was one of the first Indians to win fame in combat. Tinker, commander of the Hawaiian Air Force after Pearl Harbor, was lost in action during the Battle of Midway. "Ignoring the dangers and refusing to assign to anyone else the task, he personally led the squadrons of bombers which supplied the American spearhead of the attack."[7]
- The Navajo "code talkers," marines who used their native language, embellished with new military terms, to transmit secret messages during combat in the Pacific. The code was never broken by the Japanese.[8]
- Ira Hamilton Hayes, "the most famous Indian soldier of the Second World War."[9] Hayes, a Pima marine, was photographed with five others raising the American flag on Mount Suribachi during the battle of Iwo Jima. The dramatic shot, which won photographer Joe Rosenthal a Pulitzer Prize, made celebrities and heroes of Hayes and the other two men who survived. For the self-effacing Hayes, the notoriety arguably contributed to his alcoholism and death at the age of thirty-two in 1955.[10] His life and death came to symbolize both the bravery of Indian servicemen and the perils they encountered when they were plucked from their reservations and tossed into the white world.[11]

But Native Americans' war service had a larger impact on both Indians and whites. Indians' first-hand contact with the world beyond the reservation opened new vistas of what life could hold—for good or ill. Whites who served with Indians in the military or in defense plants—or who read about their exploits in the press—gained a new awareness of contemporary Native Americans.[12]

Some opponents of the policies of John Collier, the energetic and controversial commissioner of Indian affairs who served from 1933 to 1945, used the image of Indians' heroic wartime service to undermine his policies. Collier's Indian New Deal sought to preserve native cultures and "group life" by ending the loss of reservation lands to whites, giving Indians a greater measure of self-determination, and making education more relevant to native cultures and communities, among other measures. Collier's opponents argued that these policies amounted to segregating Indians in rural reservation-ghettos and discouraging them from assimilating with white society. They pointed to Native Americans' heroic wartime service as an argument that native people should be "freed" from federal ties and could succeed on their own in the white world.[13]

At the time of World War II, Native Americans, most of whom lived on isolated, rural reservations, numbered fewer than 400,000 in a national population of some 132 million. Though the war brought increased contact, there was still scant opportunity for most Euro-Americans to form opinions of Indians based on first-hand knowledge. Thus the news media had both the opportunity and challenge to provide accurate information for audiences to weigh against the prevailing myths and stereotypes of Native Americans.

IMAGES OF INDIANS IN THE WARTIME PRESS

In the 1940s press, the well-worn good Indian or noble savage image became the good Indian warrior, who used his superior gifts of hunting, tracking, bravery, and endurance against the nation's enemies. A related image was the Indian as loyal patriot. This image occasionally required some elaborate rationalization because Indians' mistreatment at the hands of the government and white society was so well known. On the homefront, Indians-as-patriots were portrayed as loyal supporters of the war effort who would sacrifice greatly for their country.

Another frequent image was that of the ancient, exotic Indian who spoke a secret language (as in the Navajo code talkers) and performed strange religious rituals to assure success in battle. Elements of the "bad Indian" image, the cunning, savage warrior so vividly depicted in Western movies, took on a heroic aspect as that perceived cunning and savagery was now being used to defend America from its enemies.

The Good Indian Warrior

In World War II, Indians were portrayed as patriotic warriors who were eager to fight to defend the country that had brought them to the brink of physical and cultural extinction. Article after article repeated and embellished the image of innate warriors and scouts who were instinctively superior fighters. Magazine and newspaper stories generalized to all Indians an impressive list of bellicose attributes: "American Indians are crack marksmen. They excel as scouts and trailsmen and lookouts," wrote Richard L. Neuberger.[14] "A natural fighter, tough and self-reliant," added Elizabeth Shepley Sergeant in the *New Republic*.[15] An article in *American Mercury* asserted that "Indians have muscles that endure the most rigorous strain . . . Their sensory perceptions are very highly developed, making them the perfect scouts, and they are unexcelled in the ability to sustain themselves in fighting condition on minimum water and rations."[16]

Secretary of the Interior Harold L. Ickes wrote in *Collier's* that "The Indian . . . has endurance, rhythm, a feeling for timing, co-ordination, sense perception, an uncanny ability to get over any sort of terrain at night, and, better than all else, an enthusiasm for fighting."[17]

An article in *Reader's Digest* said:

> The red soldier is tough. Usually he has lived outdoors all his life, and lived by his senses; he is a natural Ranger. He takes to Commando fighting with gusto. . . . At ambushing, scouting, signaling, sniping, [Indians are] peerless. Some can smell a snake yards away and hear the faintest movement; all endure thirst and lack of food better than the average white man.[18]

The *New York Times* reported that Indians who were specially trained for jungle fighting "employed the wiles of their ancestors and the Japanese simply could not take it."[19] An article in the *Arizona Republic* began, "Hang onto your scalps, Hitler, Hirohito and Mussolini, for twenty-nine red-blooded young Americans are on the warpath . . . ready to cut fancy capers in this conflict. Uncle Sam's first all-American platoon—twenty-nine full-blooded Navajo Indian warriors—has ended Marine corps training and is ready for assignment."[20]

Indians' many attributes as warriors were summed up in a quote from a major who said, "They are the best damn' soldiers in the Army."[21]

Indians were also portrayed as superior tacticians who, for instance, had devised the blitzkrieg. "The redskin . . . invented—or employed—the blitzkrieg," wrote Stanley Vestal, an expert on Plains Indians. "Being well mounted and extremely mobile, the Indian was usually able to outrun his enemy, and therefore seldom attacked unless he had the advantage of numbers and surprise." Vestal also wrote that white frontiersmen learned another lesson from Indians applicable to World War II: "From such Indians, the Plainsmen learned that appeasement was fatal, and that the only warfare worthy of the name was offensive warfare." Thus not only was the Indian a "realistic soldier; he knew that war meant killing, and he never gave quarter or expected it," but he taught whites tactics and attitudes that were useful on the twentieth-century battlegrounds in Europe and the Pacific.[22] Vestal, as had others before him, generalized from a particular tribe and moment in history to all Indians, presumably, in their three-century struggle against Euro-Americans.

Though many of the articles cited, particularly those from magazines, went on to give examples of brave feats by individual Indians and to identify them by tribe, all of the three hundred or so disparate tribes and groups were swept into the overall generalizations. If such descriptions sounded like racial stereotyping echoing that of Hitler, the point was not made in the articles. Only one author hinted there might be hyperbole, if not stereotyping, in the repeated warrior images: "The differences between Indians and other soldiers . . . may be exaggerated. The Indians themselves are amused at being classified as persons apart."[23]

Other magazine and newspaper articles contained no such qualifications. Rather, they baldly asserted, without evidence or attribution, that Indians as a group were exceptional fighters. The ancestry of such a notion on the part of whites was not hard to discern. These modern fighters were, in the white imagination, the descendants of the eighteenth- and nineteenth-century warriors who terrorized settlers, defeated Custer, and spawned a genre of Western movies. This is not to say Native-American servicemen did not acquit themselves bravely during the war. They undoubtedly did. Some have even suggested that Indians were given more frequent combat assignments because they were believed to have a "warrior instinct."[24] The point is that, by characterizing Indians exclusively as superwarriors, the press depictions reinforced a stereotype that resonated far beyond the individual acts of heroism that took place.

Ira Hayes

In the case of Ira Hayes, it was a news image that changed his life and quite possibly doomed him. It was chance—not valor—that put Hayes in the photograph shot by Joe Rosenthal on Mount Suribachi. That twist of fate apparently weighed heavily on the marine when he was subsequently brought home to boost war bond sales. He felt he was letting down the buddies who sacrificed more than he:

> [Hayes] was ordered to return stateside [for] the nationwide bond selling tour. He was frightened of the publicity. . . . He was nervous and apprehensive about the future. . . . Now they were calling him a hero. A hero for what? He only helped to raise a flag. He felt ashamed because of all this adulation being showered upon him.[25]

His conflicts, however, did not fit in the scenario he had been chosen to play:

> Because he was an Indian, Hayes received extra attention. His struggle to raise the Stars and Stripes appealed to the sentiments of white America—Hollywood could not have created a better advertisement of a people united against a common foe. . . . [H]e personified the hoped-for assimilation of Indians into the mainstream of American life.[26]

The shy, inarticulate young man was ill-equipped to deal with the unrelenting attention thrust on him by an admiring press and public. This shyness was noted sympathetically by a newspaper in his native Arizona: "The raw courage that helped a full-blood Pima Indian lad fight the battle of Iwo Jima and raise the Stars and Stripes over Mt. Suribachi failed him today when one thousand tribesmen honored him. Pfc. Ira H. Hayes . . . bashfully declined to speak at a deeply religious ceremony arranged at his homecoming today."[27]

The same paper in an editorial linked Hayes' bravery to a tribal warrior heritage. While describing Pimas as "peacefully inclined, industrious and friendly," the editorial went on to say, "[T]he Pima fought back when attacked by the marauding Apache. He acted as scout and guide for white troops. His ability as a warrior is written in many a frontier record. Now . . . Pfc. Hayes writes an added page into the saga of his tribe."[28]

In other press accounts, Hayes and the two other survivors were portrayed in headline-ese as "Iwo Heroes" or "Flag Heroes of Iwo Jima." The trio were paraded around the country, reenacting the flag-raising at bond drives as thousands cheered.[29]

Stories about the bond tour portrayed all three survivors—Hayes, Pvt. Rene Gagnon, and Pharmacist's Mate John Bradley—as heroes, but only

Hayes was always described as an Indian. The others were identified by their home towns. When the Congress of American Indians feted Hayes at a luncheon in Chicago, the *Daily News* described him as a "redskin hero of World War II."[30] Thus Hayes, tormented by guilt at becoming a celebrity when so many of his comrades had died, was additionally burdened by being made a symbol of the stereotypical Indian warrior. He was not just Ira Hayes, but Ira Hayes, "full-blooded American Indian."

Indian Enlistments

Collier, a consummate publicist, portrayed Indians as eager to fight for the nation that had slaughtered, demoralized, and pauperized them. Such a depiction, presumably, would ratify the benefits of his controversial policies as commissioner of Indian affairs. Thus Indians who were patriotic and eager to join the war effort would demonstrate that his policies of cultural pluralism were indeed helping to bring Indians into the mainstream, rather than trapping them in traditional cultures. "Strange as it may seem, the Indians have responded earnestly and even enthusiastically from the challenge of the war," he wrote.[31]

The number of Indian enlistees in the armed forces in 1942, while relatively small, "represents a larger proportion than any other element of our population," he continued.[32] This statement, which may have been true only of the first rush of enlistments after Pearl Harbor, was repeated in a number of other articles, thus adding to the image of Indians as eager, patriotic warriors. Later scholars, looking at Native American participation over the length of the war, observed that "the Indians' role in the military scarcely stands out."[33] But during the war years, the image of Indians as eager enlistees resonated widely.

Writing in the *Saturday Evening Post*, Richard L. Neuberger declared that Indians had "more voluntary enlistments than any other population group." He cited military officials as saying that "had the percentage of volunteers been as high in the rest of the country as among the Indians, there would have been no need for Selective Service."[34] Neuberger made the same point in an earlier article in the *New York Times*.[35] In the *New Republic* Elizabeth Shepley Sergeant wrote that "a large proportion" of Indians going into the armed forces were enlistees. "The Indian was hell-bent, as soon as the draft started, to join up," she wrote.[36] "The Amerinds [American Indians] have put 15,000 braves into our fighting forces—more per capita than any other racial group in the country, white, yellow or black," wrote Donald Culross Peattie in the *Reader's Digest*.[37] "Indians lead the rest of the country in percentage of volunteers for the armed forces and in purchase of War Bonds," a *New York Times* article began.[38]

Although late in the war an article by Interior Secretary Harold L. Ickes put the enlistment figures more modestly ("In enlistments, [Indians] equal the per capita contribution of any racial group"[39]), the earlier impression refused to die. "[Indians] are making contributions to our war effort far out of proportion to their numbers," wrote Burnet Hershey in the *American Mercury* late in 1944.[40] A 1945 *New York Times* story said that "out of the racial minority groups in the United States the American Indian is making the largest per capita contribution to winning the war," attributing the statement to the president of the National Congress of American Indians.[41]

The overall impression readers of these articles were apt to get was that all Indians, regardless of tribe or geographic origins, had racial characteristics that made them unusually good fighters who were eager to jump into the fray against the Axis. The centuries-old image of the Indian as bloodthirsty warrior, embellished in Western movies, was thus resurrected to suit the new circumstances of the war. Though it could strike today's readers as contradictory that such wholesale racial generalizing took place at a time when the Allies were fighting against totalitarians who engaged in derogatory stereotyping of Jews and other minorities, the point does not seem to have been made in the 1940s press.

The Loyal Patriot Indian

Indians were depicted as examples to other colonial peoples in their loyalty and eagerness to fight on behalf of their colonizers: "Our Indians are an important symbol to colonial peoples all over the world," wrote Richard L. Neuberger in *Asia and the Americas*. "[O]ur Indians . . . regard the war with hope. They believe it will lead to more opportunity and less inequalities for the people of China, India, South America and the island nations, and that in any such readjustment the American Indian will benefit, too."[42] This theme was elaborated on to depict Indians as true and original democrats who naturally would be moved to fight on the side of the democracies. Collier actually used the Indians' fight against whites who tried to extinguish their cultures as a rationale explaining why Native Americans were now fighting for their former enemies:

> It may not be too great a stretch of the imagination to suggest that the Indians have identified the struggle of democracies the world over with their own struggle of the last century. It may be that they see in a victory of the democracies a guarantee that they too shall be permitted to live their own lives.[43]

This image of Indians as patriots who were willing to overlook their mistreatment at the hands of whites to fight the totalitarian enemy was heightened when it was reported that the Nazis had predicted—incorrectly—that Indians would revolt if asked to fight.[44] "No Indian loyalties are divided. They were amused at attempts of some Axis agents to foment an Indian 'revolt' against their 'oppressors,' " wrote Burnet Hershey in the *American Mercury*.[45]

Stories of Indians who resisted the draft, which might have detracted from their patriotic image, did not figure prominently in national magazine articles though they were reported in local and national newspapers. Instances that were widely reported involved the Papago (now Tohono O'odham) tribe of Arizona and members of the Tuscarora and Onondaga tribes of the Iroquois Confederacy of New York state. In these cases, those resisting the draft did so because they did not recognize the authority of the United States to force them to serve. None of the Indians was portrayed as not wishing to fight.[46]

More prevalent were images of Indians on the homefront, doing their bit for the war effort. Inspirational stories abounded: of a Navajo family who brought the reservation superintendent $350 in a cigar box for defense bonds;[47] of the Navajo former tribal chairman who collected $300 for the Red Cross from fellow tribesmen in the form of "a sack of corn, a quarter of beef or mutton, or a rug";[48] of the Crow tribal council that voted to turn over the reservation's buffalo, oil, coal, and mineral resources to the government;[49] of Chippewa women forming rifle brigades to combat any enemy invasion;[50] of the Colville tribe that postponed a lawsuit against the government "for the duration"; and of the Columbia River fishermen who set aside a portion of the income from their salmon catch for the servicemen.[51]

Headlines over small stories in the *New York Times* conveyed the image of Indians as patriots: "California Indians Support War,"[52] "Crow Indians Offer All,"[53] "Shoshones Buy War Bonds,"[54] "Indians to Aid Bond Sale,"[55] "Indians Aid War Effort,"[56] "Indians Real Patriots."[57]

Arizona papers carried articles in a similar vein. Among them: "Navajo Assist In War Effort";[58] "Navajo Show Value In War Plants, As Fighting Men";[59] "Navajo Family Helps In War";[60] "Indians Hurry To Draft Day";[61] "Papago Reservation Exceeds Bond Quota By 600 Percent."[62]

All of these vignettes, some of which were repeated several times in different publications, contributed to the image of Indians as not only fierce warriors but also loyal patriots on the homefront, sacrificing greatly for the war effort. In the context of World War II, they were good Indians because they were allied with whites against a common enemy. Indians were folded into the national propaganda effort to rally support for the war.

This is not to suggest that Indians were not patriotic supporters of the war effort. The point to be made is how this patriotism was publicized in the mainstream press. In short, Indians were depicted as part of the united national effort to win the war.

The Ancient, Exotic Indian

The selection of language and descriptive details in stories often contributed to the image of Indians as some exotic amalgam of museum exhibit and circus act. In so doing, articles often trivialized and distorted, for instance, native religious practices.

A 1942 *Newsweek* article on an Indian radio station began, "Decked in gay red shirt and with braided hair reaching to his belt, the chief stomped his feet to the thump of tom-toms and led his tribesmen in haunting chants. They sang the raiding songs of their ancestors, brought up to date with references to Pearl Harbor." The article, about a Comanche war ceremonial broadcast on the radio, was laced with references to "an old-time scalping song," "war whooping," and "fuss and feathers."[63]

While superficially accurate, by leaving out the larger context of the place of such ceremonies—indeed, the place of ritual warfare—in Comanche life, the article presented the familiar image of "redskins" "on the warpath," though this time on behalf of Uncle Sam. The article said nothing about the tradition of warfare in Plains Indian life in which feats of individual bravery ("counting coup") rather than wholesale slaughter were valued. Nor did it explain that scalp-taking was widely used by whites also.[64]

Similarly, short items about Plains Indians performing the Sun Dance, a ceremony central to their religion, contained no background or context that would explain the ritual's place in Plains Indian life. For example, one single-paragraph item began, "Sioux braves, committed to forty-eight hours of rigorous dancing without food, set up their Sun Dance pole near here on the hot prairie today to make medicine against the Axis and pray for safe return of their own warriors."[65]

The item, typical of several that appeared in newspapers,[66] made no mention of the place of the ritual in traditional Plains culture or the fact that this religious observance was banned by the government until the 1930s. No one can realistically expect that one- or two-paragraph snippets culled from wire service dispatches would even begin to interpret the complex belief systems of Plains tribes. Nonetheless, the appearance of these short, unexplained items contributed to the overall image of Indians as exotic people who worshipped strange, pagan gods by means of outlandish ceremonies. By selecting such stories, thereby denoting them as news, the press contributed to the image of Indians as ancient and exotic beings.

The popular war correspondent Ernie Pyle, in one of his last dispatches before he was killed in the Pacific, wrote with respect of Navajo marines performing religious ceremonies prior to the landing at Okinawa:

> Before the convoy left . . . the Navajos . . . put on a ceremonial dance. The Red Cross furnished some colored cloth and paint to stain their faces and they made up the rest of their Indian costumes from chicken feathers, sea shells, coconuts, empty ration cans, and rifle cartridges. Then they did their own native ceremonial chants and dances out there under the tropical palm trees with several thousand marines as a grave audience. In their chant they asked the great gods in the sky to sap the Japanese of their strength. . . . They put the finger of weakness on the Japs, and they ended their ceremonial chant by singing the Marine Corps song in Navajo.[67]

Though the dispatch did not explain the traditions or beliefs that underlay the ceremony, Pyle's sensitive handling of the subject, and reporting the singing of the Marine Corps song in Navajo, linked Indians to the larger group effort, rather than setting them apart. It dignified the observance, rather than trivializing it.

Though the Navajo code talkers were the most celebrated of the Native Americans who used their tribal languages as codes, others, including Oneidas, Chippewas, Sac and Fox, and Comanches were assigned to similar signal corps work.[68] The enthusiastic stories of Indians using their native languages as codes to baffle the enemy conveyed dual messages. On the one hand, Indians such as the Navajo code talkers were portrayed positively as making unique contributions to the Allied victory. But a more subtle point made by the stories was that these Indians were a people apart, so removed from mainstream civilization that few outside their group even recognized their language. Thus, Indians were portrayed as both a part of mainstream America (aiding the war effort) and a separate, alien group (speaking an unknown language) simultaneously.

DISCUSSION

Overwhelmingly, Indians who served in World War II were portrayed in the press as the quintessential braves on the warpath. The old image of the bloodthirsty savage was transformed into that of a noble warrior for the Allied cause. The stereotypical notions of Indians as implacable fighters, unusual in their daring and endurance, were transplanted to the twentieth-century global conflict. In addition to elaborating and reinforcing the warrior image, Indians were also portrayed as exotic beings who practiced ancient ceremonies. Tribal warrior traditions and religious practices were briefly reported, often without context, so their religious setting was lost or trivialized. Indians' homefront contributions to the war were portrayed in a positive light that made them out to be unswervingly patriotic and loyal to the American cause.

Without doubt Native Americans served bravely and patriotically, both in battle and at home. However, the positive and enthusiastic images in the press may have also conveyed the image that all Indians were ready and eager for assimilation into postwar white society when this was not the case. As historian Donald Fixico wrote:

> Unfortunately, the Indians' dedication and involvement during the war was not an accurate barometer of their readiness for assimilation that later proved detrimental to them. The public supported the view that the war experience had sufficiently introduced Indians to mainstream society, a view that added to the momentum for Native American assimilation. . . . Despite the beliefs of the public and the government, Indians did not readily assimilate into mainstream society.[69]

Nevertheless, the images of Indian bravery and patriotism were used by whites who promoted policies aimed at withdrawing federal support and services from the tribes.[70] For example, Oswald Garrison Villard, writing in the *Christian Century*, took note of Indian wartime exploits and asserted that "there is a movement among them and their friends" seeking "an entirely new status" for Indians. This movement, Villard wrote, "nowise desires to destroy (Indian cultures) but only to build up." Nevertheless, the thrust of the article was a strongly worded argument for assimilation.[71] Another article advocating the withdrawal of federal services from Indian tribes was pegged on the supposed dissatisfaction of returning servicemen with what the author viewed as the paternalistic policies of Collier and the New Deal.[72]

The eventual result of the movement to "free" Indians from federal wardship was the infamous "termination" policies of the 1950s that caused economic and social dislocation for a number of tribes (see next chapter). The press' image of Indians as eager and patriotic participants in the war effort thus contributed to the postwar movement to withdraw government support from tribes, a policy that was detrimental to many native people and groups.

NOTES

1. Tom Holm, "Fighting a White Man's War: The Extent and Legacy of American Indian Participation in World War II," in Peter Iverson, ed., *The Plains Indians of the Twentieth Century* (Norman: University of Oklahoma Press, 1985), 151.

2. Alison R. Bernstein, *American Indians and World War II* (Norman: University of Oklahoma Press, 1991), 22.

3. John Collier, "The Indian in a Wartime Nation," *Annals of the American Academy of Political and Social Science* 223 (Sept. 1942): 29.

4. Bernstein, 35.

5. Ibid., 23–24, 40–41.

6. Ibid., 43.

7. Collier, 30; Richard L. Neuberger, "The American Indian Enlists," *Asia and the Americas* 42 (Nov. 1942): 630.

8. Murray Marder, "Navajo Code Talkers," *Marine Corps Gazette*, reprinted in *Indians in the War* (Chicago: United States Bureau of Indian Affairs, 1945), 25–27; see also, *New York Times*, Sept., 19, 1945, 9; *Arizona Star*, Aug. 14, 1982, n.p.

9. Bernstein, 49.

10. This argument is made in Albert Hemingway, *Ira Hayes, Pima Marine* (Lanham, Md.: University Press of America, 1988), 129–159; see also Donald L. Fixico, *Termination and Relocation: Federal Indian Policy, 1945–1960* (Albuquerque: University of New Mexico Press, 1986), 3–4.

11. Holm, 155.

12. Fixico, 14.

13. Ibid.; see also O. K. Armstrong, "Set the American Indians Free!" *Reader's Digest*, Aug. 1945, 47–52.

14. Neuberger, "American Indian Enlists," 630.

15. Elizabeth Shepley Sergeant, "The Indian Goes to War," *New Republic*, Nov. 30, 1942, 708.

16. Burnet Hershey, "Indians on the Warpath Again," *American Mercury*, Oct., 1944, 478.

17. Harold L. Ickes, "Indians Have a Name for Hitler," *Collier's*, Jan. 15, 1944, 58.

18. Donald Culross Peattie, "Braves on the Warpath," *Reader's Digest*, July 1943, 79.

19. *New York Times*, Jan. 19, 1944, 3.

20. *Arizona Republic*, July 5, 1942, sec. 2, p. 1.

21. Ickes, 58.

22. Stanley Vestal, "The Plains Indian and the War," *Saturday Review of Literature*, May 16, 1942, 9–10.

23. Hershey, 278.

24. Bernstein, 61.

25. Hemingway, 129–130.

26. Bernstein, 51.

27. *Arizona Star*, May 2, 1945, 16.

28. *Arizona Star*, Apr. 16, 1945, 8.

29. See, for example, *Chicago Daily News*, May 21, 1945, 4; *Chicago Tribune*, May 20, 1945, 21.

30. *Chicago Daily News*, May 19, 1945, 3.

31. John Collier, "The Indian in a Wartime Nation," *Annals of the American Academy of Political and Social Science* 223 (Sept. 1942): 29.

32. Ibid.

33. Bernstein, 40.

34. Richard L. Neuberger, "On the Warpath," *Saturday Evening Post*, Oct. 24, 1942, 79.

35. *New York Times*, Aug. 30, 1942, sec. IV, p. 7.

36. Sergeant, 708.

37. Peattie, 78.

38. *New York Times*, Feb. 9, 1943, 5.

39. Ickes, 58.

40. Hershey, 477.

41. *New York Times*, Jan. 23, 1945, 6.

42. Neuberger, "American Indian Enlists," 629–630.

43. Collier, 30.

44. The prediction was reported in several publications, including *Saturday Evening Post*, Oct. 24, 1942, 79; *Asia and the Americas*, Nov., 1942, 628, and *American Mercury*, Oct., 1944, 478. See also *New York Times*, Apr. 25, 1942, 6.

45. Hershey, 478.

46. *New York Times* Feb. 22, 1941, 8; May 15, 1941, 14; May 20, 1941, 7; Oct. 21, 1941, 25; *Arizona Star*, Oct. 7, 1940; Oct. 16, 1940; May 20, 1941; May 21, 1941, n.p.

47. *Arizona Republic*, Dec. 20, 1941, 16.

48. *Arizona Republic* (?), Feb. 21, 1942, clipping in the file "Indians of North America—Navajo—Military Service," Arizona Historical Society, Tucson.

49. *New York Times*, Jan. 8, 1942, 44; Hershey, 480.

50. *New York Times*, Dec. 18, 1941, 36.
51. Neuberger, "On the Warpath," 79.
52. *New York Times*, Dec. 30, 1941, 38.
53. *New York Times*, Jan. 8, 1942, 44.
54. *New York Times*, Apr. 22, 1942, 12.
55. *New York Times*, May 9, 1942, 20.
56. *New York Times*, Jan. 3, 1943, 29.
57. *New York Times*, Feb. 9, 1943, 5.
58. *Arizona Republic*, Oct. 20, 1943, n.p.
59. *Arizona Republic*, Aug. 16, 1943, n.p.
60. *Arizona Republic*, Dec. 20, 1941, n.p.
61. *Arizona Star*, Feb. 16, 1942, n.p.
62. Undated clipping in the file "Indians of North America—Tohono O'odham—Military Service," Arizona Historical Society, Tucson.
63. "Radio Warpath," *Newsweek*, Apr. 20, 1942, 60.
64. Harold E. Driver, *Indians of North America*, 2d ed., revised, (Chicago: The University of Chicago Press, 1969), 320–323, 520; Ruth M. Underhill, *Red Man's America* (Chicago: University of Chicago Press, 1953), 159–163.
65. *New York Times*, Aug. 8, 1942, 14.
66. See, for example, *New York Times*, Aug. 6, 1945, 17; June 21, 1946, 25.
67. The dispatch, distributed to newspapers through the Scripps-Howard syndicate, was reprinted as "Ceremonial Dances in the Pacific" in *Indians in the War*, pp. 12–14. The editors of that publication noted that in addition to Navajos, Sioux, Comanche, Apache, Pima, Kiowa, Pueblo, and Crow servicemen also participated in the ceremonies. The story was also reprinted in Ernie Pyle, *Last Chapter* (New York: Henry Holt and Company, 1946), 133–135.
68. Bernstein, 46.
69. Fixico, 15.
70. Holm, 150.
71. Oswald Garrison Villard, "Wardship and the Indian," *Christian Century*, Mar. 29, 1944, 397–398.
72. Armstrong, 47–52.

5

The 1950s: Termination and Relocation

After World War II several forces, political and economic and social, converged to promote legislation to withdraw federal services from Native Americans. The political arguments for withdrawal of funds and services went back to the assimilationist policies of the nineteenth and early twentieth centuries that held that the only way to deal successfully with the Indian "problem" was to force or persuade Native Americans to become like whites. That doctrine had been put aside during the New Deal years when John Collier as commissioner of Indian affairs promoted policies designed to protect native cultures.

Now, in the postwar years, new rhetoric was brought to bear. Promoters of this new assimilation spoke of "emancipation" and "setting the Indian free" of any special relationship with the federal government. Or, to put it negatively, the new policies sought "termination" of federal responsibilities.

The rhetoric resonated on several levels. In Cold War America, words such as "freedom" and "liberty" took on extra meanings that implied individualism and, ultimately, anticommunism. They were pitted against anything that smacked of collectivism or socialism, words increasingly associated in the public mind with Soviet communism. Thus some native communal practices and institutions were denounced as being somehow subversive. And, federal benefits to Indians were viewed by many as government handouts that promoted dependency. It was largely ignored or unknown that these benefits often were provided under treaties between the tribes and the government.

While popular rhetoric supported individualism against collectivism, there was also in the 1950s a promotion of the "American way of life," a unified view of a society that shared values, beliefs, aspirations, and lifestyles—in other words, conformity. Under this view, the idea of Indians maintaining a separate identity was incomprehensible. It was widely assumed that, given proper incentives, Native Americans would readily reject their cultures and assimilate into the white world.[1]

Opponents of termination also used Cold War rhetoric. Oliver LaFarge, president of the Association on American Indian Affairs and one of the most vocal critics of termination, noted the similarities between schemes to force assimilation of Native Americans and Communist attempts to stamp out ethnic pride in Eastern Europe.

"One of our howling errors is ignoring the fact that you cannot make a people over against their will and contrary to their aspirations. We all recognize this simple fact eagerly and emphasize it when it comes to Hungarians or Poles, but somehow we refuse to apply it to American Indians," he wrote.[2]

Also, words such as "emancipation" and "integration" were associated positively with the civil rights movement to end racial discrimination and segregation of African Americans. Thus, when traditional Native Americans resisted assimilation, they and their supporters were condemned for supporting "segregation."

In fact, one of the most energetic proponents of termination, Sen. Arthur V. Watkins, Republican of Utah, likened termination for Indians to the Emancipation Proclamation for African Americans. In 1957 he wrote, "Following in the footsteps of the Emancipation Proclamation of ninety-four years ago, I see the following words emblazoned in letters of fire above the heads of the Indians—*THESE PEOPLE SHALL BE FREE!*"[3]

While the calls for freedom in the early civil rights movement meant freedom for blacks to be treated equally in a white-dominated society, Indians were seeking to remain separate from the larger society. The differences between the demands of the two groups often went unnoticed by whites, however.[4]

The economic rationale for the thrust toward termination came in the postwar emphasis on reining in "big government" by cutting costs and shrinking bureaucracies. Also, the postwar West was experiencing an economic boom. Local governments and businesses wanted access to Indian lands both to exploit them economically and to put them on the tax rolls.[5] But, as Native American veterans and war industry workers returned to their reservations, unemployment and poverty became severe, making any cutbacks in federal funds or services unlikely.[6] This situation fueled the drive for setting Indians "free" of government programs, to fend for themselves in the larger society and economy. As the overline and headline for a *Reader's Digest* article put it: "Our treatment of the original Americans seems designed to perpetuate poverty and dependence: Set the American Indians Free!"[7]

The article restated opponents' arguments against the Indian New Deal, and misled the public, critics charged. Dr. Haven Emerson, president of the Association on American Indian Affairs (AAIA), wrote:

> Had it appeared in some local journal, [it] should merely have been deplored as an ill-informed rehash of old fallacies and sentimentalities concerning our Indians. With the authority of the *Reader's Digest* behind it, however, the article becomes a potential danger to the very freedom which it demands. No one can be free unless he is independent.[8]

Emerson's criticisms, however, appeared in the AAIA's journal, which had a fraction of the circulation of the *Reader's Digest*, one of the highest circulation magazines of the time.

Similar motives drove the move to relocate Native Americans in cities far from their reservation homes. Veterans returning after World War II often found poverty and unemployment on the reservation. And, their experiences in the outside world had, federal officials believed, fitted them to compete successfully with other Americans for jobs off the reservation.[9] Other Indians, too, were attracted to the cities by stories of wealth and adventure and by harsh conditions at home. By the early 1950s, relocation was becoming linked with termination as a way of breaking Indians' ties to the federal government. If Indians could be drawn to work in cities, the reasoning went, they would live, work, and go to school with non-Indians and eventually assimilate into the dominant culture.

TERMINATION LEGISLATION

The seeds of termination were sown in 1947, two years after John Collier resigned as commissioner of Indian affairs. When a U.S. Senate committee asked the Bureau of Indian Affairs how its expenses could be cut, Acting Commissioner William Zimmerman, Jr., came up with three lists of tribes. On the first list were tribes that, in Zimmerman's view, were ready to have federal services withdrawn immediately. On the second list were tribes for whom services could be withdrawn within ten years; those on the third list would need more than ten years to function without federal support services, according to Zimmerman's rationale. The "Zimmerman plan" was often cited by terminationists in Congress to support measures withdrawing support from certain tribes, though Zimmerman insisted he had not intended to draw up a blueprint for termination.[10]

The first measure establishing termination as official policy was House Concurrent Resolution 108, which stated that it was "the policy of Congress, as rapidly as possible, to make the Indians . . . subject to the same laws and entitled to the same privileges and responsibilities as . . . other citizens of the United States, and to end their status as wards of the United States."[11]

The resolution, which marked a major shift in Indian policy, was adopted on August 1, 1953, without significant debate.

HCR 108 also called for withdrawal of federal control and supervision over a number of tribes, including the Menominees of Wisconsin, the Klamaths of Oregon, and Indian groups in California, Florida, New York, and Texas.[12] Other bills followed in 1953 and early 1954 mandating termination for more tribes. Still other legislation repealed nineteenth-century laws prohibiting liquor on reservations, banning sale of munitions, and restricting livestock transactions by Indians.[13]

More controversial was Public Law 280, a measure that would have given the states of California, Minnesota, Nebraska, Oregon, and Wisconsin jurisdiction over Indians living there, with the exception of the Red Lake Chippewas of Minnesota, the Warm Springs Band of Oregon, and the Menominees. Other states could assume jurisdiction over Indians just by passing legislation. Indian consent was not required. Indian groups, their supporters, and others such as the American Civil Liberties Union protested the measure. Though President Eisenhower called the bill "unchristian" and said he hoped it would be amended to require tribal consent, he signed it anyway in August 1953.[14]

In all, a total of 288 bills and resolutions on Indian affairs were introduced in the Eighty-Third Congress, and forty-six of them became law. This was more legislation affecting Native Americans than had been considered by any other Congress.[15]

In 1954 Congress took up bills to terminate specific tribes. The Indians and their allies were allowed their say in hearings held in February and March of that year. Their arguments that tribal lands and federal services were guaranteed by treaties and were not a matter of charity were largely ignored.[16]

THE PRESS

In the 1950s newspapers and magazines were still key sources of information for most people, though television news was beginning to make inroads. Neither newspaper editors nor television executives saw television as a competitor at news gathering. Relatively few viewers watched the fifteen-minute evening newscasts.[17] Many local communities had daily newspapers, often afternoon ones. In addition, bigger papers provided coverage for larger communities and sometimes regions. Though there were few truly national newspapers, the *Christian Science Monitor* served a national audience, and the *New York Times* was regarded as the paper of record. Readers in all parts of the country also had access to nationally circulated magazines. National and international news was available through wire services such as the Associated Press and United Press, which served small and large news outlets.

The debate among journalists on the relative merits of objectivity and interpretative reporting, begun in the 1930s, continued in the 1950s. Objective reporting, as journalists defined it, meant excising all opinion from stories, relying on provable facts, and attributing most information, preferably to official sources such as public officials. Interpretative reporting, ideally, explained events and situations without engaging in opinion. Critics of objective reporting said it relied too heavily on official sources and did not explain the facts. Critics of interpretation charged it was a guise for injecting opinion into the news columns.

The wire services, which served many newspapers of varying political views, were generally recognized as being scrupulously objective, removing all opinion (and sometimes, it was argued, explanation) from their dispatches.[18] For reporters, whether filing for the wires or writing for a newspaper, objectivity was the goal. A 1952 college journalism text said, "For more than a century, American newspapermen have tried to develop the most factual, objective, uncolored, and accurate news writing to be seen anywhere in the world. They have glorified their objective reporting and their complete separation of fact and comment—leaving the latter to the editorial page."[19]

Many stories about Native Americans in both the national and local press were objective "hard news" stories. These stories, often from wire services, did not describe or characterize Indians. While this practice avoided stereotypes, it also served to denude native people of their distinctive cultures and to obscure the complexities of treaties that made Indians legally, as well as culturally, distinct from other Americans. Readers of such stories might well have asked: If Indians are just like everyone else, why should the government give them special services? Why shouldn't they pay taxes and stand on their own feet the way other Americans do?

Besides event-oriented hard news stories, newspapers ran colorfully written feature articles. When such articles depicted Native Americans, they frequently fell back on superficial descriptions of clothing and tribal practices that didn't get at the realities of native lives and cultures. Instead, such stories often perpetuated well-worn Indian imagery.

By the late 1940s and 1950s, the press was beginning to pay increased attention to its coverage of racial minorities. Evidence of this came from college journalism textbooks and from the report of the prestigious Commission on Freedom of the Press, known as the Hutchins Commission. For example, a 1949 textbook, which described itself as a "reporter's handbook," noted a "general trend away from use of racial identification." It then enumerated cases where racial identification was permissible, using an example involving the Seneca nation of the Iroquois Confederacy.[20] Journalism textbooks cautioned against the gratuitous use of race in reporting crime news. Most often the warning was made in reference to African Americans.[21]

At least two of the five "requirements" for the press proposed by the Hutchins Commission's report, *A Free and Responsible Press*, related to the treatment by the news media of those outside the mainstream. The first of the commission's requirements was for "a truthful, comprehensive, and intelligent account of the day's events in a context which gives them meaning." The third requirement called for "the projection of a representative picture of the constituent groups in the society."[22]

Discussion of reporting on minority groups, particularly African Americans or "Negroes," also became increasingly frequent in *Nieman Reports*, "the first academically based journalism review,"[23] which began in 1947. *Nieman Reports* was published by the Lucius Nieman Foundation, which brings journalists to Harvard University for a year of study. The first volumes of *Nieman Reports* in 1947 and 1948 contained an account of the first African American Nieman Fellowship recipient. After that, articles about black journalists and reporting on blacks appeared with increasing frequency. The second volume contained an article on the *Cherokee Phoenix*, the first Native American newspaper. The article did not, however, relate this history either to contemporary Native American journalism or to coverage of Native Americans.[24] This was the only article found about Native Americans in the early volumes.

Another indictment of the way the press treated minority groups, African Americans in particular, came from the Nieman class of 1946, who collectively wrote a book, *Your Newspaper*, criticizing the press and offering some remedies. The book chastized newspapers for

> their shameful treatment of those whom they seem to regard as second-class citizens—the members of minority groups. Negroes are special victims of this discrimination.
>
> . . . North and South, most newspapers are consistently cruel to the colored man, patronizing him, keeping him in his place, thoughtlessly crucifying him in a thousand big and little ways. . . . As pictured in many newspapers, the Negro is either an entertaining fool, a dangerous animal or . . . a prodigy of astonishing attainments, considering his race.[25]

PORTRAYALS OF NATIVE AMERICANS

Though examples of stories using the imagery of Indians seen in literature and popular culture for centuries were not hard to find in the 1950s press, these images were often overlaid with the dominant cultural concerns of the time. Thus, "good Indian" stories conveying positive images of Indians turned the image on its head and depicted them as people who had rejected their traditional cultures and integrated into white society. Rather than being noble savages or children of nature, they had put the natural world aside and embraced the materialism and competitiveness of the mainstream. Such an image reflected the 1950s celebration of conformity. Whereas in the 1920s the good Indian might be depicted as someone who possessed secrets of serenity, tranquillity, and oneness with the natural world that were envied by harried, materialistic whites, the 1950s good Indian was someone who fitted in.

This image emerged clearly in an article in the *Christian Science Monitor* that began, "The picturesque, beaded, feathered, and quaint American Indian has just about vanished from the lands of his ancestors. In his place stands Mr. Indian, modern American citizen. Clad in a business suit, his keen black eyes view the passing scene with growing understanding and appreciation of his rights and obligations."[26]

The article went on to quote Oliver LaFarge that the "new" Indian "understands the American scheme, has caught the American dream. . . . He intends to participate in them fully, and he revolts ever more fiercely and ever more strongly against any measure that blocks his progress towards full equality."[27]

The image of "bad Indians," that is, bloodthirsty savages, would seem out of place in depictions of contemporary Native Americans. Yet, the image of Indians "on the warpath" was invoked, often humorously, when a conflict involving Native Americans arose.

The related image of degraded Indians was seen often. This image depicted Indians as desolate, poverty-stricken people. Sometimes they brought it on themselves through improvidence or laziness, and sometimes they were victims of forces beyond their control. Stories conveying the degraded Indian image tended to describe—accurately and often quite vividly—what Indians lacked *vis-à-vis* white society without mentioning the strengths of Native American cultures. Usually the deficiencies were in material comfort, health care, and education.

As a *Christian Science Monitor* editorial succinctly put it, "the 'Indian problem' can be summed up in two words: poverty and ignorance (of matters necessary to get on in a white man's country)." Earlier, the editorial made the valid point that Indian policy "affects a great many more human beings than the few that Eastern tourists see selling necklaces and pottery as the Sante Fe [*sic*] pauses at Albuquerque." But those other human beings were nowhere described, characterized, or portrayed. The image the reader got, then, was a vaguely negative one of a downtrodden people.[28]

Another *Christian Science Monitor* story, about a boarding school for Navajo children, was headlined "Navajo Youths Enthusiastic / Learning White Man's Way." The story carried a bleak picture of Navajo life:

> [T]he black-eyed children are largely illiterate, undernourished and timid. The archaic society they left behind has taught them extreme humility. . . . Besides learning their "three R's," [in the school] they must also become familiar with the proper method of washing their feet, how to clip their finger nails, and how to brush their teeth.[29]

The article went on to assert that the "fiercely earnest students" were working to learn "the fundamentals of living in white society, and to make an honest living with dignity and respect. . . . If they are to raise their living standards above perpetual poverty—standards lower than any other group in the United States—they must assimilate the white man's culture."[30]

The assumption was that not only was the reservation bereft of material comforts but that dignified, respectable work was also unavailable; that the only "proper" way to eat, wash, and groom oneself was the white way. The downside of assimilation, that is, the loss or denial of traditional cultures, values, and practices, was not mentioned.

Degraded Indians were also portrayed as lazy and dependent people who had allowed themselves to be robbed of initiative by a paternalistic federal government. This image surfaced repeatedly in articles on termination. An article in *Commonweal* stated:

> [C]ontact with the white man's world and the protracted state of tutelage have inevitably weakened the Indian's society and sapped his moral fiber. These wards of the state have grown content with letting others take care of them. And when big money has come their way they have shown a talent for speedily throwing it to the four winds.[31]

The article not only portrayed Indians as lazy spendthrifts but also ignored the considerable differences in tribes' circumstances and treatment by whites.

Images of Indians as ancient and exotic were abundant in stories that emphasized the trappings of tribal culture without going into its reasons or meanings. Stories expressed amazement at anachronisms such as traditionally dressed Indians wearing glasses or chewing gum. A story about a pow wow in Chicago noted that "even in the midst of their traditional dances . . . the Indians unwittingly showed many evidences of being modern, up-to-date Americans."[32]

It mentioned Indian "girls, in beautifully beaded buckskin, were all that one imagines Indian damsels of long ago to have been—except that several had acquired permanent waves in their naturally straight heavy black hair."[33]

Sometimes images of Indians as both exotic and degraded were combined in the same story. A four-paragraph wire service story about an Indian exposition in Oklahoma described the Indians attending as "wearing bright headdresses, beaded belts, moccasins and other traditional finery" but also said: "Fourteen persons were arrested for drunkenness in some 'preliminary' celebrations."[34] That a short wire service story out of Oklahoma carried in a New York newspaper mentioned fourteen drunkenness arrests in a crowd of two thousand Indians could not help but reinforce the image of degraded Indians as alcohol abusers. It seemed Indians were victims of a self-fulfilling prophesy. If there was an Indian gathering, the number of arrests for drunkenness was automatically newsworthy.

Considering the 1950s preoccupation with conformity, it was not surprising that many stories portrayed Indians as involved citizens who were—or sought to be—as individualistic and competitive as whites. In contrast to earlier decades, stories glorifying Indian traditions were less frequent.

Finally, the ideology and terminology of the Cold War intruded even on something as internal to the United States as Indian affairs. For example a travel article on an improved highway on the Navajo reservation noted that the Indians welcomed tourists. "No longer is Navajoland behind an iron curtain of its own."[35] A story on an Indian festival in Manhattan quoted the mayor of New York as saying that the Indians assembling at Union Square were "the only reds who really belong here."[36]

In a more serious vein, Cold War paranoia colored even consideration of a Congressional report that Navajos had an average life expectancy of less than twenty years, compared with more than sixty-eight years for whites. The story quoted a Congressman who noted that Russian visitors had visited the Navajo reservation with cameras: "No doubt they took those pictures back to Russia and told them that was the way Americans live."[37]

Each of the stories appeared factually accurate. Yet the selection and use of such stories may have contributed to a generalized inaccuracy by reinforcing stereotypical images of Indians in the minds of readers who had few real-life encounters with native people to modify the pictures they received in the press.

TERMINATION CASE STUDY: THE MENOMINEES

The Menominees, an Algonquian-speaking people, had lived in Northern Wisconsin at least five thousand years. Unlike many North American tribes, they managed to retain some of their original lands, a reservation of some 235,000 acres. It was a small remnant of their original territory of 9.5 million acres. The Menominees resisted allotment, which had caused much of the lands of neighboring tribes to pass from Indian to white hands in the early twentieth century.[38]

The Menominees' main source of income was a sawmill that processed wood from the tribe's forest, harvested on a sustained-yield basis. The business brought the tribe enough prosperity that it paid for most of its own community services, such as schools and health care. When Indian Bureau personnel mismanaged the lumbering operation, the Menominees sued in the U.S. Court of Claims. In 1951, seventeen years after the suit was filed, the Menominees were awarded a $7.65 million judgment.[39]

The Menominees decided to take some of the money in one-time per capita payments of $1,500 to each member. To do this, however, required an act of Congress. Such a bill passed the House, but in the Senate it ran into the terminationist views of Senator Watkins, who sought to tie the payments to an agreement that the Menominees would allow termination of all federal services. On June 20, 1953, Senator Watkins spoke before the Menominee General Council and indicated he would not approve per capita payments until the Menominees agreed to termination within three years. After he left, the council voted 169 to 5 for termination.[40]

According to several accounts, the vote did not reflect the views of Menominee people about termination. Rather, some likely believed they were voting only for the per capita payments. Others voted for the termination resolution believing it was inevitable anyway. Still others voted yes out of fear of the consequences if they resisted. Many more of the 3,200 tribal members expressed their negative views by refusing to vote at all.[41]

The Menominees wanted more time to prepare for termination than Senator Watkins was willing to give. They sought five years, but Senator Watkins insisted that it be accomplished in three. He wrote the three-year provision into the Senate version of the bill that would also give the tribe its per capita payments. The matter was held up in the House, due principally to the efforts of Rep. Melvin Laird, Republican of Wisconsin; it was put over to the next session of Congress. During that session, beginning in early 1954, Menominee representatives appeared before a joint Senate-House committee.[42]

Eventually, on June 17, 1954, President Eisenhower signed the Menominee Termination Act. The measure gave the tribe most of the longer time frame Representative Laird had fought for, calling on the tribe to submit a plan for management of its assets by the time federal services were to be terminated—in 1958. It also gave the tribe its per capita payments and closed tribal rolls to future enrollment.[43]

From 1954 until termination finally took effect—after several delays—in 1961, the Menominees went through the painful process of dismantling the familiar and comfortable reservation structure and replacing it with complex, costly, and burdensome institutions. The whole termination exercise was viewed by Menominees as "disastrous" and "a failure."[44] The eventual result was that people who had been largely self-sufficient were plunged into unemployment and poverty and had to rely on state welfare agencies. The reservation territory became a county—Wisconsin's newest and poorest. In some cases tribal land was sold to outsiders to pay taxes. Many Menominees left for cities, trading rural poverty for urban poverty.[45]

As early as 1964 some tribe members petitioned Congress to repeal the termination act. Eventually, in 1973 after years of lobbying by Menominees and their supporters, Congress adopted the Menominee Restoration Act, reversing termination.[46]

Menominee Images

In the case of the Menominees, the imagery in the press was subtle and complex. Their story was covered extensively by the *Shawano Evening Leader* (1953 circulation: 7,463)[47] the community paper of Shawano, the town closest to the reservation. Papers in the larger, more distant towns of Green Bay and Milwaukee covered the story to a lesser extent.

In the Shawano paper, the Menominees were depicted as involved Indian citizens, community members who were neither exotic relics of the past nor degraded victims but who were set upon by outside forces—the federal government. Beyond Shawano, they were depicted—when their stories appeared at all—as good Indians who had made "progress" and were "ready" to be "free" of federal supervision, though the costs of such "freedom" were not explained.

For example, when Senator Watkins visited the Menominee reservation to urge termination on the tribe, he was quoted in the *Green Bay Press-Gazette* as telling them, "You Menominees have been doing very well. . . . You have a much better reservation than some of the other Indian tribes" and expressing pleasure that almost all could speak English.[48] A story in the *Milwaukee Journal* said members of the tribe "already enjoy high standards of living in comparison with some other tribes."[49]

The only article found outside Wisconsin that touched on Menominee culture was a 1953 *Chicago Tribune* story that portrayed the tribe as prosperous and culturally indistinct from whites.

> In wealth, they are second only to the Oklahoma oil-rich Indians. . . . The Menominees are industrious and thrifty, generally educated in the lower schools, quite a few in high schools, and some in colleges. . . .
>
> Keshena [a town on the Menominee reservation] is a typical small town, with scattered houses and buildings. About 95 percent of the Menominees are Catholic.[50]

Thus, if readers outside Wisconsin had any image of Menominees at all, it was of a people who were well-off and integrated into the mainstream, people for whom termination would pose no problems. The implication readers would likely draw from such stories was that no need existed for the federal government to provide anything to the tribe.

Menominees were not depicted as exotic and colorful or as downtrodden victims. In fact, they lacked a clear image in the press outside their community. This lack of a vivid image, added to the characterizations of the Menominees as self-sufficient and well-off, gave weight to Senator Watkins' assertion that the Menominees were "ready" to take on their own destinies.

Senator Watkins's Visit

The visit of Senator Watkins to the Menominee reservation on June 19–21, 1953, to urge the tribe to accept termination provided an opportunity to see how various publications portrayed the tribe and the issue.

The *Shawano Evening Leader* covered the event extensively. An advance story on the eve of Senator Watkins's visit explained clearly that the tribe's predicament arose from its "recent attempt . . . to obtain payment from tribal funds on deposit in the United States Treasury of $1,500 to each enrolled member of the tribe." The article noted that the government paid the money "in settlement of claims brought by the tribe against the federal government."[51]

It went on to explain how Senator Watkins, head of the subcommittee to which the payment bill was assigned, balked at letting the tribe have its own funds without strings attached "because of his conviction that, [following the claims settlement] the federal government should be relieved of the responsibility of continuing supervision over the Menominee Reservation."[52]

Both the terminology and the emphasis were different in accounts that appeared in more distant papers, such as in Green Bay and Milwaukee.

The news story in the *Green Bay Press-Gazette* after the tribe's meeting with Senator Watkins said the Menominees "rejected a plan . . . that offered [the tribe] immediate and complete independence from the United States government." The Menominees, it said, "declared they are perfectly content to remain wards of the federal government for the present. They also told officials they expect the government to pay their claims in full."[53]

The words used here conveyed a far different image of the Menominees. Rather than being a local group seeking funds rightfully owed them, as in the *Shawano Evening Leader* account, they were portrayed as dependent, and perhaps even indolent. In the postcolonial era, when international news was full of accounts of peoples in Africa and Asia seeking independence from their colonizers, the idea of an Indian tribe being offered "independence" and turning it down must have struck readers as strange.

Also, by describing the tribe as being "perfectly content to remain wards" of the government, the story conveyed the image of the Menominees as complacent and unambitious, a subtle reflection of the stereotype of lazy Indians living off government handouts. By calling on the government to "pay their claims in full" the article conveyed the notion that these Indians were not only lazy but grasping or greedy as well.

The article never clearly explained that the Menominees' $1,500 payments were from money that already belonged to the tribe. Instead, it left the impression that the funds were somehow federal charity or a reward for "independence." It quoted Senator Watkins as saying, "You had a just complaint on your Indian claims and Congress has adjusted it." Later it referred to funds "which the government wants to turn over to the Menominees." It would take extremely careful reading to understand that the tribe actually owned the funds.[54]

The *Milwaukee Journal* carried an Associated Press wire service account on June 23, 1953, of Senator Watkins's visit. Unlike the stories in the smaller papers, this one carried a Washington dateline. The image it conveyed differed even more starkly from those in the Shawano paper. The story began, "A Wisconsin tribe finally has agreed that legal machinery should be set in gear to give its members freedom from federal control, a goal sought by American Indians for decades."[55]

The story went on to say the tribe agreed to Senator Watkins's move "to take the group from under Uncle Sam's wing" and that Senator Watkins would set up "an emancipation timetable." This timetable was linked in the fourth paragraph of the story to the distribution of the $1,500 per capita payments. The explanation that the payments were from the tribe's own funds didn't appear until near the end of the story, in the thirteenth of a total of fifteen paragraphs. The story also said Senator Watkins proposed to make arrangements for the tribe to "become full citizens and graduate from its status of ward of the government."[56]

The image of the Menominees in this story was of a people who were dependent and reluctant to leave the nest, to continue the avian metaphor used by the AP. Words such as "freedom" and "emancipation" conjured up a desirable objective—an image of people being liberated from burdensome conditions. It did not mention the treaties under which the conditions were imposed or the costs and responsibilities that the government would escape by cutting its ties to the tribe. By saying in the lead paragraph that "freedom from federal control" was "a goal sought by American Indians for decades," the story alluded to Native Americans' centuries-long struggles to retain their lands, livelihoods, and cultures. In fact, in the case of the Menominees in the 1950s, the tribe had not actively sought elimination of federal controls and certainly not under the terms laid down by Senator Watkins.

Terms such as "freedom" and "emancipation" carried a greater resonance in 1953 than today. Readers might well have been perplexed that a people would be reluctant to become "free," especially if the readers did not know that the Menominees were, indeed, "free" to vote, to leave the reservation, and to exercise most of the perquisites of citizenship. That information was omitted from virtually all of the stories, especially those in papers beyond Shawano, Wisconsin.

The hopeful and positive tone conveyed by the Associated Press story out of Washington was strikingly dissimilar to the account of the meeting between Senator Watkins and the Menominees carried by the Shawano paper. That story had an air of grimness, almost resignation. The story, noting that Menominee "freedom" "appeared certain," mentioned the treaty tying the tribe to the government in the third paragraph of the story, which was the longest and most prominent article on the front page that day.

Rather than implying that the government was magnanimously liberating the tribe, the story said that the government "insisted that the tribe go on 'its own.' "[57] Senator Watkins was described, not as a benevolent emancipator, but "an earnest advocate of Indians' taking over their own affairs, [who] has much power over Indians' affairs in the U.S. by virtue of his chairmanship of the Senate's Indian subcommittee." The story also showed the threatening nature of Senator Watkins's remarks, quoting the senator as saying it would be "unwise" of the Menominees not to respond to Congressional prodding to take over their own affairs.[58]

In the *Shawano Evening Leader* story, the Menominees were portrayed as involved Indian citizens—well-informed, articulate, and sometimes hostile to the senator, portrayals that were not seen elsewhere. It quoted tribal representatives as asking Senator Watkins why he was holding up the per capita payments, and asserting that the senator did not understand the tribe's problems. It described a woman "firing verbal shots" at the senator for delaying the per capita payments. Yet another Menominee was quoted as asking if it wasn't "Congressional discrimination" to block the payments.[59] None of these images of the Menominees as concerned, well informed, and apprehensive of the consequences of termination resonated in the press beyond Shawano.

Interestingly, the terminology used in the *Shawano Evening Leader* before Senator Watkins's visit described the proposed separation of the Menominees and the federal government as allowing the government to be "relieved of the responsibility of continuing supervision over the Menominee reservation."[60] But when Senator Watkins arrived, the paper adopted—temporarily, at least—the senator's terminology, referring to separation as giving "the tribe full independence from the U.S. government" and as "full freedom from government."[61]

The paper chronicled in detail the Menominees' efforts to stall termination but did not report extensively, in 1953 and 1954 at least, on dissension within the tribe over who was and was not eligible for per capita payments. That dissension, as well as the perils that lay ahead for the tribe, was detailed in a series in the *Milwaukee Sentinel* in August and September 1954 after the tribe was terminated and after the per capita payments were distributed.[62]

Menominees as Community Members

Aside from the termination issue, Menominees were frequently in the news in the *Shawano Evening Leader*. They were depicted as involved Indian citizens with multifaceted lives. The *Evening Leader* ran stories about Menominee community activities that did not differ significantly from those of others in the community: Menominee beauty queens, obituaries, and church festivals all received space in the Shawano paper. A reader who had no independent knowledge of the people and events the paper wrote about would see the Menominees as citizens integrated into the fabric of the community, people who were depicted as neither exotic nor downtrodden. They clearly were shown as distinct and separate, but they were not portrayed as either superior or inferior.

For example, the paper put out a special edition commemorating the centennial of the founding of the reservation, complete with a history of the tribe and congratulatory advertisements from local businesses.[63]

Ada Deer, who was later to lead the Menominee restoration effort and eventually to become assistant secretary for Indian affairs, was in 1953 an eighteen-year-old high school graduate who was one of five Indian girls to win a trip to Hollywood and a bit part in a movie. The *Shawano Evening Leader* recorded her accomplishment with apparent hometown pride. "Shawano businessmen have made arrangements to honor Miss Ada Elizabeth Deer, eighteen-year-old Keshena girl who leaves next Monday for Hollywood to take part in the filming of the Columbia picture 'Golden Stallion.' " The article included, in the manner of community journalism of the time, the names of Deer's parents and siblings, her high school honors, and college plans.[64]

The Menominee tribe's yearly summer pageant also was portrayed positively as a source of civic pride in the newspaper. A news story about the event struck a booster-ish tone:

> The pageants, which are based on highlights in tribal history or the colorful legends of the Menominees, are entirely the product of Menominee minds and ingenuity. The Menominees are proud of their pageants; proud because this event, which had its beginning some ten years ago, has grown steadily in popularity until today it has statewide acclaim as an outstanding dramatic event.[65]

Obituaries of Menominees apparently got the same treatment as those of other members of the community. In fact, if a reader did not know Menominee family names or the towns and hamlets on the reservation, it would be impossible to tell if the subject of an obituary or, for that matter, news of clubs or schools, was Indian or not.[66]

OTHER IMAGES OF INDIANS IN THE TERMINATION CONTROVERSY

In early 1954 while Congress considered their fate, the Menominees were virtually invisible in the national press. Their story did not catch the public's eye as had that of the Pueblos in the 1920s. Other Indian legislation, however, got national coverage. Papers such as the *New York Times* carried numerous staff-written and wire service stories that chronicled the progress of various termination bills through Congress as well as other issues. The *Times*, particularly, also ran stories of protests by Indians and their allies against the bills. National magazines such as the *New Republic* and *Commonweal* likewise carried articles on the legislation. These publications were not unsympathetic to the peril to tribes implicit in the bills.

One of the first collective statements explaining the Indians' position came in late February 1954 when representatives of forty tribes met in Washington to protest what they saw as abrogation of treaty rights. The *New York Times* quoted the group as saying:

> We feel that many of our fellow Americans do not know that we are citizens, free to move about the country like everyone else. We fight for our country, and we pay taxes like everyone else, except on the land and property our ancestors retained by agreement with the United States government.[67]

This paragraph, on page twenty-five, was virtually the only collective statement asserting Native American treaty rights that was found in the press during this time. Though individual Indians and their supporters appeared before the committee and argued for equity, the legal argument was seldom seen in the press accounts. In contrast, when the protest of the white-dominated Association on American Indian Affairs was reported, the story emphasized the plight of Indians who would become victims of "homeless poverty" if termination bills were passed. The three-paragraph story did mention treaty rights, but the emphasis was on Indians as victims of "ill-advised, untimely and off-target Abandonment bills."[68]

When Senator Watkins, the instigator of termination, was quoted, the image of Indians was of dependent tax avoiders who must be forced to fend for themselves. He was quoted as saying, "It is distasteful to me to have anyone be a ward of the government unless he is incompetent," and "in nine out of ten cases . . . it comes down to the fact they don't want to pay taxes."[69] And, later, "[W]e don't intend to deprive them of their God-given right to make a few of their own mistakes in managing their own affairs."[70]

What appeared, then, were images that varied with the source: Indians, speaking for themselves, emphasized their treaty rights. White "friends" of Indians spoke of their plight. Senator Watkins spoke of Indians as dependent tax avoiders. The image of Indians making the legal argument for their treaty rights, however, was the least prominent of the three.

One reason for this may lie in the origins of the stories. Most were reports of speeches, hearings, or meetings, often arranged by government officials. When Native American views appeared in print, they likely came from testimony in hearings. There was little evidence found of reporters seeking out other Indians for comment. Thus readers were more likely to see Indians depicted as pitiable victims or lazy freeloaders.

Editorials in the *New York Times* and the *Washington Post* and a column in the *Christian Science Monitor* questioned the wisdom of the legislation and urged Congress to consult the Indians before sealing their fates. However, sometimes the imagery used perpetuated familiar stereotypes. For example, Josephine Ripley, writing in the *Christian Science Monitor*, used stereotypical, trivially exotic terms such as "heap much trouble," "braves have hit the warpath," and "smoke signals," while taking Congress to task for its termination bills. Ripley noted that the "freedom" being imposed on tribes by Congress would impose heavy taxes on their lands and resources and would thrust them into business competition for which they were unprepared. Yet the column's message was diluted by patronizing its subjects with demeaning terms.[71]

In these accounts, the Menominees were mentioned only briefly or by oblique reference. Their arguments were not detailed. No interpretive or feature stories explained who the Menominees were or where they lived or why they had agreed to termination. One might speculate that the Menominees might have been more newsworthy if they were seen as conforming to the familiar images of Indians as exotic and "colorful" or as degraded victims.

Though the *New York Times* devoted several stories each to Congressional efforts to terminate Western tribes such as the Paiutes of Utah and the Flatheads of Montana, it devoted only a paragraph to news that President Eisenhower had signed the bill for Menominee termination—the first such legislation for any tribe.[72] That story was followed a few days later by a short item relating Eisenhower's gaffe during the signing ceremony in June. The president, noting the date and apparently believing all Indians, ancient and contemporary, Western and Woodlands, were interchangeable, asked the Menominees, "What was the date in '76 that you fellows nicked Custer?"[73]

MENOMINEES' PER CAPITA PAYMENTS

It was not until August 1954, when the $1,500 per capita payments were distributed to the Menominees, that the *Times* ran a stand-alone story and photograph about the tribe. The article showed an interesting intersection of news values and Indian imagery. At least since the stories of oil-rich Oklahoma Indians appeared in the 1920s, stories of "rich" Indians were deemed newsworthy. Often the stories chronicled the ways Indians, unused to a money economy, squandered their windfalls and sank back into poverty. The image such stories conveyed was of degraded Indians: vulnerable, childlike, improvident people who could not cope with the white man's money.

The *New York Times* story, from the Associated Press, showed the Menominees using their money wisely but indicated that this was surprising. "What happens when sudden wealth hits an Indian reservation? A buying spree is the logical answer," the article said. It also reported that authorities had invoked a federal law barring salesmen from the reservation to protect tribe members from unscrupulous peddlers.[74]

The image of "rich" Indians as improvident and degraded was stronger in the *Milwaukee Journal*, which reported an "air of watchful expectancy hanging over Shawano as residents waited for the impact of nearly $5 million to sink in" at the nearby reservation. It also reported that law enforcement officials were "taking a wary attitude about celebrating," although there had been no incidents.[75]

The newspaper's only other reports on the distribution of per capita payments were about Indians running afoul of the law. "Menominee Indians have invaded Milwaukee, tossing currency instead of tomahawks," one story began. It said twenty-one Indians had been arrested since the per capita payments began and quoted a local judge as saying, "I've seen more Indians here in the last ten days than in the three months previous. . . . Our skid row taverns are reaping a harvest."[76]

Reports in the *Shawano Evening Leader* conveyed a different image. An article reporting the paper's own survey of Indians' buying habits related that "recipients of the $1,500 per capita checks are spending wisely and cautiously." The story was larded with phrases such as "very good judgment," "acted very responsibly," "conservative buying," "taking care of the home first."[77]

The paper reprinted a neighboring newspaper's editorial praising the *Leader's* survey and noting that it served "the tribe's cause nobly by pointing out that Indians can be and usually are just as responsible as anyone else in similar economic circumstances."[78]

It is impossible to know which image was more accurate, that of Indians going to the city and getting drunk or that of Indians buying wisely and putting money in the bank. Probably both had elements of truth. The point, however, is that stories in papers outside the Menominees' community seemed more likely to invoke the familiar rich Indian image than did the local press.

RELOCATION

Relocating Indians to work in cities was first seen by federal officials as a way to ease overpopulation on reservations. Later it was viewed as a way to help termination work. If Indians left the reservations in sufficient numbers and assimilated into the urban mainstream, there would eventually be no need for reservations, some believed. This optimistic view was illustrated by the headline on a *Saturday Evening Post* story that said, "Indian Reservations May Some Day Run Out of Indians."[79] A *New York Times* story began, "If you want to see an Indian on a reservation, you still have plenty of time. But for your children or grandchildren, it may be a different story." The article came close to declaring victory for assimilation by saying, "a generation from now the red man in his historic milieu will take some seeking out."[80]

Throughout the 1950s, the Bureau of Indian Affairs helped Native Americans move to cities by paying transportation one-way from the reservation, helping them find jobs and housing, paying for groceries and rent until the first paycheck arrived, and buying such accommodations to urban culture as an alarm clock to help workers get to their jobs on time.[81] By the mid-1950s, various vocational training programs were added to give Indians skills to live and work in cities.[82] The program, officials emphasized, was entirely voluntary. Critics disputed this. Nevertheless, it attracted Indians' attention. Between 1952 and 1957 a total of seventeen thousand to twenty thousand persons were relocated with federal assistance. Interestingly, that number was only a quarter of the total who left reservations between the end of World War II and 1957.[83] The number of Indians staying in the cities and the number returning to the reservation were hotly disputed, as was the quality of the lives they made for themselves in the cities.

Stories about the relocation program generally drew sharply different images of the Indians who were its beneficiaries or victims, depending on one's viewpoint. Articles based primarily or entirely on government sources drew sunny pictures of relocated Indians' new lives. One called the program "a rainbow of hope."[84] Indians in such articles were generally characterized as good Indians who were eager to adapt to the white mainstream. A Sioux man was quoted as saying, "I'm tired of little odd jobs around Rosebud (reservation). I want a regular pay check!" A Navajo man, relocating with his wife and two children to Chicago, was quoted as explaining, "Too many Navajos—not enough to eat."[85]

While such articles occasionally touched on the contrast between Indians' simple reservation lives and the complexities of the city, they did not mention the deracination that was an inevitable part of relocation. A *New York Times* article noted that the newcomers often spoke little English, were bothered by city noises, feared that the tall buildings would fall on them, and were ignorant of such necessities of urban life as buses, streetcars, shopping, and operating kitchen appliances. But the general tone of the article was as optimistic as its headline: "Indians Make Good as City Migrants." The article did not say if any relocatees failed to keep jobs or returned to their reservations.[86]

Pro-relocation articles often portrayed Indians as people with special gifts or attributes that made them ideal workers. For example, a *Reader's Digest* article mentioned the "suitability of Indians for industrial occupations" and quoted various employers as saying that Indians were "particularly skillful at cutting, shaping and riveting sheet metal" and "intelligent, industrious people," that women were adept as stenographers and machine operators, that they were "neat, diligent and skillful."[87] Similarly, an article by Commissioner of Indian Affairs Glenn L. Emmons in *Nation's Business* magazine said employers "have discovered just how skillful, industrious and productive a trained Indian can be."[88]

The picture of Indians presented in the pro-relocation articles was uniformly one of people eager to work, to educate their children, and to get ahead in the sense that whites understood the term—to advance materially in an individualistic, competitive society. They were, in short, seeking success through assimilation.

A very different picture of relocated Indians was painted in articles attacking the plan. They portrayed relocated Indians as victims of a thinly disguised government scheme to deprive them of their lands. The Indians described in these articles were desolate, hopeless people who had been uprooted from their traditional ways and dumped into a hostile urban environment. An *Atlantic Monthly* article put the contrast starkly:

> Two months ago Little Light, her husband Leonard Bear, and their five children were persons of standing in a Creek Indian community in Oklahoma. They had only eighty acres of poor land and a modest cabin, but except for the hungry seasons they understood their way of life; they were at peace.
>
> Today they are slum dwellers in Los Angeles, without land or home or culture or peace.[89]

The article went on to describe the family's squalid living conditions, the husband's drinking, the wife's fear and shame, a child's illness. They were, as the article stated, "victims," poor, degraded Indians who had been wronged by the white government.[90]

Other articles portrayed relocated Indians as simple, gullible, and childlike. A *Coronet* magazine story told of a relocatee in Chicago who "was 'lost' in his room for twenty-four hours. He had lost the BIA [Bureau of Indian Affairs] address. And although he had the phone number he was 'ashamed' to ask how to dial." The article went on to describe the depression of Indian women in city apartments: "Some have locked themselves in their rooms, afraid to go out and tackle the supermarkets."[91] The Indians portrayed in such articles came close to the image of Indians as unspoiled children of nature, untutored in the ways of urban Euro-America. The image in the relocation stories, however, contained few of the glowing descriptions of the unspoiled traditional life that were seen in the 1920s and 1930s. What remained was a bleak image of Indians who were victims of urban society.

IMAGERY AND JOURNALISTIC PRACTICES

The contrast in news values between the press distant from Native American communities and a local paper such as the *Shawano Evening Leader* was evident in two papers' treatments of Indian dances. An Indian dancing contest during the Menominee centennial was reported in the *Shawano Evening Leader* as a contest, with emphasis on the winners as individuals. Each winner was briefly profiled, as in this example:

Second place winner Dewey Wynos Sr. is another Indian who has been "dancing all his life." And he learned the art from his grandparents.

A Menominee, Dewey is married and has five children. He is 38. The Wynos family resides three miles north of Neopit and Dad Wynos is employed in the woods, working as a caterpiller operater [sic] for the Menominee Mills.[92]

The dancers, thus, were portrayed as real citizens with names, families, and multifaceted lives. In structure and tone the article was not unlike one describing winners of a county fair pie-baking competition or an athletic event. Community news values that put a premium on getting local people's names in print allowed the dancers to be portrayed as real people.

In the national press, different values prevailed. An Easterner, writing about what was likely a similar event involving different tribes, a pow wow at Pawnee, Oklahoma, portrayed Indian dancing in a far more stereotypical, though vivid, fashion.

Half-naked young men with tight, hard muscles were dancing with controlled violence, repeating the ritual steps that their warrior ancestors had done generations before. . .

There was a strange confusion of past and present, of the primitive and the sophisticated. A little child in red sneakers came dancing past. A portly Indian—half naked—with a large, well-fed belly heaved past us, wearing rimless glasses, looking for all the world like an accountant at a masquerade.[93]

Indians were quoted in the story, but never named. The imagery was of strange, exotic people who were symbols rather than individuals. Again and again the author expressed wonderment that the romantic savages he remembered from Western movies were living in the twentieth century: "[T]here was . . . something defiant which pulsated beneath the accoutrements of civilized living. Call it a primitive spirit, call it the past made real. . . . It came as a happy vindication of my childhood's romantic dream about Indians."[94]

Here the emphasis was on colorful, personal writing. While that purpose produced a compelling story, it also reinforced the image of Indians as exotic and savage with only a veneer of civilization.

Even in the national press, an interpretative story and a wire service's objective account of the same incident could leave readers with starkly different images, as in the following example: In early February 1954 Sen. Hugh Butler of Nebraska proposed ending the distribution of cloth to New York members of the Iroquois Confederacy. This practice was the provision of a treaty signed in 1794 when George Washington was president. The story carried by the *New York Times* presented a very different image of the people and their insistence on the ancient practice than did the story sent out by the United Press wire service and printed in the *Christian Science Monitor*.

The *New York Times* account described the cloth distribution as an "obligation assumed in the government's earliest days" and an "ancient treaty right." It explained that the Six Nations Iroquois Confederacy "have insisted on this bounty as a symbol of their sovereignty and of title to their lands." It also provided background on the history of the relations between the Iroquois and the European settlers, noting that the Indians once "formed the balance of power" between the French and English.[95]

The image of the Iroquois in this article was of once-sovereign people who have a proud history. The distribution of cloth was not treated as either quaint or trivial. Rather it was seen as an important symbol of their treaty rights as sovereign people living in the United States.

The dispatch by the United Press wire service, which presumably was made available to all United Press newspaper clients nationwide, presented a very different image of the New York tribes. It referred to the cloth annuity as a "token handout" and a "yearly custom." Though the dispatch mentioned the treaty with the Iroquois, it did not explain why the Indians insisted upon its continuance. Instead, it indirectly quoted Senator Butler that the "practice has become outmoded as the Indians become more integrated with the white population."[96]

By failing to explain the Indians' sovereignty argument for continuing the cloth distribution, the United Press dispatch left readers with the image of the Iroquois as exotic and silly and treated the calico cloth merely as fabric rather than a symbol of treaty obligations.

When men from the Lumbee tribe in North Carolina broke up a Ku Klux Klan rally on Jan. 18, 1958, with shouts and gunfire, the story echoed across the country. Articles about the encounter made the front page of the *New York Times, Chicago Tribune,* and *Chicago Daily News* and appeared in the *Christian Science Monitor, Life, Time, Newsweek, U.S. News and World Report,* among others. The extraordinary visibility of the story showed the power both of news values that prize conflict and of Indian images.

The story fit the news formula that esteems the event over the situation, the dramatic confrontation over ambiguous discussion. It was a story that had a clear beginning, plot, and climax. Also, there was likely great interest in stories of Klan activities at this time because of the growing civil rights movement in the South. The same paper that carried the Lumbee story also reported that a stick of dynamite was found in a locker at Little Rock (Arkansas) Central High School, which had been desegregated the previous fall under federal guard.[97]

But a clear factor that made the story irresistible to the nation's press was the image of Indians as warlike. Here, again, was the centuries-old image of the bloodthirsty warrior, refined for the times. The phrase "on the warpath" occurred six times in the twelve stories examined. Stories were strewn with other phrases that brought to mind Saturday matinee movies such as "A horde of armed Indians," "Redskins stirred up,"[98] "the Indian war,"[99] "war-whooping, gun-shooting Indian raid,"[100] "a tough but fairly peace-loving lot," "ancient Indian anger," "old war cries," "Natives are restless,"[101] and "bad medicine."[102]

The story seemed to grow more vivid with the retelling. The first day's account in the *New York Times* said, "scattered shots and a few weak war whoops were heard."[103] But a follow-up Associated Press story in the *Chicago Tribune* said, "Bloodcurdling warwhoops and volleys of rifle and shotgun fire burst upon the quiet, cold evening."[104]

A first-person account by a reporter whose car was damaged in the melee repeated many of the old warlike Indian images. "Covering an Indian war is still dangerous," United Press reporter Alvin Webb wrote, "especially when the Indians and palefaces take turns shooting in your general direction." The story went on to say the newsmen "didn't spot any bows and arrows or horses—but we managed to have our car shot out from under us" and that they were "surrounded by some fifty Indians—some friendly but others hostile."[105]

Other stories explained that the Lumbee people had lived in North Carolina for centuries and variously described them as a branch of the Cherokee nation or descendants of the Croatans who may have taken in Sir Walter Raleigh's seventeenth-century colony on Roanoke Island. In any case they were far in time, place, and culture from the Plains Indians whose encounters with whites gave rise to the popular culture image in the reporter's account.

DISCUSSION

Images of Native Americans at the beginning of the termination era contrasted sharply in the local and national press. Readers of the Menominees' "hometown" paper, the *Shawano Evening Leader*, saw an image of well-informed and articulate local citizens struggling with the powerful and distant federal government. Readers of papers beyond Northern Wisconsin saw only glimpses of a people who seemed little different from the white majority, people who were ready for "freedom." While stories in both local and nonlocal papers were essentially factual, the facts, and the images they contained, conveyed very different meanings.

The local press reported the termination story in detail as a significant local issue. Its straightforward reporting depicted the Menominees as members of the community. If they had an image, it was of involved Indian citizens.

But the termination of the Menominees took place almost entirely outside the national spotlight. Though the national press covered in general terms Congressional efforts to terminate federal responsibilities toward Native Americans, it virtually ignored the Menominees until well after their legislation was enacted. While many factors were involved, the force of familiar Indian imagery as an index of newsworthiness undoubtedly contributed. Menominees were not colorful and exotic enough, nor were they destitute enough, to attract the attention of the press outside Wisconsin. Because they did not fit neatly into the images often assigned to Indians, their story failed to resonate. Also, the terminology of "freedom" and "emancipation" used by Senator Watkins as he pushed termination bills through Congress conveyed a benign image that did not hint at the consequences for the Indians.

In contrast, stories that played to the familiar Indian images of exotic people doing ancient dances at a pow wow, pitiable victims of relocation, or war-whooping braves attacking the Ku Klux Klan drew prominent placement and banner headlines in publications far from the locales of the incidents.

NOTES

1. Nicholas C. Peroff, *Menominee Drums* (Norman: University of Oklahoma Press, 1982), 22.

2. Oliver LaFarge, "Termination of Federal Supervision: Disintegration and the American Indians," *Annals of the American Academy of Political and Social Sciences* 311 (May 1957): 43–44.

3. Arthur V. Watkins, "Termination of Federal Supervision: The Removal of Restrictions Over Indian Property and Person," *Annals of the American Academy of Political and Social Science* 311 (May 1957): 55.

4. Peroff, 64.

5. Larry W. Burt, *Tribalism in Crisis: Federal Indian Policy, 1953–1961* (Albuquerque: University of New Mexico Press, 1982), 4–5.

6. Francis Paul Prucha, *The Great Father* Volume II (Lincoln: University of Nebraska Press, 1984), 1024.

7. Article by O. K. Armstrong, *Reader's Digest*, August, 1945, 47–52.

8. Quoted in Prucha, 1024.

9. Donald L. Fixico, *Termination and Relocation: Federal Indian Policy, 1945–1960* (Albuquerque: University of New Mexico Press, 1986), 134.

10. Prucha, 1026–1028.

11. Quoted in Fixico, 93–94.

12. Fixico, 97–99; Burt, 22–23.

13. Burt, 23–24.

14. Ibid., 24–25.

15. Fixico, 106.

16. Peroff, 72–73.

17. James L. Baughman, *The Republic of Mass Culture* (Baltimore: Johns Hopkins University Press, 1992), 60.

18. Grant Milnor Hyde, *Newspaper Reporting* (New York: Prentice Hall, Inc., 1952), 203.

19. Ibid., 67.

20. John Paul Jones, *The Modern Reporter's Handbook* (New York: Rinehart & Co., Inc., 1949), 63.

21. See, for example, Hyde, 434.

22. Commission on Freedom of the Press, *A Free and Responsible Press* (Chicago: University of Chicago Press, 1947), 20–29. The other requirements were: "2. A forum for the exchange of comment and criticism. 4. The presentation and clarification of the goals and values of the society. 5. Full access to the day's intelligence."

23. Marion Marzolf, *Civilizing Voices: American Press Criticism 1880–1950* (New York: Longman Publishing Group, 1991), 172.

24. Charles W. Gilmore, "The Cherokee Phoenix," *Nieman Reports* 2, no. 3 (July 1948): 13–14.

25. Leon Svirsky, ed., *Your Newspaper: Blueprint for a Better Press* (New York: The Macmillan Company, 1947), 22–24.

26. *Christian Science Monitor*, Apr. 19, 1952, E5.

27. Ibid.

28. *Christian Science Monitor*, Nov. 19, 1953, E2.

29. *Christian Science Monitor*, May 15, 1953, 7.

30. Ibid.

31. *Commonweal*, Aug. 28, 1953, 505.

32. *Christian Science Monitor*, Mar. 11, 1953, 17.

33. Ibid.

34. *New York Times*, Aug. 16, 1954, 19.

35. *New York Times*, May 9, 1954, sec. X, p. 37.

36. *New York Times*, June 21, 1953, 56.

37. *New York Times*, Mar. 1, 1954, 27.

38. Deborah Shames, ed., *Freedom With Reservation: The Menominee Struggle to Save Their Land and People* (Madison: National Committee to Save the Menominee People and Forests, 1972), 1–3.

39. Ibid., 3.

40. *Shawano Evening Leader*, June 22, 1953, 1.

41. Shames, 7–8; Peroff, 53–55; Fixico, 95–96.

42. *Shawano Evening Leader*, Mar. 4, 1954, 1.

43. Shames, 8–9; Peroff, 56–58.

44. Shames, x.

45. Ibid., 10–11.

46. Peroff, 197.

47. R. Bruce Jones, ed., *N. W. Ayer & Son's Directory of Newspapers and Periodicals 1953* (Philadelphia: N. W. Ayer & Son, Inc., 1953), 1066.

48. *Green Bay Press-Gazette*, June 22, 1953, 19.

49. *Milwaukee Journal*, June 23, 1953, 9.

50. *Chicago Tribune*, Aug. 5, 1953, part 1, p. 16.

51. *Shawano Evening Leader*, June 18, 1953, 1.

52. Ibid.

53. *Green Bay Press-Gazette*, June 22, 1953, 19.

54. Ibid.

55. *Milwaukee Journal*, June 23, 1953, 9.

56. Ibid.

57. *Shawano Evening Leader*, June 22, 1953, 1.

58. Ibid.

59. Ibid.

60. *Shawano Evening Leader*, June 18, 1953, 1.

61. *Shawano Evening Leader*, June 20, 1953, 1.

62. *Milwaukee Sentinel*, Aug. 15, 1954, E1; Aug. 22, 1954, E1; Aug. 29, 1954, E1; Sept. 5, 1954, E3.

63. *Shawano Evening Leader*, Aug. 6, 1954, Menominee Indian Reservation Centennial Edition.

64. *Shawano Evening Leader*, Aug. 20, 1953, 1.

65. Ibid.

66. See, for example, obituary for Theodore Neconish, *Shawano Evening Leader*, Aug. 4, 1953, 1.

67. *New York Times*, Mar. 1, 1954, 25.

68. *New York Times*, Mar. 26, 1954, 9.

69. *New York Times*, Feb. 26, 1954, 8.

70. *New York Times*, Feb. 27, 1954, 30.

71. *Christian Science Monitor*, Mar. 4, 1954, E5. See also *New York Times*, Apr. 4, 1954, sec. IV, p. 8, and *Washington Post*, Apr. 12, 1954, 8.

72. *New York Times*, June 18, 1954, 17.

73. *New York Times*, June 21, 1954, 14.

74. *New York Times*, Aug. 7, 1954, 15.

75. *Milwaukee Journal*, Aug. 4, 1954, 1.

76. *Milwaukee Journal*, Aug. 13, 1954, 1.

77. *Shawano Evening Leader*, Aug. 7, 1954, 1.

78. *Shawano Evening Leader*, Aug. 16, 1954, 1.

79. *Saturday Evening Post*, Nov. 23, 1957, 10.

80. *New York Times*, Oct. 9, 1955, 60.

81. Fixico, 136; see also Elaine M. Neils, *Reservation to City* (Chicago: University of Chicago Department of Geography Research Paper No. 131, 1971).

82. Fixico, 143.

83. Ibid., 148, 235.

84. O. K. Armstrong and Marjorie Armstrong, "The Indians Are Going to Town," *Reader's Digest*, Jan. 1955, 41.

85. Ibid., 40.

86. *New York Times*, May 18, 1953, 23.

87. Armstrong and Armstrong, 42.

88. Glenn L. Emmons, "Give Indians a Chance," *Nation's Business*, July 1955, 42.

89. Ruth Mulvey Harmer, "Uprooting the Indians," *Atlantic Monthly*, Mar. 1956, 54.

90. Ibid., 54–57.

91. Madelon Golden and Lucia Carter, "New Deal for America's Indians," *Coronet*, Oct. 1955, 74–76.

92. *Shawano Evening Leader*, Aug. 14, 1954, 1.

93. *New York Times*, Aug. 23, 1953, 21.

94. Ibid.

95. *New York Times*, Feb. 3, 1954, 1.

96. United Press dispatch in the *Christian Science Monitor*, Feb. 4, 1954, 6.

97. *Chicago Tribune*, Jan. 21, 1958, 6.

98. *Chicago Tribune*, Jan. 19, 1958, 1, 4.
99. *U.S. News and World Report*, Jan. 31, 1958, 14.
100. *Newsweek*, Jan. 27, 1958, 27.
101. *Time*, Jan. 27, 1958, 20.
102. *Life*, Jan. 27, 1958, 26–27.
103. *New York Times*, Jan. 19, 1958, 1.
104. *Chicago Tribune*, Jan. 21, 1958, 4.
105. *Chicago Daily News*, Jan. 20, 1958, 10.

6

The 1960s and 1970s: Direct Action for Self-Determination

In the predawn hours of November 20, 1969, a group of Native Americans, many of them San Francisco-area college students, landed on Alcatraz Island and "claimed" it for Indians.[1] Their occupation of the island, which lasted until June 1971, captured public and media attention nationwide. The seizure of the barren, rocky former prison island in San Francisco Bay in a sense opened an era in which activist Native Americans put themselves prominently on the mainstream news agenda. The 1970s was the "high-water mark" of native activism, with more than one hundred political events, including the occupation of Bureau of Indian Affairs (BIA) headquarters in Washington in 1972 and the seventy-one-day standoff at Wounded Knee, South Dakota, in 1973.[2] It was an era when public interest in things Indian was higher than at any time since the 1920s when John Collier and his allies had called on the nation to "save the Pueblos."[3] However, in contrast to the 1920s, the instigators of action in the 1960s and 1970s were Native Americans themselves, with whites in supporting roles.

If Alcatraz was a beginning, it was also a culmination of forces that had been building since World War II. Then, thousands of Indians left their reservations for the first time to serve in the military or work in defense factories. When they returned to the reservation, they brought their experience of the outside world and found at home poverty and unemployment.[4] Later, in the 1950s, Congress' asserted intent to end all federal services to Indians and its actual termination of several tribes caused many to fear they would be next. Termination led the National Congress of American Indians (NCAI), the main pan-Indian organization of the time, to denounce bitterly the policies that threatened tribal existence without consulting the Indians themselves.

The companion policy to termination, relocating reservation Indians in cities, spurred an urban migration that brought some one hundred thousand Native Americans to cities between 1953 and 1972. Thousands more relocated on their own. This migration had the unintended effect of spawning a generation of relatively worldly, sophisticated urban Indians who were more independent of tribal strictures, more accepting of pan-Indian ideas, and more politically active and militant than their elders.[5] The postwar era also saw far more Native Americans going to college than ever before, and by the 1960s they were coming of age. They could not help but notice the gains being made by blacks as they confronted segregation in the civil rights movement. Activist Native Americans took lessons from the confrontational tactics of black civil rights leaders and proclaimed "red power" for themselves and their people.

Standing Rock Sioux author Vine Deloria, Jr., wrote that many Indians were ambivalent about joining with or adopting the tactics of the civil rights movement, some because of natural reticence and others because of ideological considerations. Native Americans, after all, were seeking to maintain their ancestral lands and cultures, not to integrate into the white world. But in the confrontational atmosphere of the 1960s, Deloria contended, "Indians were forced to adopt the vocabulary and techniques of the blacks in order to get their grievances serious consideration by the media."[6]

According to Stephen Cornell, tactics of direct action appeared sporadically in the late 1950s with Mohawks and Tuscaroras in New York state and the Lumbees who routed a Ku Klux Klan rally in North Carolina (see previous chapter). By the 1960s incidents such as "fish-ins" in the Northwest and other direct actions were becoming frequent. Cornell counted more than sixty major events in the decade.[7] Indian activism was spurred by the meeting in 1961 of the American Indian Chicago Conference, organized by University of Chicago anthropology professor Sol Tax and the National Congress of American Indians, which drew together nearly five hundred Indians from sixty-seven tribes.[8] Young, more militant Indians at the conference formed the National Indian Youth Council (NIYC) and took a major role in drafting the conference's statement of purpose.[9]

Both the conference's statement of purpose and, later, the NIYC's statement of policy repudiated assimilation and endorsed tribal nationalism or self-determination. The "Declaration of Indian Purpose" of the American Indian Chicago Conference said:

> We, the Indian people, must be governed by high principles and laws in a democratic manner, with a right to choose our own way of life. Since our Indian culture is slowly being absorbed by the American society, we believe we have the responsibility of preserving our precious heritage; recognizing that certain changes are inevitable. We believe that the Indians should provide the adjustment. . . . We

believe in the inherent right of all people to retain spiritual and cultural values, and that the free exercise of these values is necessary to the normal development of any people.[10]

The "Statement of Purpose" of the National Indian Youth Council stated:

The Indian people are going to remain Indians for a long time to come. However, every ethnic group of people who are to live within a changing world of good and bad influences must possess a sense of security within their own group. Being of Indian origin should always be held in high regard but never as a disadvantage. American Indians rightfully hold an esteemed and influential position based on their past and present record. . . . [T]here is and always will be need for the Indian people themselves to protect our birthright.[11]

The Kennedy and Johnson administrations had endorsed the idea of increasing Indian self-determination and had funneled significant funds to reservations through various antipoverty programs. However, tribal governments, which were designed by the New Deal Indian Reorganization Act and which offended tribal traditionalists by their subservience to the BIA, largely administered the funds. For most, traditional power structures changed little.[12] During the 1968 presidential campaign, Richard Nixon repudiated termination and endorsed the principle of self-determination. He made good on his rhetoric in a message to Congress in 1970 that "called for self-determination without termination."[13] However, the legislation he proposed was not immediately enacted, and Indians by 1973 denounced the administration for inertia in implementing its promises.[14]

If the rhetoric of the 1950s celebrated assimilation and conformity, the self-determination movement of the following decades emphatically rejected that notion in favor of Indians' asserting control over their own institutions and celebrating traditional cultural expressions and values. Even as pan-Indian movements were gaining prominence, traditionalists of many tribes were calling for a return to the old ways of governing and religious practices.[15]

To the chagrin of many Native Americans and to the economic benefit of others, portions of the mainstream culture appropriated Indian accouterments, and for a while in the late 1960s and early 1970s, radical chic meant wearing Indian jewelry and garments and displaying one's sympathy for Native Americans. One reason for the public interest in Indian culture and causes was the highly-charged mood of the 1960s and 1970s. The nation was reeling from political assassinations, urban riots, an increasingly unpopular foreign war, antiwar demonstrations, and the colorful antics of disaffected youth. Change was in the air. The public seemed eager to hear the complaints of the downtrodden and move for reform. It appeared that Native Americans thus joined blacks, Chicanos, migrant workers, and others as yet another disadvantaged group seeking its due. If definitions of newsworthiness included conflict and the unusual, Native American activism was newsworthy indeed.

THE PRESS

By the 1960s, the news media had become acutely aware of its responsibilities to racial and ethnic minorities. Some of the awareness was thrust upon it by the era's big stories such as the Southern school integration conflicts that began in the 1950s, the nonviolent direct action against segregation laws in the South such as boycotts and protest marches, and the riots in northern cities. Most of the reporters covering the Southern civil rights movement for the mainstream Northern press were white men. By the late 1960s, however, when riots erupted in black areas of Los Angeles, Newark, Detroit, and other cities, editors began to see clearly that it was in their self-interests to have multiracial staffs and to pay attention to news from communities of color.

The press' inadequacies in covering racial issues and the black community were driven home by the stinging criticism in Chapter 15 of the *Report of the National Advisory Commission on Civil Disorders* (the Kerner Commission). The commission was appointed by President Lyndon B. Johnson after the disastrous 1967 riots in Detroit, Newark, and elsewhere. It was charged with finding out not only what happened but how future riots could be prevented (see Chapter 1 of this book). The report said the news media

> have failed to analyze and report adequately on racial problems in the United States and . . . to meet the Negro's legitimate expectations in journalism. . . . The media report and write from the standpoint of a white man's world. The ills of the ghetto, the difficulties of life there, the Negro's burning sense of grievance are seldom conveyed. Slights and indignities are part of the Negro's daily life, and many of them come from what he now calls "the white press"—a press that repeatedly, if unconsciously, reflects the biases, the paternalism, the indifference of white America.[16]

The report also called on the news media to report the broader subject of race relations in context, to cultivate diverse sources among blacks, to hire more blacks, and to integrate black news into all parts of the paper.[17]

The Kerner Commission report was a milestone in press criticism and a benchmark by which coverage of racial and ethnic groups has been measured ever since. Its publication, plus the upheavals of the times, led to numerous conferences, symposia, and publications on coverage of racial issues.[18] A survey of news media executives taken shortly after the report's publication showed that many of those responding agreed that the media's coverage of race was flawed, that they were trying to improve, and that there were not enough blacks in journalism.[19] Coverage of those outside the mainstream had clearly caught the attention of the mainstream press.

Journalism educators, according to one study, were slow to respond to the call for more and better coverage of racial issues and the companion need to train journalists to do this coverage. A study of reporting textbooks published before and after the Kerner report said, "There has always been some compassion for minorities (even when paternalistic in texts), but the evolution toward adequate discussion and guidance for students has been slow."[20] The article noted wide variance in texts' attention to coverage of minorities.

One book that did devote considerable space to coverage of minorities was *Reporting the Citizens' News* by Ralph S. Izard, which dealt with many aspects of journalism and groups outside the mainstream, including Native Americans. The book devoted about three pages to advising students on how to cover American Indians, telling them to study texts and scholarly analyses, to talk to experts, and especially to spend time with people on the reservations or in urban neighborhoods.[21] The book also warned against use of words such as "pow wow" for a discussion involving Indians and "on the warpath" when Indians took issue with authorities. Such terms, it said, "have become stereotypes and may be used to classify groups of individuals in a way which denies their individuality." It also said, "The fact that groups or individuals are honestly sensitive about a certain label should be given consideration. But that does not mean automatic acceptance."[22]

The Kerner Commission dealt only with the coverage of African Americans—"Negroes." Most criticism of the coverage of racial matters framed the matter along black-white lines. Some, however, sought to apply its criticisms and recommendations to the coverage of Native Americans. In the *Columbia Journalism Review* survey of news executives cited earlier, one respondent, James Kuehn of the *Rapid City Journal* in South Dakota, responded in terms of his paper's coverage of Indians, not blacks: "We have an Indian settlement . . . that is not very inviting. I do not feel our employees understand their plight or problems."[23] That statement was prophetic in view of the occupation of nearby Wounded Knee about five years later.

In their groundbreaking history of the Native American press, James E. Murphy and Sharon M. Murphy wrote that the Kerner Commission's criticisms "could have easily been applied to the media treatment of Indians." Coverage of the direct actions of the 1970s, they wrote earlier, was "crisis-activated and did little to further the ongoing story of Indian life and needs."[24]

Even as it was reassessing its coverage of minority groups, the press in the 1960s and 1970s was looking anew at its own values and practices. The assault on objectivity that dated from the 1930s now took on a more political aspect. According to Michael Schudson, critics in the 1960s said "objective" reporting "reproduced a vision of social reality which refused to examine the basic structures of power and privilege. It was not just incomplete, . . . it was distorted. It represented collusion with institutions whose legitimacy was in dispute."[25] Schudson listed three criticisms of objectivity articulated in the 1960s. First, such news stories rested on certain assumptions about government and society. In other words, the starting point of objective stories was an assumption of the validity of the essential status quo. Second, objective stories were biased toward the "observable and unambiguous," toward an "impersonal narrative style" and "inverted pyramid" organization, toward conflict, and toward "events rather than processes." Third, such stories favored the passive recording of official viewpoints.[26]

Those concerned with the shortcomings of objectivity pointed to a term coined in 1961 by Daniel Boorstin—the "pseudo-event"—as an illustration of the way objectivity allowed the press to be manipulated. A "pseudo-event," Boorstin explained, was something that was not spontaneous, as was a train wreck or an earthquake, but took place "for the immediate purpose of being reported or reproduced." Its success, he wrote, "is measured by how widely it is reported."[27] Pseudo-events, Boorstin wrote, "have blurred the edges of reality. . . . are neither true nor false in the old familiar senses. . . . [T]he images—however planned, contrived, or distorted—[are] more vivid, more attractive, more impressive, and more persuasive than reality itself."[28] Stories written within the constraints of the objective form could be manipulated by the planners of pseudo-events because the objective form left little room for interpretation.

One could argue that the Native American activists who invited the press to cover their takeovers of Alcatraz Island and Wounded Knee, whether unwittingly or by design, were participating in elaborate pseudo-events. If this was the case, it was also true that the federal authorities who were the activists' adversaries were using the objective press' traditional reliance on official sources to get across their side of the story.

As Schudson and others have indicated, the critique of objectivity, along with other factors such as the increasing influence of television news, led to expansions of news definitions and forms. The media, particularly larger newspapers, provided more room for investigative and "enterprise" reporting and allowed journalists more leeway in how they presented the news, whether through interpretation or more personalized feature writing.[29]

The popularity of the "new journalism," that is, using certain literary devices in the writing of nonfiction, led some journalists to experiment with that highly descriptive, sometimes personal, form in column and feature writing.[30] Investigative reporting, too, was increasingly popular and widely practiced. It was spurred by the upheavals of the time that called into question government credibility and brought to public attention injustices toward many groups.[31]

IMAGES

The 1960s and 1970s brought important changes both to Native Americans and to journalistic practices. Did these changes lead to different images of native people in the press? This chapter will examine articles that illustrate images in general, then examine the actions at Alcatraz and Wounded Knee as reported by the local and national press.

Newspapers and magazines ran numerous stories about Indians in the 1960s and 1970s that contained some new images and revisited old ones. Generally stories of the era differed from previous times in the attention they paid to Indian voices. These voices—often militant and angry—came from people with names, personalities, and causes, people who were often taking on the white establishment, people who required the press to deal with them on their own terms. Native Americans, in their press portrayals, seemed less distant from the reader than before. Nevertheless, stereotypical images and language turned up frequently. However sensitive journalists were becoming to minority issues, they still, on occasion, found Indian subjects to trivialize and demean.

For example *Newsweek*'s heavy-handed attempt at humor belittled the important 1961 American Indian Chicago Conference:

> It was the first time since Hiawatha was knee-high to a tall papoose that braves grown gray had come from every tribe . . . to sit around a mystical council fire. To indulge the white man's notion of the red man (and satisfy their own passion for ethnic distinction), they first passed around and puffed at the calumet.[32]

The image of the good Indian as noble savage was reborn in the 1960s and 1970s to depict Native Americans as prophets and saviors who would show whites the way back to a humane, earth-centered existence. The image fit well with the newly-popular concern for the environment. Such stories often treated the diverse tribal cultures and beliefs as a single entity and spoke of "the Indian way." For example, in 1971, *Life* magazine, which once banned stories about Indians on the whim of a managing editor,[33] ran a special issue on American Indians. One passage stated:

> America is only now beginning to learn how valid this [Indian] way was, how relevant to man's needs. And barely in time, for the white man's actions which brought the Indian close to extinction today seem destined to curse the whole environment. From its Indian citizens the United States may yet learn some lessons about restoring the balance between man and his surroundings.[34]

The same year *Mademoiselle,* a fashion magazine for young women, published an interview with Vine Deloria, Jr., the Standing Rock Sioux author of the popular *Custer Died for Your Sins* and other works. Deloria was quoted as saying:

> There's got to be a recognition that you can't go on and on exploiting the earth. . . . There's got to be a return to some kind of meaningful relationship with natural things, such as Indians have had. . . . [T]here's got to be an owning up—not just saying that Indians were right and whites were wrong, but an understanding that

the earth . . . can't stand the greed and exploitation which are built into Anglo values.[35]

An *Esquire* profile on Wallace Mad Bear Anderson, the Tuscarora traditionalist, said "he spreads the word of an Indian rebirth: as the white man destroys his own world with guns and garbage, the Indians will inherit the land once again."[36]

The image of Indians in such stories was once again as it had been in the 1920s and 1930s, of the unspoiled children of nature who held the key to salvation of decadent white society by their closeness to the natural world and communal institutions. Native Americans' legitimate and traditional reverence for the earth was often romanticized and overly generalized in such stories.

A corollary image was one that predicted great progress for tribes that had seized their own resources and exploited them in their own Indian way. In contrast to the 1950s image of Native Americans as successful only if they cast off their cultures and assimilated into the white mainstream, the 1960s-1970s image embraced a capitalistic self-determination. This highly optimistic "shrewd Indian" image was exemplified in a *U.S. News and World Report* article that likened Navajos to oil-rich Arab nations as tough bargainers for development of their resources.[37] Another article in the same vein, by Marvin L. Franklin, assistant to the secretary of the interior for Indian affairs, said a program of "bringing industrial plants to Indian communities is creating jobs and lifting standards of living for the 'original Americans.' "[38]

But the hopeful stories were easily offset by those bemoaning the Indians' plight. The degraded Indian image, a staple of Indian depictions since at least the nineteenth century, was now elaborated on in heart-rending detail in exposes of the "plight" of Indians—their schools, their lives on reservations, their lives in urban ghettos. Articles bore such titles as "Hope Has Little Meaning for Blackfoot Indians,"[39] "The Lagoon of Excrement,"[40] "The 50,000,000 Acre Ghetto,"[41] "Our Shameful Failure with America's Indians."[42] Frequently the stories recited the statistical litany of Indian deficiencies, such as these from the *Reader's Digest*: an average yearly income of $1,500, less than half the national poverty level; life expectancy of forty-four years, versus sixty-six years nationwide; an infant mortality rate three times the national figure; 70 percent of housing substandard; school dropout rates twice the national average; a teen suicide rate five times the national average.[43]

Beyond the figures, the image of Indians as degraded and destitute was reinforced by descriptions such as this from a *New York Times* story on the Blackfeet tribe in Browning, Montana:

Many Indians live in squalid shacks that look like they had been transported out of the Dust Bowl of the Depression. About one-third have no indoor plumbing, and the water is frequently so contaminated no one can drink it. Only one street in the entire town is paved. . . . What pervades this town is a feeling of shame, to the point of self-loathing.[44]

A *Newsweek* story on urban Indians said their condition "represents a new dimension in wretchedness."[45] Even a story about a relatively wealthy tribe, the Jicarilla Apaches of New Mexico, described them in terms of their deficiencies. Asking the question, "Is a multimillionaire Apache tribe really rich?" the article described the tribe's ventures into land deals; movies; gas, oil, and timber leases. But it also mentioned widespread alcoholism and individual poverty. "[T]he immediate impression is of nearby shacks, hulks of abandoned cars. . . . There is a sense of sadness, withdrawal, coolness, depression despite the flickering wit and enthusiasm of [tribal council president] Charlie Vigil. . . . The reservation looks poor despite public affluence."[46] Thus even Indians supposed to be well-off were seen as poor, both materially and in spirit.

Two themes developed another image of Indians, that of an ancient and exotic people, a people of the past. One theme played up the popularity of Indian cultural artifacts—jewelry and garments—which became fashion items sold in upscale department stores such as Saks Fifth Avenue. A *Newsweek* story titled "Tribal Chic," began, "With the plight of the American Indian high on the latest list of liberal causes, it was only a matter of time until Indian artifacts became the latest word in fashion."[47] Or, as *Time* magazine put it, "On the fad level, a budding renaissance of Indian cultural accouterments has inspired pot-smoking teen-agers and high-fashion socialites to don beaded necklaces, fringed jackets, Indian belts, bikinis and feathers."[48]

Charlotte Curtis of the *New York Times* used pointed wit to skewer liberal socialites who held a cocktail party at a Southampton, Long Island, mansion to aid American Indians.

"They aren't to be believed," the taxicab tycoon's wife said as she looked at the motley fashions out across the lawn. "Did you ever see such get-ups?" . . . What Mrs. Scull was seeing was Indians in coats and ties and paleface Southampton women in beads, feathers, fringed leather and all the other bits and pieces of what passes for Indian fashion.[49]

Thus Native American material culture, and sometimes religious items, became status symbols for those who wanted to appear "with it." The fact that the jewelry and garments derived from a place and time remote from mainstream Euro-American culture helped give them commercial value. The clothing and jewelry were depicted as exotic oddities, the fad of the moment.

Another evocation of the image of Indians as ancient and exotic came in the press attention given to traditional Indian religious practices. Rather than being seen as pagan, immoral, or curious as they had been in previous times, such practices were now depicted as being admired and embraced by members of the counterculture and at least treated with some respect by others.

A two-page article on the "revival of American Indian religion" in *Newsweek* stated that "Indians are finding new significance in their ancient religious heritage" and that tribal religions "are becoming a powerful source of Indian solidarity."[50] The article commented positively on such formerly condemned rites as the Sun Dance of the Plains Indians and the use of peyote in the Native American Church.

The *Life* magazine issue on Indians described Hopi kachinas respectfully, without skepticism or reference to Christianity:

> [The San Francisco Peaks] are the home of the kachinas, the spirit forces of the universe. In February the kachinas descend from the peaks into the villages to help bring on the rain. They cannot be seen, but during festivals, the Indians believe, the kachinas enter into the dancers and inform their ceremonial masks with spiritual powers.[51]

When the federal government returned the sacred Blue Lake in the Sangre de Cristo Mountains of New Mexico to the Taos people in December of 1970, a number of articles described the religious practice that dictated native use of the lake.

Articles such as these, while they dealt respectfully with Native American religions, at times portrayed the people as mystical and almost otherworldly, people whose exotic and ancient religions gave them insights unavailable to whites.

Perhaps the most distinctive image to come out of the era was that of Indians as angry and militant. This image generally depicted Indians as people who had suffered in relative silence for generations and finally were seeking redress. As Oliver LaFarge, a well-known author and defender of Indians, put it, "The temper of American Indians has reached the boiling point."[52] In essence this image was a variation on that of the noble savage. Some articles romanticized the efforts of Indians to speak for themselves and control their own destinies. For example, an article in *Mademoiselle* began, "Hokahne! 'It's a good day to die,' the old Sioux war cry, is the call to arms for today's young Indian women, who feel they have only three hundred years of repression to lose and everything to gain."[53]

In some versions, the image depicted Indians as politely confrontational, less menacing than activists of other ethnic groups. A *New York Times* story about Thomasine Ruth Hill, Miss Indian America, quoted her on the subject of "red power" as saying, "[T]here is a good side to [red] power and a bad side. I feel that Indians would not resort to violence to achieve their goals. We've learned from past history that it doesn't pay off."[54] Other articles portrayed angrier Indians, as in this *Time* story:

After more than a century of patience and passivity, the nation's most neglected and isolated minority is astir, seeking the means and the muscle for protest and redress. . . . [T]he new American Indian is fed up with the destitution and publicly sanctioned abuse of his long-divided people. . . . [T]he newly aroused Indian is no longer content to play the obsequious Tonto to the white man's Lone Ranger.[55]

The image sometimes depicted a legendary warrior, fighting a modern conflict to preserve the ancient rights of his people. Such an image was seen in a *Ramparts* article on efforts of militant Washington Indians to enforce their salmon-fishing rights. One member of the Nisqually tribe was described:

Tall and sinuous, with fine features, his black shoulder-length hair secured with a red headband, Bridges cuts a flamboyant figure. . . . He has been arrested 21 times since becoming involved in the fishing rights and has a 15-year sentence on appeal; over the years, when few other sources of dignity were available, he has come to take pride in the ability to fight back, as he says, "so that it takes three or four of them to get the handcuffs on."[56]

Thus militant Indians were generally depicted sympathetically as romantic figures who were saving not only their own people but a failing white society by resurrecting the ways of the past. As *Look* magazine put it:

Indians—perceiving today a certain falling apart of our society—are becoming freshly attuned to their own culture and old sayings. The upshot is a wholly new thing: pan-Indian nationalism. . . . And with this new awareness has grown new militancy—a determination to judge life according to their own values, as well as to retain an Indian identity while participating in an industrial economy.[57]

This positive image, however, was offset by a counterimage after militants took over institutions, brandished weapons, and left material ruin in their wake. Two such actions are described in the following sections.

ALCATRAZ

The takeover of Alcatraz Island, the derelict federal prison in San Francisco Bay, was, essentially, fueled by the increasing urbanization and education of Native Americans. It showed their acute awareness of their ill-treatment by whites and their yearnings to resurrect traditional tribal cultures. Richard Oakes, a Mohawk and former steel worker then living in San Francisco, was one of the leaders of the action. Oakes was one of the first students in San Francisco State College's Native American Studies program. He wrote that he proposed the invasion at a statewide meeting of Indian college students. His rationale, he explained, was that the island, having been closed as a prison, was being considered for a number of uses, including a theme park and a cemetery.[58] Indians involved in the takeover cited a nineteenth-century federal law that gave some tribes permission to reclaim unused federal land that had been taken from them.[59] After an initial landing in which fourteen Indians stayed overnight on the island, then allowed themselves to be removed by federal authorities, about eighty arrived in force on November 20, 1969.

Using wry irony, they claimed the island "by right of discovery" and offered to buy it from the government for "$24 in glass beads and red cloth, a precedent set by the white man's purchase of a similar island three hundred years ago." Alcatraz was well-suited for Indians, they said, because it was "isolated from modern facilities . . . has no fresh running water . . . has inadequate sanitation facilities" and its inhabitants had "always been held as prisoners and kept dependent on others." Thus, the Indians proclaimed, "this place resembles most Indian reservations."[60]

The young Indians saw the takeover as "symbolic of a spiritual rebirth" and "a first step towards rebuilding the land base" usurped by whites. But it was also, "an experiment in self-determination" and an exercise in public relations, that is, of "educating the general public to the Indian condition [by] breaking . . . into the public news media."[61] The invisibility the Indians felt was put this way in the "Alcatraz Newsletter," a publication of the early months of the occupation: "Before we took Alcatraz, people in San Francisco didn't even know that Indians were alive, and if that's a sample of what the local people knew, . . . then there are people across the nation who never knew that Indians were alive or ever even knew our problems."[62]

Certainly the nationwide news coverage generated by the takeover made Native Americans visible. The young Indians on the island initially invited the press to accompany their landings and visit their makeshift habitations. The news media, in turn, covered the story extensively, publicizing virtually without question the Indians' demands that the island be turned over to them and used for a Native American cultural-educational center; the visits from celebrities; the pow wows, conferences, and pronouncements.

The occupying Indians expected federal officials to force them from the island. Instead the government cut off water and electricity and waited for the Indians to give up. The standoff continued thus through two winters while the dwindling number of Indians endured physical hardships, internal dissension, disorganization, alcohol and drug abuse, and violence.[63] Finally, on June 11, 1971, federal marshals removed the remaining fifteen Indians and retook the island.[64]

In the early months of the occupation, stories in both the local San Francisco press and national publications portrayed the Indians sympathetically and almost light-heartedly. "The Indian uprising that worked," headlined a *Look* magazine article. "[T]here exists here a sense of something exalted and superbly primeval," William Hedgepeth wrote in the article, "Scents of victory fill the air. . . . [T]his invasion amounts to THE symbolic act of Indian awareness. . . . The beginning of the warpath!"[65] Kay Boyle, writing in *The New Republic*, called it a "stunning act of the imagination and the will."[66]

In the San Francisco newspapers, the "invasion" was front page news. The "cheerful occupation" of the Indians was reported in vivid detail that sounded like a school field trip or camp-out. "All seemed in good spirits, including at least four children who played hide-and-seek in the tiny cellblocks . . . ," one story said. It went on to report about the Indians watching football on television and playing softball and Frisbee.[67] Another article said the Indians painted signs saying the island was "Indian Land," and some "lounged around the fire while others gathered around the big tom-tom for ceremonial sings."[68]

National magazines and the *New York Times* also portrayed the landings sympathetically. Earl Caldwell, writing in the *New York Times*, evoked images of elemental nobility and innocence in his descriptions of the Indians on the island, such as the "husky youth . . . with the wind sweeping his long black hair" and the "muscular Indian youths, most of them teenagers" who were unloading donated food while "the women romped with their children in the prison yard." The article described a well-organized community: "They have their own security force. They have teams that fish for food. They are converting the old guard houses and administrative buildings into living quarters. And they keep devising plans for the day when someone attempts to evict them." Alcatraz's new residents, Caldwell wrote, were "young and strong with long black hair and determined not to leave."[69]

Caldwell's accounts were more personal and evocative of the scene, in the way of the "new journalism" genre, than was ordinarily the case in *New York Times* news stories. One Caldwell story began, "In the afternoon they sit at the wooden tables in the dining hall and pass the time playing cards and listening to their music. Most of them are teenagers who have been living on Alcatraz for nearly three months and there is nothing left for them to explore."[70]

Images of the Indians as physically attractive were frequent. Richard Oakes, the Indians' spokesman in the early days of the occupation, was described as a "handsome, dark-haired and broad-shouldered" man "who resembles [movie star] Victor Mature."[71] A woman, the granddaughter of athlete Jim Thorpe, was described as "a pretty, blond college girl," and a man on the Indians' council was "a serious, intelligent Sioux."[72]

The stories depicted the Alcatraz occupiers romantically as good Indians, idealistic and noble, dedicated to restoration of their traditional lands and cultures. In the noble savage tradition, they were seeking communion with nature, even if they had not found it.

As the occupation wore on, the portrayals changed. The romantic portrayals of 1969 and early 1970 were replaced by menacing images of violence and savagery. Thus the good and noble Indian images were superseded by a revival of images similar to early views of bad Indians as brutal savages. The first article to suggest this change came just six weeks into the occupation. It noted factionalism, alcohol abuse, fights, and vandalism. Ironically, the parallel it drew was not to aboriginal "savages" but to the degenerate English schoolboys in William Golding's *Lord of the Flies*.[73] Nevertheless, the dark image of people bereft of civilization was clear.

Stories late in the occupation portrayed the Indians as potentially violent and warlike. A *San Francisco Chronicle* story said, "A year ago the talk was of evading a government force, now the talk is of active resistance."[74] *Time* magazine quoted one of the remaining Indians on the island as saying, "We will never give Alcatraz back. . . . And if they try to force us, we will fight to the death to keep our land."[75]

Other articles described the bleak conditions on the island in terms that recalled the image of the degraded Indian who had created his own problems. A *Time* magazine article created the impression of incompetence as it described a donated boat that nearly sank, an "ill-maintained" electric generator, buildings destroyed by accidental fires, and rusted or jammed plumbing. "A graver problem," the article went on, "is the pervading sense of anomie, a social disintegration."[76]

After the Indians were ousted from the island, a *San Francisco Chronicle* story described "scenes of ruin" and "an unrelieved vista of squalor, filth, systematic pilfering and mindless destruction." It also mentioned a death threat to the island's only teacher and the savage rape of a twelve-year-old girl.[77] The impression was clear that such violence and destruction was the work of uncivilized brutes. No Indians were quoted in the story, though in a later, shorter story the Indians denied deliberate destruction.

For the most part, the stories of the Alcatraz occupation were descriptive and did not make sweeping judgments. Nevertheless, by the end of the siege of Alcatraz, readers of news coverage were inevitably left with images of Indians as savage and, if not warlike, certainly unafraid of violence, people who were incompetent to organize a tidy and efficient community.

WOUNDED KNEE

The climax of Native American direct action came in the symbolically powerful confrontation at Wounded Knee in 1973, in which members of the American Indian Movement (AIM) and their supporters seized the Wounded Knee settlement on the Pine Ridge Sioux reservation and held off federal marshals, Federal Bureau of Investigation agents, and backers of the elected tribal chairman for seventy-one days.

Wounded Knee, in the isolated, windswept hills of Southwestern South Dakota, was the scene in 1890 of the last major bloodletting of the Indian wars. That incident grew out of whites' fears of the popularity of the messianic Ghost Dance religion and Indians' alarm at increasing white repression. In the incident, a band of Minneconjou Sioux, led by Chief Big Foot, were fleeing from one reservation to another when they were intercepted, surrounded, and fired upon by Seventh Cavalry soldiers. In the ensuing gunfire, hundreds of Sioux—estimates ranged up to 300—many of them unarmed women and children, were mowed down and later buried in a mass grave.[78] The name Wounded Knee was in the minds of many in 1973 because of the popularity of Dee Brown's *Bury My Heart at Wounded Knee*, a best-selling chronicle of the nineteenth-century Western Indian wars from the Indian point of view.[79]

A great deal has been written about Wounded Knee II, as the 1973 matter came to be called, both about the standoff itself and the worldwide media coverage it generated.[80] Rather than retelling those tales, this research will look at the images contained in print coverage in the local and national press.

However, a brief summary of the incident is necessary to put the press coverage in context. The Wounded Knee takeover had its roots in the rise of militant, urban Indians in the 1960s and 1970s. The American Indian Movement, an organization formed in Minneapolis in 1968 to protect Native Americans against police harassment, had helped organize the Trail of Broken Treaties, a 1972 Indian rights demonstration in Washington, D.C., that ended up with the takeover of the Bureau of Indian Affairs building. In early 1972 and again in 1973, AIM had mobilized hundreds of Indians—mostly Sioux from the Rosebud and Pine Ridge reservations—to demonstrate against leniency toward white offenders in the murders of two Sioux men in reservation border towns. On February 27, 1973, a group of AIM supporters, led by Russell Means (Oglala Sioux) and Dennis Banks (Chippewa), took over a church, trading post, and other buildings at the historic Wounded Knee village. Their motives included calling attention to Indians' dismal conditions, seeking enforcement of treaty rights, and ousting the tribal government, led by Richard Wilson. The AIM faction contended the Wilson administration was corrupt and subservient to the Bureau of Indian Affairs.

The conflict revealed splits among Indians along generational and social, as well as ideological, lines. Some AIM supporters were not Sioux and were urban Indians. A good many, though, were reservation Indians, including fullblood traditionalists who had long opposed the tribal government dominated by more assimilated mixedbloods, as well as others who disliked the tribal government. The takeover brought federal marshals and FBI agents to the reservation, who sealed off the tiny Wounded Knee settlement. Wilson's tribal police and vigilante supporters added a third element to those arrayed against the insurgents. All were well armed; sporadic firefights cost the lives of two Wounded Knee Indians and seriously injured a federal marshal. Dozens of others were less seriously injured. Wilson supporters were accused by the AIM faction of harassment and intimidation, including the fire bombing of an AIM leader's home. After protracted negotiations, aided by representatives of the National Council of Churches, the militant Indians stood down on May 8.

A good deal of criticism was leveled at the news media's performance at Wounded Knee, particularly the television coverage. Partisans on all sides of the complex matter criticized the press from their own viewpoints. Some of those who covered the confrontation also were critical. Occupiers complained that news reporters were ignorant of the background and issues that led to the takeover and accepted the government's assertions at face value. News reporters complained that AIM leaders manipulated the press and staged events for television cameras and that the government cut off access to the AIM encampment. Government officials complained that the overwhelming news media presence prolonged the siege.[81]

The present analysis approaches the print coverage from different angles. It will look at the images of Indians, the differences between the local and national press, and the uses of journalistic conventions and practices.

Images at Wounded Knee

As in the Alcatraz takeover, images of the occupiers of Wounded Knee were more sympathetic in the early days than later. One reason for this may be that early in the occupation, reporters were able to sneak around federal officials' roadblocks and into the village to report first hand what they saw. Later the village was at times effectively sealed off from the outside, and most information came from the government.

An image appearing in some publications early on was a romantic view of the Indians as heroic, noble warriors trying to hold out against a superior federal force. For example, *New York Times* reporter John Kifner apparently was in the first group of mainstream news reporters to visit the insurgent Indians at Wounded Knee after the takeover. His story described a young Indian on sentry duty armed with a ".22–caliber rifle with a stock held together by tape" and only one bullet. It described the Indians' armaments as ordinary hunting rifles, small-bore shotguns, pistols, knives, screwdrivers, and Molotov cocktails made from soda pop bottles.[82] This was contrasted with the government's arsenal: "M-16 and other high-powered rifles, submachine guns, two armored personnel carriers, night-vision Starscopes and powerful searchlights."[83]

Another story said, "[A] band of young Indians and their allies are dug in, armed and painted for war, while on the hillsides around them a federal force of armor and automatic weapons stands nervously."[84]

The heroic nature of the Indians' takeover was depicted in a quotation from Russell Means: "We have bet with our lives that we could change the course of Oglala history on this reservation and the history of the rest of Indian America." An old Oglala woman was quoted invoking the Oglalas most revered warrior: "[H]ow did Crazy Horse put it? . . . Oh, yes—'It's a good day to die.' "[85]

Those occupying the village were portrayed in a nonthreatening, almost humble way, such as in the *New York Times* story describing a group of Indian women fixing and serving breakfast. The story quoted an elderly woman named Elizabeth Fast Horse as telling younger women, "Mind the elderly and mind your bosses and everything will be all right."[86]

This positive image was not sustained at Wounded Knee partly because of the inability of the insurgents to get consistent access to the press and partly because the situation itself was so complicated. While Alcatraz had been a clearcut effort to publicize and gain redress for Indians' terrible treatment by white government and society, the Wounded Knee Indians' complaints were more complex. The Wounded Knee insurgents sought reform of the BIA and enforcement of treaties they contended the government abrogated, but they also wanted to oust the elected Oglala Sioux tribal government headed by Richard Wilson, who they charged was repressive and corrupt. This factional dispute, the *New York Times* said, "was worthy of a political feud in New York's Tammany."[87] Such complex messages did not lend themselves to short slogans or simplistic stories.

While the *New York Times* and the news magazines generally gave equal weight to all the occupiers' demands, not all reporters did so. An article in the *Chicago Daily News* began, "A second front has opened in the siege of Wounded Knee—the renewal of a decades-old confrontation of Indian against Indian, tribe against tribe. The battle had started as Indian against white man."[88] However, initial dispatches from the scene and later accounts by participants indicated that the demands were listed together from the start. Also, some accounts suggested Oglalas who opposed the Wilson administration invited AIM to the reservation to help oust it.[89] Interestingly, the author of the *Daily News* story, Terri Schultz, later wrote a much-cited article for *Harper's* magazine taking the press to task for inaccurately reporting the incident.[90]

Some have noted that coverage seemed to be from a "war correspondent's perspective," as though Wounded Knee II were a military engagement.[91] Certainly many stories could have come from the Vietnam war with only a change of place names. For example, early in the occupation, the *Rapid City Journal* quoted an eyewitness who said, "It was a commando raid in the most accurate sense, well organized and lightning fast, and executed in almost total darkness."[92]

The Associated Press account of the firefight that resulted in the first fatality of the occupation, an Indian named Frank Clearwater, contained these sentences:

> [T]he gunfire began about 7 a.m. . . . when Indians fired on a government helicopter that was on a reconnaissance mission on the outskirts of the village. The helicopter was not hit . . . although it drew "much fire."
>
> "About a half hour later three government roadblocks came under heavy fire," [Charles] Cadieux [an Interior Department official] said, and an hour later the marshals and FBI agents at the blockades were given the order to return fire. He said the gunfire exchange was continuing about 10 a.m. . . . at three of the six federal roadblocks.[93]

Such terminology, however, was not unique to Wounded Knee. It was regrettably frequent in the 1960s and 1970s as news media reported violent incidents such as the May 1970 firing on antiwar demonstrators by the National Guard at Kent State University that left four dead and the December 1969 police raid on Chicago Black Panther headquarters in which two Black Panther leaders were shot. When applied to Indians, however, the framing and terminology of the stories resurrected Western movie images of bloodthirsty warriors.

This Western movie depiction of the bad Indian—the marauding "hostile" Indian preying not only on whites but on "pacified" Indians—was seen in the frequent references not only to the insurgents' militancy, but the references to armaments and military activities and to Western movies themselves. *U.S. News and World Report*, for example, termed the takeover a "replay of a 'wild West' conflict" in which "members of the militant American Indian Movement, held as hostages for two days eleven white residents . . . seized guns and ammunition at a trading post, fired on approaching cars and planes, and sent out a list of demands."[94]

Time also invoked Western movie images when it said Wounded Knee "was overrun . . . by roughly two hundred armed members of the American Indian Movement (AIM), a militant group . . . The protesters set up headquarters in a Roman Catholic church and ransacked a trading post. They took eleven hostages."[95] The bad Indian image was also fostered, no doubt, by some of the occupiers heavy-handed staging of dramatic tableaux in which they brandished guns.[96]

A related portrayal was of the occupiers as renegades—possibly subversive agents of a larger conspiracy. A *Chicago Tribune* columnist who visited Wounded Knee and wrote at least eleven columns on it floated leftist conspiracy theories that portrayed the Indians as duplicitous or at least dupes of the radical left. Bob Wiedrich, the columnist, asserted that "about one thousand white radicals" had drifted through the Pine Ridge reservation since the Wounded Knee takeover and had "helped the Indians prolong their takeover . . . by furnishing technical know-how of modern warfare." The column said the "radicals" were engaging in "resupply missions mounted from lairs in Rapid City, South Dakota, an even one hundred miles away."[97]

An Associated Press story questioning where the occupiers got heavy armaments also hinted at conspiracy:

> The American Indian Movement occupation of Wounded Knee began with weapons normally used to hunt squirrels, rabbits and pheasants and evolved to armaments used for bigger game, including people.
>
> The question of how the occupation force of Indians came by their weapons has never been fully explained.[98]

The Indians occupying Wounded Knee thus were portrayed as not only bloodthirsty and hostile but as possibly disloyal, too.

Imagery was also reflected in the terms used to describe the Indian factions. The people who occupied Wounded Knee were frequently referred to in the *Chicago Tribune* as "militant Indians," or "armed Indian militants"[99] or "a small band representing the hard-line American Indian Movement."[100] An editorial made the paper's image of AIM as bad Indians explicit, calling them "A group of armed insurrectionists" with "a flair for publicity and no scruples." It described AIM leaders Means and Banks as "self-acknowledged outlaws" and "gun-toting and gun-firing criminals." The point of the editorial was that the government had not been resolute enough in dealing with the Indians.[101]

A different image was conveyed by the *New York Times*, which called the occupiers "militant" on occasion, but also used labels such as "dissident Indians"[102] and, more frequently, "insurgents."[103] This term conveyed the idea of Indians who were rebels, perhaps revolutionaries, without making value judgments about their cause. A *New York Times* editorial, taking the opposite tack from the *Tribune*, urged patience on the part of the government and said the Indians "must be regarded as insurrectionists, however quixotic their uprising."[104]

Those who took over Wounded Knee were discredited in stories that characterized their action as a "pseudo-event" that was staged for the news media.[105] Such an image undermined the validity of the Indians' claims. Stories about the occupation referred to drama and theatrics frequently, thus conveying the notion that the action was somehow make-believe. It would be easy for the audience to conclude that the issues were also fictional. The action was thus variously described as a "media maneuver,"[106] having "all the elements of bad theater" including "outmoded makeup (war paint) and melodramatic lines ('Massacre us or meet our human needs')";[107] a "pathetic drama" that "resembled guerrilla theater more than guerrilla warfare."[108]

Sometimes essentially the same information was used to convey different images. In a long article that recounted the historical, political, and social roots of the conflict, the *New York Times* described "a bleak picture of some of the worst poverty in America. Abandoned, rusted cars cluster around tumble-down shacks and litter the prairie hills. . . . Hopeless, drunken men lurch about the streets at mid-morning."[109]

That depressing image of reservation life contrasted strongly with that in the *Chicago Daily News*, which said residents of Pine Ridge "don't seem to mind what most strangers notice first: the poverty and the dust. Even in winter the old Indian men sit all day along a low brick ledge on Main Street, dreaming of better days gone forever."[110] By saying reservation residents "don't seem to mind" being poor, the story portrayed them as degraded Indians who were satisfied with conditions others would not tolerate.

A similar image was painted by *Time* magazine, which described Indians coming to Pine Ridge in "the dilapidated cars with crunched fenders that are the Indians' trademark"—a description that made it appear Indians chose to drive such vehicles.[111] And, according to the *Chicago Tribune*, "The average Oglala . . . is generally happy on the reservation and goes out of his way to be friendly to white men."[112]

Images in a Local Paper

The local press, represented by the *Rapid City Journal*, covered the occupation in great detail. Stories appeared on the front page most of the seventy-one days of the siege.[113] A great many of the daily stories updating developments, or simply reporting nothing new had happened, came from the Associated Press wire service. The newspaper staff also contributed feature and "enterprise" stories that filled gaps in the daily coverage. It is through these stories that one can see a different image of the occupation than appeared in the distant press.

The image of the Wounded Knee insurgents that emerged from the Rapid City paper was of usurpers and renegades—outsiders who had invaded an unsuspecting village and caused great disruption and damage. The image came less from explicit language than from a cumulative impression. Wire service stories were fairly straightforward news accounts that did not delve into description or interpretation. However, they relied more on government sources than those of AIM, probably because Wounded Knee was inaccessible to the press at times.

In addition to the wire service stories, the paper ran features, often citing unnamed sources, that displayed local residents' anger toward AIM. One story, for example, cited an unnamed white rancher, who cast AIM in a sinister role. "Indian families . . . are gathering together at night in groups at various ranches out of fear of being attacked by members of the occupying American Indian Movement. They are maintaining guard all night," he was quoted as saying.[114]

Another story reported on a meeting of clergy and other local residents who criticized a Lutheran denomination for giving a grant to AIM. "Consensus was that AIM members are 'a bunch of renegades,' that they do advocate violence, do not represent the Oglala Sioux Nation, and should not receive church support," the story said.[115]

Still other articles described the travails of displaced Wounded Knee residents, the destruction they found after the siege was over, and how the occupation might cut into the region's tourism revenues.

There were a few stories that conveyed a different impression. One described a "young mother of six" who was circulating petitions to dissolve the tribal government. The woman, who "described herself as a sympathizer who has relatives inside Wounded Knee," was not identified because of fear she would lose her job.[116]

Such stories were scarce, however. This selection of stories, then, left a cumulative image of AIM as outsiders, armed interlopers who had descended on a peaceful village and dispossessed the residents, upsetting the tranquillity and economy of the region. They were depicted, in the parlance of Western movies, as "renegade" or "hostile" Indians who had attacked the "pacified" village.

DISCUSSION

The 1960s and 1970s marked a turning point in coverage of Native Americans. The changes in journalism that allowed more description and interpretation were reflected in daily news stories. Longer magazine pieces contained vivid description and were sometimes linked to advocacy, as had been the case earlier. Supporters of Native Americans wrote eloquently in the pages of the *New York Times Magazine* and other publications, including, interestingly, magazines for young women such as *Seventeen* and *Mademoiselle*. Furthermore, the advocate-author was likely to be an Indian, such as author Vine Deloria and Mohawk activist Richard Oakes. Indians now had some access to the mainstream press to tell their own stories.

The militants' bold demonstrations caught the attention of the press and politicians. This time, in contrast with previous eras, Native Americans themselves conceived and initiated the action. At Alcatraz they brilliantly used a pseudo-event to attract public attention to their cause. Their action drew reporters from around the country and succeeded on a scale not seen for decades in dramatizing their call for self-determination and restoration of tribal lands and cultural identities.[117] The cross-country trip and costumed dances of the Pueblos that John Collier staged in the 1920s were not unlike the militant Indian takeovers of Alcatraz and Wounded Knee in their attention-getting qualities.

By early 1973, when AIM and others hunkered down behind barricades at Wounded Knee, the press should have been experienced if not adept at covering confrontations by militant groups. Certainly there were enough examples, ranging from the urban riots of the mid-1960s to literally dozens of direct actions, demonstrations, takeovers, standoffs, sit-ins, and the like staged by activists of many causes. Also, the Kerner Commission report of 1968 had given the press a clear set of standards and guidelines for covering civil disorders involving racial or ethnic groups.

Ironically in this era of investigative reporting, the press seemed at times all too willing to accept the activists' or the government's claims at face value without the skepticism that good reporting is supposed to require. For example, no stories were found in the mainstream publications examined at the time of Wounded Knee II that thoroughly investigated AIM's charges against the Wilson administration. Nor was there much thorough investigation of AIM's origins and personnel.

Positive images of Native Americans seemed a newer version of the noble savage: These Indians were portrayed as idealistic and wise. They were depicted as people uniquely attuned to the earth who could save society from destroying the planet and itself, if only whites would listen. Initially their sometimes naive and grandiose plans were reported at face value without examination, as in the early days of the Alcatraz takeover. Later, at Wounded Knee, occupying Indians complained of unfair treatment by a press too willing to give credence to government claims.

The negative image that emerged was also a variation on earlier images. It was a resurrection of the Hollywood version of the bad Indian as brutal and uncivilized. The occupation of Wounded Knee put images of armed Indians on front pages nationwide. Stories used military terminology that could have come from Vietnam—or a John Wayne Western. In the local press, AIM insurgents were portrayed as "hostiles" who disrupted reservation life.

Far from being a "vanishing race," Native Americans were prominent on the news agenda in the late 1960s and early 1970s. From the plethora of stories, a variety of images emerged. Images of Indians as militants who spoke for themselves and took direct action to advance their cause were added to popular culture images of Indians as spiritual guides and ecological saviors. Real Indians became celebrities as musicians, authors, and aggressive activists. Indian culture and clothing became widely fashionable. It was perhaps due to the "consciousness-raising" of previous Indian direct actions and of the new sensitivity of the press to ethnic groups that less of the shopworn stereotypical language of past eras appeared in the stories examined.

Still, some of the old images of bloodthirsty warriors and noble savages were revisited and elaborated. While readers of the mainstream press had access to a greater variety of stories, many of them by or about articulate Native Americans who were driving the story, vestiges of the old images endured.

NOTES

1. *San Francisco Chronicle*, Nov. 21, 1969, 1.

2. Stephen Cornell, *The Return of the Native: American Indian Political Resurgence* (New York: Oxford University Press, 1988), 189–190.

3. Francis Paul Prucha, *The Great Father*, vol. 2 (Lincoln: University of Nebraska Press, 1984), 1085, 1115–1116.

4. Stan Steiner, *The New Indians* (New York: Delta Books, 1968), 17–27.

5. James S. Olson and Raymond Wilson, *Native Americans in the Twentieth Century* (Provo, Utah: Brigham Young University Press, 1984), 163–166.

6. Vine Deloria, Jr., *Behind the Trail of Broken Treaties* (New York: Delacorte Press, 1974), 24–25.

7. Cornell, 189.

8. Prucha, 1115; Olson and Wilson, 158–159.

9. Steiner, 28–38.

10. Quoted in Alvin M. Josephy, Jr., *Red Power* (Lincoln: University of Nebraska Press, 1971), 37–38.

11. Quoted in Steiner, 305.

12. Alvin M. Josephy, Jr., *Now That the Buffalo's Gone* (Norman: University of Oklahoma Press, 1984), 225–228.

13. Prucha, 1112.

14. For assessments of Indian views of the Nixon administration see Alvin M. Josephy, Jr., "What the Indians Want," *New York Times Magazine*, Mar. 18, 1973, 18–19, 66–82, and "Real Goals of the Restless Indians," *U.S. News and World Report*, Apr. 2, 1973, 26–30.

15. Olson and Wilson, 166.

16. National Advisory Commission on Civil Disorders, *Report of the National Advisory Commission on Civil Disorders* (New York: Bantam Books, 1968), 366.

17. Ibid., 382–386.

18. For examples, see Carolyn Martindale, *The White Press and Black America* (New York: Greenwood Press, 1986).

19. Woody Klein, "News Media and Race Relations: A Self-Portrait," *Columbia Journalism Review*, Fall 1968, 42–49.

20. Gene Burd, "Minorities in Reporting Texts: Before and After the 1968 Kerner Report," *Mass Comm Review* 15, nos. 2 and 3 (1988): 45–60, 68.

21. Ralph S. Izard, *Reporting the Citizens' News* (New York: Holt, Rinehart and Winston, 1982), 322–326.

22. Ibid., 333–334.

23. Klein, 42–49.

24. James E. Murphy and Sharon M. Murphy, *Let My People Know: American Indian Journalism, 1828–1978* (Norman: University of Oklahoma Press, 1981), 14, 7.

25. Michael Schudson, *Discovering the News* (New York: Basic Books, 1978), 160.

26. Ibid., 184–185.

27. Daniel Boorstin, *The Image* (New York: Atheneum, 1962), 11. See also Schudson, 170–171.

28. Boorstin, 36.

29. Schudson, 163.

30. For a discussion of the "new journalism," see Tom Wolfe, *The New Journalism* (New York: Harper and Row, 1973), 3–52.

31. For a discussion of investigative reporting in the 1970s, see Leonard Downie, Jr., *The New Muckrakers* (Washington: New Republic Book Co., Inc., 1976).

32. "In Wild Onion Town," *Newsweek*, June 26, 1961, 32.

33. *Life*, July 2, 1971, 38.

34. Ibid.

35. Peter Collier, " 'White Society Is Breaking Down Around Us . . . Even Its Myths—Like the Melting Pot—Are Dead' An Interview with American Indian Writer Vine Deloria," *Mademoiselle*, Apr. 1971, 202–204.

36. Roy Bongarz, "Three Meanies 1. The New Indian," *Esquire*, Aug. 1970, 107–108, 125–126.

37. Kenneth R. Sheets, "American Indians Bargain 'Arab Style' to Cash In on Resources," *U.S. News and World Report*, June 3, 1974, 53–54.

38. Marvin L. Franklin, "Payrolls: An Answer to the Indian Militants," *Nation's Business*, June 1974, 54–58.

39. *New York Times*, May 6, 1969, 49.

40. Robert Sherrill, *Nation*, Nov. 10, 1969, 500–503.

41. Roul Tunley, *Seventeen*, Oct. 1960, 122–123, 177–181.

42. *Reader's Digest*, Apr. 1970, 104–109.

43. Ibid.

44. *New York Times*, May 6, 1969, 49.

45. "An Indian in the City," *Newsweek*, June 14, 1971, 94–100.

46. Herbert Gold, "How Rich is a Rich Apache?" *New York Times Magazine*, Feb. 13, 1972, 18.

47. "Tribal Chic," *Newsweek*, Apr. 2, 1973, 80, 83.

48. "The Angry American Indian: Starting Down the Protest Trail," *Time*, Feb. 9, 1970, 14–20.

49. *New York Times*, July 13, 1970, 35.

50. "Indians: The Great Spirit," *Newsweek*, May 14, 1973, 71–72.

51. "Our Indian Heritage," *Life*, July 2, 1971, 44.

52. Oliver LaFarge, "The Indians Want A New Frontier," *New York Times Magazine*, June 11, 1961, 12.

53. Nancy Axelrad Comer, "Hokahne!" *Mademoiselle*, Oct. 1970, 158–159, 195–198.

54. *New York Times*, Feb. 4, 1969, 30.

55. "The Angry American Indian: Starting Down the Protest Trail," *Time*, Feb. 9, 1970, 14–20.

56. Peter Collier, "Salmon Fishing in America: The Indians vs. the State of Washington," *Ramparts*, Apr. 1971, 29–31, 39–45.

57. William Hedgepeth, "America's Indians: Reawakening of a Conquered People," *Look*, June 2, 1970, 23–43.

58. Richard Oakes, "Alcatraz Is Not An Island," *Ramparts*, Dec. 1972, 35–40.

59. Josephy, *Buffalo's Gone*, 229.

60. *San Francisco Chronicle*, Nov. 10, 1969, 1; Nov. 11, 1969, 1; Nov. 21, 1969, 1.

61. Steve Talbot, "Free Alcatraz: The Culture of Native American Liberation," *Journal of Ethnic Studies*, Fall 1978, 83–96.

62. Quoted in Talbot, 90.

63. *San Francisco Chronicle*, June 12, 1971, 2.

64. *San Francisco Chronicle*, June 12, 1971, 1.

65. William Hedgepeth, "Alcatraz: The Indian Uprising that Worked," *Look*, June 2, 1970, 44–45.

66. Kay Boyle, "A Day on Alcatraz with the Indians," *New Republic*, Jan. 17, 1970, 10–11.

67. *San Francisco Examiner and Chronicle*, Nov. 23, 1969, 1, 18.
68. *San Francisco Chronicle*, Nov. 22, 1969, 1, 18.
69. *New York Times*, Dec. 10, 1969, 37, 43.
70. *New York Times*, Feb. 22, 1970, 75.
71. *San Francisco Examiner and Chronicle*, Dec. 7, 1969, A13.
72. John A. Coleman, "Lords of the Rock," *America*, May 2, 1970, 465–467.
73. *San Francisco Chronicle*, Jan. 8, 1970, 4.
74. *San Francisco Chronicle*, Mar. 15, 1971, 5.
75. "Anomie at Alcatraz," *Time*, Apr. 12, 1971, 21.
76. Ibid.
77. *San Francisco Chronicle*, June 14, 1971, 1.
78. Deloria, *Behind the Trail*, 65–68; Prucha, 728–729.
79. Dee A. Brown, *Bury My Heart at Wounded Knee* (New York: Holt, Rinehart and Winston, 1971). Brown's account of the 1890 massacre is on 415–417.
80. See Prucha, 1119–1120; Josephy, *Buffalo's Gone*, 215–255; Deloria, *Behind the Trail*, 63–83; Peter Matthiessen, *In the Spirit of Crazy Horse* (New York: Penguin Books, 1983, 1991), 58–82; Rolland Dewing, *Wounded Knee: The Meaning and Significance of the Second Incident* (New York: Irvington Publishers, Inc., 1985); Bill Zimmerman, *Airlift to Wounded Knee* (Chicago: Swallow Press, Inc., 1976); Stanley David Lyman, *Wounded Knee 1973* (Lincoln: University of Nebraska Press, 1991); Robert Burnette and John Koster, *The Road to Wounded Knee* (New York: Bantam Books, 1974), 220–254; John Koster, "American Indians and the Media," *Cross Currents*, Summer 1976, 164–171; *Voices from Wounded Knee, 1973* (Mohawk Nation, via Rooseveltown, N.Y.: Akwesasne Notes, 1974); Edward Justin Streb, "The Rhetoric of Wounded Knee II: A Critical Analysis of Confrontational and 'Media Event' Discourse" (Ph.D. diss., Northwestern University, 1979).
81. See Streb; "Trap at Wounded Knee," *Time*, March 26, 1973, 67; Desmond Smith, "The Media Coup D'Etat," *Nation*, June 25, 1973, 806–809; Terri Schultz, "Bamboozle Me Not at Wounded Knee," *Harpers*, June, 1973, 46–56; Koster, 164–171; Burnette and Koster, 228–231; Ted Elbert, "Bury Me Not at Wounded Knee," *Quill*, May, 1973, 23–25.
82. *New York Times*, Mar. 5, 1973, 1, 26.
83. Ibid.
84. *New York Times*, Mar. 24, 1973, 1, 14.
85. *New York Times*, Mar. 5, 1973, 1, 26.
86. Ibid.
87. *New York Times*, May 13, 1973, sec. IV, p. 3.
88. *Chicago Daily News*, Mar. 2, 1973, 6.
89. See, among many, Josephy, *Buffalo's Gone*, 216–217.
90. Schultz, 46–56.
91. Streb, 119–128.
92. *Rapid City Journal*, Mar. 2, 1973, 1.
93. *Rapid City Journal*, Apr. 8, 1973, 1.
94. "Behind a Modern-Day Indian Uprising—," *U.S. News and World Report*, Mar. 12, 1973, 36.
95. "Raid at Wounded Knee," *Time*, Mar. 19, 1973, 21.
96. Photographs of Indians brandishing weapons appeared, among many, in *Time*, Mar. 12, 1973, 21; Mar. 19, 1973, 17; *Newsweek*, Mar. 12, 1973, 27; *Chicago*

Tribune, Mar. 11, 1973, sec. 2, p. 1; Mar. 12, 1973, 1; *New York Times*, Mar. 24, 1973, 1; *Rapid City Journal*, Mar. 5, 1973, 1.

97. *Chicago Tribune*, Apr. 10, 1973, 12.

98. *Rapid City Journal*, Apr. 5, 1973, 8.

99. *Chicago Tribune*, Mar. 3, 1973, 3, for example.

100. *Chicago Tribune*, Mar. 11, 1973, sec. 2, p. 1.

101. *Chicago Tribune*, Mar. 13, 1973, 10.

102. *New York Times*, Mar. 28, 1973, 1.

103. *New York Times*, Apr. 6, 1973, 1; Apr. 8, 1973, sec. IV, p. 3.

104. *New York Times*, Mar. 15, 1973, 42.

105. Streb, for example, examining both the print and broadcast media, wrote that the occupation fulfilled Boorstin's qualities for a "pseudo-event," see 92–98. See also Smith, 806–809.

106. "Return to Wounded Knee," *Newsweek*, Mar. 12, 1973, 27.

107. "A Suspenseful Show of Red Power," *Time*, Mar. 19, 1973, 16–18.

108. "The Siege of Wounded Knee," *Newsweek*, Mar. 19, 1973, 22–23; see also *Chicago Tribune*, Apr. 8, 1973, sec. 2, p. 4; Apr. 12, 1973, 26; May 11, 1973, 18.

109. *New York Times*, Mar. 24, 1973, 1, 14.

110. *Chicago Daily News*, Mar. 3, 1973, 3.

111. "A Suspenseful Show of Red Power," *Time*, Mar. 19, 1973, 16–18.

112. *Chicago Tribune*, Mar. 4, 1973, 29. In fairness it should be noted that this statement was amended in a later article which said, "[C]onditions can be deceiving. On the surface the Oglala Sioux are docile and seemingly happy. But underneath, they endure a frustration that leads to the Pine Ridge Reservation's biggest problem—drunkenness," *Chicago Tribune*, Mar. 18, 1973, 6.

113. *Rapid City Journal*, Jan. 26–May 21, 1973.

114. *Rapid City Journal*, Mar. 15–16, 1973, 8.

115. *Rapid City Journal*, Apr. 5, 1973, 10.

116. *Rapid City Journal*, Mar. 23, 1973, 3.

117. Olson and Wilson, 169–170.

7

The 1980s and 1990s: Talking Back to the Media

The militant direct actions of the early 1970s had retreated into memory and the vogue for Indian fashions had faded by the time Ronald Reagan became president in 1981. However, that splash of public attention to Native American concerns left legacies that would be felt into the last decades of the century. The conflicts put Indian grievances forcefully before the public and made it clear that Native Americans were committed to regaining their rights.[1] Importantly, the actions were initiated by Native Americans themselves. They became, in the words of Stephen Cornell, "major actors in their own drama."[2]

By the time Reagan took office, the philosophy of self-determination for Indians had been articulated by four successive presidents, although exactly what that meant in practice changed with the times, office holders, and circumstances. Reagan, too, rhetorically backed self-determination. In practice, the Reagan policies severely cut back or eliminated funds for Indian education, health, housing, and human services, a practice critics called "termination by accountants."[3] It was estimated that cutbacks affecting Indians were ten times greater than those affecting others.[4] The cutbacks caused privation in Indian Country. For example, according to Stephen Cornell, cancellation of a Comprehensive Employment and Training Act (CETA) program on the Ponca reservation in Oklahoma eliminated around two hundred jobs virtually overnight. The Navajo tribe reported in 1982 that yearly per capita income had dropped 25 percent from 1980.[5]

The Reagan administration advocated privatization of economic development on reservations but, critics argued, threw economic and bureaucratic roadblocks in the way of tribes when they tried to compete with local governments or business interests. On the positive side, it backed a 1982 law that gave tribal governments certain tax exemptions as well as the right to tax in limited circumstances.[6] However, with unemployment reaching 95 percent on some reservations,[7] and with the country in recession, these moves did not make serious dents in tribal economic problems.

In the post–World War II era, development of energy resources was seen as economic salvation for some tribes. Some Western tribes that had large deposits of coal, oil, uranium, and other minerals leased the right to extract the materials to large corporations. Often the leases provided royalties to the tribes on a fixed basis. Thus, when the energy crisis of the late 1970s hit and prices skyrocketed, Indians were still paid at low rates. More ominously, the coal and uranium extraction led to air and water pollution on reservations, which caused disease and death for miners and other tribespeople. Particularly hard-hit were Navajos who mined uranium.[8]

Native Americans were in a decidedly disadvantageous bargaining position when approached by large corporations seeking to exploit their resources. Given the destitution and high unemployment on reservations, as well as tribal leaders' inexperience in negotiating leases, it was not surprising many agreed to contracts that were exploitative. On the other hand, traditionalists often opposed development on grounds that it was despoiling the sacred earth and leading the people away from Indian ways.

Some reservations considered becoming hazardous waste storage sites. As in the development of energy resources, those favoring the immediate benefits of jobs and tribal revenues were pitted against traditionalists and environmentalists who feared the effects on the land.[9]

Despite the ups and downs of public policy, by the last two decades of the century some believed Native Americans were probably better off legally than they had been in the past.[10] A bedrock issue that underlay all others was Native American sovereignty and treaty rights. This was exemplified in controversies between Indians and nearby whites over fishing rights and water and land use. An American Indian Freedom of Religion Act was passed in 1978, but later court decisions seemed to limit some religious practices, such as the use of peyote, and removed protection from some sacred lands. However, the Native American Graves Repatriation Act required museums and other institutions to return human remains and other objects to the tribes.[11]

In 1994 President Bill Clinton also endorsed self-determination and a "government to government" relationship between the federal government and Indian tribes. The president summoned leaders of all 547 federally recognized tribes to the White House for a meeting, the first such event since 1822.[12]

A potentially far-reaching development was the rise in casinos and other gambling enterprises on tribal lands. In 1979 a bingo hall opened on Seminole lands in Florida and was promptly closed down by state officials.

Later its legality was upheld by the courts. By 1987 nearly fifty tribes had bingo operations.[13] In 1987 the Supreme Court ruled that any form of gambling permissible in a state could be done on Indian lands. This opened the way for slot machine gambling and casinos in some states. The 1988 Indian Gaming Regulatory Act imposed federal regulations on Indian gambling.[14] By 1993 Indian gambling grossed $5 billion, and 200 tribes had some sort of gaming.[15] For the first time a number of tribes achieved economic clout in their communities because of their gambling operations. Indian gambling enterprises became major employers of Indians and non-Indians in states like Connecticut and parts of Wisconsin and Minnesota. Gambling revenues paid for roads, water systems, health care, and education for some tribes.

Indian gambling was not without problems. State governments sought to limit the operations.[16] Disputes arose in some small tribes over who was and was not a member and thus entitled to casino profits.[17] Some tribes were cheated out of gambling profits by the outside casino operators they employed.[18] Rivalries between pro- and antigambling factions led to bloodshed in a few cases.[19] Nevertheless, gambling remained a significant and growing engine of economic development.

Native American protests were also raised on the emotional and symbolic issue of the use of Indian representations for sports teams. Critics contended such logos and mascots were racist and demeaning to Native Americans. "Indians are people, not mascots," wrote Lakota editor and publisher Tim Giago. He quoted activist Charlene Teters as saying, "Mascots disgrace Indian people. . . . When a static symbol is used to represent a group of people, it gives off a one-dimensional image and devalues the living individuals."[20] Another activist said the mascot issue "represents the core of institutional racism. As long as we tolerate these types of images, attitudes towards jobs, social welfare, progress, and important issues will continue to be dealt with at a surface level."[21]

Stanford University and Dartmouth College did away with their Indian mascots in the 1970s, and numerous other colleges and high schools did so later. Others, including the University of Illinois, professional football teams such as the Washington Redskins and Kansas City Chiefs, baseball teams such as the Atlanta Braves and Cleveland Indians, and hockey teams such as the Chicago Blackhawks, clung stubbornly to what they saw as tradition or profitable marketability.

THE PRESS

The press, too, changed in the last two decades of the century. By then it was clear that print media no longer exclusively set the news agenda as first broadcast television, then other news media entered the marketplace. Both numbers of newspapers and their circulations relative to the population declined.[22] In efforts to keep and win readers, some newspapers emulated television through use of bright colors, flashy graphics, shorter stories, and a punchy, personal style of writing. A prototype of this kind of journalism, which was widely imitated, was *USA Today*, a national newspaper launched in 1982.[23] Growing numbers of newspaper editors allowed writers more latitude beyond the traditional "inverted pyramid" form that put all important facts at the beginning of the story. After all, the editors noted, most readers had probably already learned of an event via television.

The mass circulation consumer magazines such as *Life*, *Look*, and the *Saturday Evening Post* died or were faint shadows of their former selves though others, such as *Reader's Digest* and the *New Yorker*, survived. Mass magazines devoted to celebrities, sports, and entertainment, such as *Sports Illustrated* and *People*, became widely popular.[24]

The press paid greater attention to those outside the mainstream than in previous decades. This was due partly to a sense of social responsibility, partly to the realization that the population and workforce were becoming increasingly diverse, and partly to the increasing voices of journalists of color. Newspapers made well-publicized efforts to diversify their staffs and to widen definitions of news. One of the most vocal in this regard was *USA Today*, which emphasized not only hiring a diverse staff but striving for news coverage that reflected the diversity of the nation.[25]

Criticisms of news media coverage of racial and ethnic groups generally fell into several areas that echoed the criticisms of the Kerner Commission more than twenty years earlier:

- Not enough people of color were on staffs of mainstream media. Still fewer were in decision-making roles.
- Traditional definitions of news distorted coverage of people of color. Definitions emphasized conflict, the unusual, the extremes in life; they gave credence to sources with power and money; they emphasized events more than situations or trends. Such definitions did not lead to meaningful coverage of communities of color, which were often on the peripheries of power and wealth.
- The ordinary lives and community activities of people of color were not covered to the same extent as those of whites.
- Sources of news were too seldom drawn from non-whites.[26]

While much attention went to larger groups such as African Americans and Hispanics or Latinos, increasingly Native Americans' views were heard on treatment of their people in the news media. Generally their criticisms echoed those of the larger groups, but in addition, Native Americans criticized the use of imagery.

They complained of use of stereotypical terms such as "circle the wagons," "on the warpath," "pow wow," and "wampum" in the news. They also complained that stories about Native Americans too often were negative ones that reinforced stereotypes of alcoholism and poverty. They said journalists failed to understand Native American cultures, history, and treaty rights and misrepresented them when reporting conflicts such as those over fishing. They criticized mainstream reporting on the rise of Native American casinos for not describing adequately the tribal sovereignty that made them possible. Finally, mainstream coverage was cited for too often depicting Native American people and communities as historical artifacts or museum pieces who had no contemporary existence.[27]

Journalism educators, too, paid attention to preparing their students to work in a multicultural world. Again, though more notice was given to the larger African American and Latino or Hispanic groups, Native American concerns also surfaced. These generally sought to remind students of the complex cultural and legal issues surrounding news about Native Americans, and to explore the nature of stereotyping in the media.[28]

IMAGES

Given all this attention to accurate portrayals of diverse communities, was the press more sensitive to images of Native Americans embodied in its stories? Did journalistic practices that sought to broaden definitions of news and ways of telling it affect the portrayals of Native Americans?

As in the 1960s and 1970s, the variety of Indian images in the press increased. But, perhaps in keeping with the hard-nosed "me" orientation of the 1980s and public cynicism of the 1990s, there were fewer romantic images. Stories depicting Native Americans as exotic people from the past or degraded Indians who were beset by poverty and social problems persisted, though modified to fit the times.

Although Native Americans were not routinely identified as "braves," "squaws," and the like in the mainstream press, stereotypical language continued to crop up. It seemed to appear more often in stories in which Indians were peripheral to the action than in stories specifically about their concerns.

The story selection also reinforced imagery. Despite attempts to broaden the definition of what was considered news, stories of conflict, the unusual, and the bizarre still rated prominent placement. When these values were applied to stories about Native Americans, a numerically small group with little political or economic power, mundane but significant stories about their communities were less likely to see print.

This imagery-by-selection was illustrated by the author of a 1990 op-ed column in the *New York Times*:

> The only news to travel from Indian Country to the major media in 1990 has been news of disaster: a violent standoff between Mohawks and government officials in Quebec; fatal gun battles over casino gambling at the St. Regis reservation in New

York State; the ignoble fall of Peter MacDonald from the helm of the Navajo Nation. America has been saturated with images of incompetent Indian leadership and harebrained business schemes. As much as Native Americans seek understanding, this has been a year when many would just as soon the press had ignored them.[29]

The author of the column, Robert H. White, went on to describe several promising Native American economic development ventures.

NATIVE AMERICAN CRITICS

While it was not hard to find stories that perpetuated misleading images of Native Americans in the 1980s and 1990s, it was also possible to read Native Americans' criticisms of their treatment in the press.

For example, when an unknown virus struck down a number of people in the Southwest in May of 1993, it was incorrectly linked to the Navajo Nation. Headlines suggested that the mystery disease, later found to be a strain of hantavirus, was peculiar to the Navajos. A front page story in *USA Today* was headlined, "Navajo Flu Claims 11; Search for Cause Intense."[30] The following day the disease story was in the center of the paper's front page. The main headline read, "Medical Mystery / Tracking Cause of Navajo Flu."[31] A one-column headline in the *Chicago Sun-Times* declared, "Navajos' Epidemic A Puzzle."[32] The headline over a *Time* magazine story read, "Evil Over the Land / A deadly illness plagues the Navajo nation."[33] However, despite the headlines, even early articles pointed out that not all victims of the disease were Navajos. Of the first twenty-five victims, seven were not Navajo.[34] Eventually the disease struck sixty-nine people in seventeen states.[35]

The headlines and stories drew an image of Navajos as somehow diseased and—when the cause was suspected to come from rodent droppings—unclean. Navajo people complained that they were ostracized and isolated by others who feared contracting the disease. The tribal council passed a resolution saying that news coverage of the disease led to "discriminatory attitudes and activities against Navajo people."[36]

Navajo people faulted the press on several counts in addition to misleading coverage. They objected to reporters, "sometimes in noisy groups," invading Navajos' privacy and interrupting families' traditional four days of deep mourning. During this time the dead person's name is not mentioned, yet journalists "aggressively sought to interview relatives" and tried to get the names of the dead. Reporters and photographers also were condemned for trying to photograph secret sacred objects and ceremonies, in violation of the Navajo belief that reproduction of the images diminished the power of the ceremony.[37]

According to the *Washington Post*, Navajo President Peterson Zah said the journalists "brought shame to the Navajo Nation" with reports that "touched a chord of racism."[38] Beyond the direct effects of the coverage, the image linking an unknown and deadly disease to the Navajos contributed to the stereotype of Indians as degraded, in this case, diseased and dirty.

The clash of cultures showed how journalistic practices can lead to flawed images and coverage. Reporters from many states descended on the sprawling, isolated reservation to cover the story. Some were Native Americans, but not necessarily Navajos. All were under deadline pressure. They could not observe the Navajos' traditional four days of deep mourning and still get their stories. Also, journalism required facts, in this case, names. Journalists felt compelled to intrude on privacy and tradition to get their stories.

The damaging generalizations were certainly not new in the coverage of Native Americans. Nor was it the first time journalists had run roughshod over traditional practices. The significant aspect was that Navajo leaders spoke out and condemned the media and that their views were reported in the mainstream press. The complaints appeared in the *Washington Post* and the *Quill*, a nationally-circulated journalism review published by the Society of Professional Journalists, among others.

Native American journalists criticized another story that, they said, misrepresented Indian beliefs and propounded the view that "Native traditions are historic curiosities." The story, which ran in the *Washington Post*, dealt with the 1994 birth in Wisconsin of a white buffalo calf, which many tribes consider sacred. The Native American Journalists Association (NAJA) gave the story, headlined "The Great White Hope," its 1995 "Columbus" award for "perpetuating ignorance and stereotypes about Native Americans." The journalists took issue, among other things, with the headline that was a reference to a group of white boxers, and with terminology that depicted the white buffalo as "mythical."[39] The NAJA Columbus award represented another example of Native Americans speaking out on their treatment in the press.

THE "BANISHMENT" STORY

The image of Indians as exotic was reinforced by a spate of stories surrounding the 1994 case of two Tlingit youths who robbed and severely beat a pizza delivery man near Seattle. Instead of sentencing them to jail, a local judge allowed them to be released to a man who said he was a Tlingit tribal judge for banishment to a remote Alaskan island. Stories in papers across the country chronicled the controversy over the tribal judge's authenticity, whether or not Tlingit judicial tradition called for banishment, and the youths' eventual fate.

While the human dimensions of the story undoubtedly made it newsworthy, the manner in which Tlingit culture and rituals were reported was at times patronizing and lacked context. The lead of an Associated Press dispatch said, "There were no lawyers, no oaths, no objections. The twelve judges drank the juice of a thorny plant, wore deerskin tunics and had the courtroom cleansed of evil spirits. This was justice, Tlingit style."[40]

Details of the procedures were filled in later in the story, but the cultural and spiritual context for the rituals was never made clear. Without such explanation, readers were left with the image of the Tlingits as strange, perhaps primitive people who had stepped out of the past.

The difference in definitions of news between the mainstream press and Native Americans was further illustrated in a *New York Times* story that noted that the tribe was then facing an issue far more consequential than the punishment of the two youths: the government's efforts to remove the Tlingits from federal recognition. Edward Thomas, president of the Central Council of Tlingit and Haida Indian Tribes, was quoted as saying, "It just clenches my jaws . . . that the banishment of two boys is getting all this attention when we have been banished as a people."[41]

This was an example of how story selection reinforced imagery, in this case, of Indians as ancient and exotic. The banishment story hit front pages across the country, while the more significant but prosaic story of the tribe's future was buried.

THE SPORTS MASCOT ISSUE

Because stories about sports team mascots were, in essence, about images, it was interesting to see how real Native Americans were depicted in such articles. In 1989 Sen. Paul Simon, Democrat of Illinois, signed a petition calling for the abolition of team mascots such as "Chief Illiniwek," the Indian mascot of the University of Illinois. Senator Simon's action made the mascot issue political news and put it on front pages and in editorial columns from the Midwest to Washington, D.C. In this chapter of the long-running Chief Illiniwek dispute, the political framing of the story pushed Native Americans to the periphery.

Once Senator Simon signed the petition calling for elimination of the mascot and the state's other senator, Alan Dixon, supported it, the story was framed as a political controversy. Other politicians weighed in on the side of the mascot, and Indians as people virtually disappeared. The dominant image was the white-mediated image of Chief Illiniwek, an ersatz Indian created by whites for their entertainment.

That image was born in 1926 when, according to one account, an assistant band director came up with the idea of having someone in Indian garb dance at halftime of a football game.[42] The Chief Illiniwek of the 1980s and 1990s did an athletic dance at halftime of football and basketball games.

The student portraying Chief Illiniwek wore a Plains-style costume that included a long turkey-feather headdress, a breastplate, and fringed garments decorated with beadwork strips. According to the *St. Louis Post-Dis-*

patch, the costume was bought in 1983 from a Sioux chief.[43] The apparent derivation of the costume was historically ironic, because the Sioux were enemies of the Illini confederation after whom the mascot was named.

The Illini, or Illinois, were Woodlands, not Plains, Indians. They were a loose confederation of Algonquian-speaking hunters and farmers who allied with the French in the seventeenth century. From the Illinis' homes on the Illinois River, the tribe was slaughtered and driven west across the Mississippi by invading Iroquois, themselves driven from their homelands by whites. The Illini refugees west of the Mississippi were in turn attacked and driven back across the river by the Sioux.[44] The Illini were weakened by these attacks and by their own raids on and attacks by other, smaller Algonquian tribes. When their French protectors withdrew from the area at the end of the seventeenth century, the Illini were effectively exterminated.[45]

Indians were marginalized in the 1989 Chief Illiniwek controversy even before it became a political issue. The imagery of real Indians could be seen in a United Press International wire service dispatch that began, "Two American Indians and a student are asking the University of Illinois to replace the Big Ten school's sixty-three-year-old mascot, Chief Illiniwek." The story went on to name the student and the "two Indians," who were Faith Smith, president of the Native American Educational Services College, and James Yellowbank, coordinator of the Indian Treaty Rights Committee. The student, Robert Honig, a non-Indian, was quoted speaking for the Native Americans, who were not quoted in the story.[46]

The story also quoted a university official and the non-Indian man who performed in the Chief Illiniwek costume. The official called the mascot "a respected figure." The man who danced as the chief said his act was an "authentic tribute to Indian Americans" and "a solemn representation of Indian culture."[47]

The depiction of the Native Americans in the story's lead gave the impression of a tiny minority, perhaps oddballs, challenging the tradition of the vast university. That they did not speak for themselves in the story added to their marginalization. The white student gave their argument: "They consider it terribly offensive." But the arguments of the other side were longer and more detailed.

In the *Chicago Tribune* story of the same meeting, the Native Americans were not named until the sixth paragraph, and they were not quoted.[48] Thus when real Native Americans appeared to challenge the image of Chief Illiniwek, they were portrayed as isolated special pleaders who had to have a non-Indian student speak for them.

Several stories used terms demeaning to Indians. A political column in the *Chicago Tribune* said Senator Simon "went on the warpath" and the state's attorney general "went off the reservation." The column's headline was, "It Looks Like a Banner Season for Silliness."[49]

In an editorial titled "Knowing When to Go on the Warpath," the same paper criticized Senator Simon's judgment and concluded by saying, "A charge on the Washington Redskins or the federal budget deficit would be a better use of the senator's war paint."[50]

The image of Native Americans in these stories was one of a symbol, a metaphor, a mascot—one that had nothing to do with real people or even real history. Such trivialization perhaps made the use of stereotypical language seem permissible. The stories were not dealing with real Native Americans; they and their views had disappeared from the coverage. Though some later stories quoted Native Americans, when the Illiniwek controversy entered the political realm, Indians were shut out.

If contemporary Native Americans were relegated to minor roles in the 1989 controversy, they were more prominent a few years later when two professional sports teams with Indian names played in Minneapolis, which has a large Native American population. Native Americans were portrayed as leaders of the effort to eliminate offensive sports mascots in 1991 when the Atlanta Braves played the Minnesota Twins in the World Series and in 1992 when the Washington Redskins played in the Super Bowl in Minneapolis. In both events, Native Americans were generally portrayed in the mainstream press as legitimate protesters whose views were to be treated seriously.

For example the *(Minneapolis) Star Tribune* story of the Super Bowl demonstration began, "About 3,000 Indians and their supporters rallied outside the Metrodome Sunday to protest the use of Indian mascot names by sports teams." It went on to report, "Many prominent state and local public officials joined American Indian Movement leaders in the protest."[51]

A story in the *New York Times* described the Super Bowl protest as "part of a cultural reawakening sweeping reservations and Indian community centers, a kind of nationalism that has made many Indians less forgiving of the routine use of their names and symbols for things like automobiles and sports teams."[52]

Native Americans staged a similar, smaller protest during the 1991 World Series between the Minnesota Twins and Atlanta Braves. In both cases, major mainstream news media treated the story seriously. Major media outlets explored the mascot issue and presented Native Americans' views to a wide audience. "It's almost like the whole world is watching," said Clyde Bellecourt, a leader of AIM, after the 1991 protest.[53]

Lakota journalist Tim Giago, writing in *Newsweek* before the 1992 Super Bowl, noted that "the national media have finally caught on to the complaints American Indians have been voicing for many years."[54] Indians thus appeared in the pages of the mainstream press as partisans of a legitimate cause who were to be taken seriously.

The press became a part of the mascots controversy later in 1992 when the editor of the *Portland Oregonian* declared the paper would no longer use nicknames of sports teams that were racially offensive. William Hilliard, the *Oregonian's* editor, wrote that he took the action because of his belief "that these names tend to perpetuate stereotypes that damage the dignity and self-respect of many people . . . and that this harm far transcends any innocent entertainment or promotional value these names may have."[55]

Hilliard, an African American, indicated he knew first-hand what it was like to suffer indignities because of one's color. "There is more to being an informative and credible newspaper than just reporting the facts. . . . We also are responsible for the consequences of our reporting," he wrote.[56]

Native Americans who had been battling against the logos were pleased, but journalists were divided. Some argued that it was courageous for a newspaper to take the lead on such an issue. Others said newspapers should not censor information they disagreed with, and chided the *Oregonian* for letting an editorial viewpoint intrude on the news columns. The *Oregonian's* action and the debate it provoked were significant because they showed a recognition of the press' role in perpetuating images.

DISCUSSION

By the late twentieth century, stories of Native Americans were finding prominent places in mainstream news publications. The images those articles presented in the news seemed more varied than in the past. While the old, stereotypical images were easily found in the press, new ones were also there. Significantly, Native American journalists and others talked back to the media, taking news organizations to task for flawed coverage. Their views also found their way into some mainstream publications, where they could resonate among journalists and the public alike.

Whether it was due to the vigilance of Native Americans or the greater economic power of a few tribes or journalism's attention to multicultural issues or expanding definitions of news or some combination of these, the images of Native Americans in the 1990s press multiplied. Stereotyping did not end, as the examples cited illustrate, but it was mitigated by a variety of other portrayals.

Indians have been patronized, romanticized, stereotyped, and ignored by most of mainstream America. The twentieth-century press has been complicit in this, seldom by design but certainly through the exercise of its own conventions and values. To be sure, journalism has reflected the images and stereotypes prevalent in the popular culture. But it has done more. The very conventions and practices of journalism have worked to reinforce that popular—and often inaccurate—imagery. Stereotyping does not depend only on the use of crude language or factual inaccuracies. It also comes from the choice of stories to report, the ways stories are organized and written, the phrases used in headlines.

Though the press has seen its role ideally as being independent of outside influence and a watchdog on government, these ideals often fell short where coverage of Native Americans was concerned. In the episodes examined in this book, it was often the loudest, most aggressive sources whose messages were reported. Too seldom did journalists look beyond the loud voices to investigate independently. Often they failed to add the layers of historical and cultural context that would truly explain the meanings of events.

The mainstream press' attention to issues of diversity in the 1990s and the increasingly resonant voices of journalists of color, including Native Americans, brought attention to these shortcomings and an opportunity for a new look at coverage of groups outside the mainstream, with an eye to more balanced, realistic depictions.

NOTES

1. W. Richard West, Jr., and Kevin Gover, "The Struggle for Indian Civil Rights," in Frederick E. Hoxie, ed., *Indians in American History* (Arlington Heights: Harlan Davidson, Inc., 1988), 284, 290–291.

2. Stephen Cornell, *The Return of the Native* (New York: Oxford University Press, 1988), 215.

3. C. Patrick Morris, "Termination by Accountants: The Reagan Indian Policy," in Fremont J. Lyden and Lyman H. Legters, eds., *Native Americans and Public Policy* (Pittsburgh: University of Pittsburgh Press, 1992), 63–69.

4. Alvin M. Josephy, Jr., *Now That the Buffalo's Gone* (Norman: University of Oklahoma Press, 1984), 257–258.

5. Cornell, 209–210.

6. Morris, 74–76.

7. Josephy, 258.

8. See, among others, Ward Churchill and Winona LaDuke, "Native North America: The Political Economy of Radioactive Colonialism," in M. Annette Jaimes, ed., *The State of Native America* (Boston: South End Press, 1992), 241–266; Donald L. Fixico, "Tribal Leaders and the Demand for Natural Energy Resources on Reservation Lands," in Peter Iverson, ed., *The Plains Indians of the Twentieth Century* (Norman: University of Oklahoma Press, 1985), 219–235; Josephy, 221–223; *New York Times*, July 24, 1990, 1; May 3, 1993, 1.

9. See, for example, the situation of the Mescalero Apaches of New Mexico in *New York Times*, Nov. 11, 1993, A8; Feb. 2, 1995, A12; Apr. 23, 1995, E6.

10. West and Gover, 291–292.

11. Peter Nabokov, ed., *Native American Testimony* (New York: Viking, 1991), 407–408.

12. *New York Times*, Apr. 30, 1994, 9.

13. Nabokov, 407.

14. David Segal, "Dances with Sharks," *Washington Monthly*, Mar. 1992, 26–30.

15. "Looking for a Piece of the Action," *Newsweek*, June 13, 1994, 44.

16. Francis X. Clines, "The Pequots," *New York Times Magazine*, Feb. 27, 1994, 49–52.

17. *USA Today*, May 13–15, 1994, 1; *Chicago Tribune*, May 28, 1994, 1.

18. *New York Times*, Dec. 19, 1993.

19. *New York Times*, Mar. 22, 1993, A9; April 3, 1995, A12; Associated Press dispatch in *Arizona Daily Star*, Jan. 2, 1994, D5.

20. Tim Giago, "I Hope the Redskins Lose," *Newsweek*, Jan. 27, 1992, 8.

21. Quoted in Cynthia-Lou Coleman, "Native Americans Must Set Their Own Media Agenda," *Quill*, Oct. 1992, 8.

22. Michael Emery and Edwin Emery, *The Press and America*, 7th ed. (Englewood Cliffs: Prentice Hall, 1992), 536–537.

23. See Peter Prichard, *The Making of McPaper* (Kansas City: Andrews, McMeel and Parker, 1987), especially 293–313.

24. Emery and Emery, 584–587.

25. Prichard, 302–304.

26. Documentation, case studies, and recommendations for change can be found, among other sources, in "Special Issue: Diversity and the Press," *Newspaper Research Journal*, Summer 1990; Erna R. Smith, *What Color Is the News?* (San Francisco: Journalism Department, San Francisco State University; New California Alliance; Public Research Institute, 1991); American Society of Newspaper Editors, *Covering the Community* (Reston, Va.: American Society of Newspaper Editors, 1993); Edward C. Pease, ed., "Race—America's Rawest Nerve," *Media Studies Journal*, Summer 1994; Jon Funabiki, project director, *News Watch: A Critical Look at Coverage of People of Color* (San Francisco: Center for Integration and Improvement of Journalism at San Francisco State University, 1994); *Extra!* (New York: Fairness and Accuracy in Reporting), July/Aug. 1992.

27. See *Covering the Community*, 37–40; *Funabiki*, 12, 16–17, 24–25, 32–33, 48–51; Tim Giago, ed., *The American Indian and the Media* (Minneapolis: National Conference of Christians and Jews, Minnesota-Dakotas Region, 1991); Richard Hill, "The Non-Vanishing American Indian," *Quill*, May 1992, 35–37; Marshall Cook, "Indian Affairs and the Mainstream Media," *Editor & Publisher*, Dec. 23, 1989, 16–17.

28. See John M. Coward, "Native Americans in Journalism and Mass Communication Education," in Carolyn Martindale, ed., *Pluralizing Journalism Education* (Westport, Conn.: Greenwood Press, 1993), 121–131 and John M. Coward, *Teacher's Guide to The Media and the American Indian* (Produced for The National Conference of Christians and Jews, Oklahoma City and Tulsa Regions, 1994).

29. *New York Times*, Nov. 22, 1990.

30. *USA Today*, June 1, 1993, 1.

31. *USA Today*, June 2, 1993, 1.

32. *Chicago Sun-Times*, June 1, 1993, 21.

33. *Time*, June 14, 1993, 57.

34. *Chicago Sun-Times*, June 1, 1993, 21.

35. *New York Times*, April 24, 1994, 11.

36. Quoted in Bob M. Gassaway, "Press Virus Strikes Navajos," *Quill*, Nov./Dec. 1993, 24.

37. Ibid., 24.

38. *Washington Post*, June 14, 1994, sec. WH, p. 12.

39. *The Native Voice* (convention publication of the Native American Journalists Association), May 25, 1995, 1; for the story, see *Washington Post*, Sept. 20, 1994, D1.

40. Associated Press dispatch in the *New York Times*, Sept. 3, 1994.

41. *New York Times*, Aug. 31, 1994, A8.
42. *St. Louis Post-Dispatch*, Oct. 25, 1991, 1D.
43. Ibid.
44. George E. Hyde, *Indians of the Woodlands* (Norman: University of Oklahoma Press, 1962), 182–184, 244–245.
45. Ibid., 272.
46. United Press International, Oct. 5, 1989.
47. Ibid.
48. *Chicago Tribune*, Oct. 16, 1989, 3.
49. *Chicago Tribune*, Nov. 12, 1989, Perspective section, p. 4.
50. *Chicago Tribune*, Nov. 8, 1989, 22.
51. *Minneapolis Star Tribune*, Jan. 27, 1992, 11A.
52. *New York Times*, Jan. 26, 1992, sec. 1, p. 14.
53. *Minneapolis Star Tribune*, Nov. 1, 1991, 2B.
54. Tim Giago, "I Hope the Redskins Lose," *Newsweek*, Jan. 27, 1992, 8.
55. William Hilliard, "Stereotypes on the Sports Page," *ASNE Bulletin*, May/June 1992, 20–21.
56. Ibid.

Selected Bibliography

BOOKS

American Indian Media Image Task Force. *The American Indian and the Media.* Minneapolis: National Conference of Christians and Jews Minnesota-Dakotas Region, 1991.

Axtell, James. *After Columbus.* New York: Oxford University Press, 1988.

Baughman, James L. *The Republic of Mass Culture.* Baltimore: Johns Hopkins University Press, 1992.

Bayley, Edwin R. *Joe McCarthy and the Press.* Madison: University of Wisconsin Press, 1981.

Berkhofer, Robert F., Jr. *The White Man's Indian.* New York: Vintage Books, 1978.

Bernstein, Alison R. *American Indians and World War II.* Norman: University of Oklahoma Press, 1991.

Blue Cloud, Peter, ed. *Alcatraz Is Not an Island.* Berkeley: Wingbow Press, 1972.

Bolt, Christine. *American Indian Policy and American Reform: Case Studies of the Campaign to Assimilate the American Indians.* London: Allen and Unwin, 1987.

Boorstin, Daniel J. *The Image or What Happened to the American Dream.* New York: Atheneum, 1962.

Brown, Dee Alexander. *Bury My Heart at Wounded Knee.* New York: Holt, Rinehart and Winston, 1971.

Brucker, Herbert. *The Changing American Newspaper.* New York: Columbia University Press, 1937.

Burnette, Robert, and John Koster. *The Road to Wounded Knee.* New York: Bantam Books, 1974.

Burt, Larry W. *Tribalism in Crisis: Federal Indian Policy, 1953–1961.* Albuquerque: University of New Mexico Press, 1982.

Cahn, Edgar S., and David W. Hearne, eds. *Our Brother's Keeper: The Indian in White America*. New York: Meridian Books, 1970.

Charnley, Mitchell V. *Reporting*. 3d ed. New York: Holt, Rinehart and Winston, 1975.

Churchill, Ward. *Indians Are Us? Culture and Genocide in Native North America*. Monroe, Maine: Common Courage Press, 1994.

Churchill, Ward, and Jim Vander Wall. *Agents of Repression*. Boston: South End Press, 1988, 1990.

Collier, John. *From Every Zenith*. Denver: Sage Books, 1963.

_____. *The Indians of the Americas*. New York: W. W. Norton and Company, Inc., 1947.

Collins, John James. *Native American Religions: A Geographical Survey*. Lewiston, New York: The Edwin Mellen Press, 1991.

Commission on Freedom of the Press. *A Free and Responsible Press*. Chicago: University of Chicago Press, 1947.

Cornell, Stephen. *Return of the Native: American Indian Political Resurgence*. New York: Oxford University Press, 1988.

Covert, Catherine L., and John D. Stevens, eds. *Mass Media Between the Wars: Perceptions of Cultural Tension, 1918–1941*. Syracuse, N.Y.: Syracuse University Press, 1984.

Crawford, Nelson Antrim. *The Ethics of Journalism*. New York: Alfred A. Knopf, 1924.

Crow Dog, Mary, with Richard Erdoes. *Lakota Woman*. New York: Grove Weidenfeld, 1990.

Debo, Angie. *A History of the Indians of the United States*. Norman: University of Oklahoma Press, 1970.

_____. *And Still the Waters Run*. Princeton: Princeton University Press, 1940.

Deloria, Vine, Jr., *Behind the Trail of Broken Treaties*. New York: Delacorte Press, 1974.

_____. *Custer Died for Your Sins*. New York: Avon Books, 1970.

_____, ed. *American Indian Policy in the Twentieth Century*. Norman: University of Oklahoma Press, 1985.

Deloria, Vine, Jr., and Clifford M. Lytle. *The Nations Within*. New York: Pantheon Books, 1984.

Dewing, Rolland. *Wounded Knee: The Meaning and Significance of the Second Incident*. New York: Irvington Publishers, Inc. 1985.

Dippie, Brian W. *The Vanishing American: White Attitudes and U.S. Indian Policy*. Middletown, Conn.: Wesleyan University Press, 1982.

Downie, Leonard Jr. *The New Muckrakers*. Washington, D.C.: The New Republic Book Company, Inc., 1976.

Drinnon, Richard. *Facing West: The Metaphysics of Indian-Hating and Empire-Building*. Minneapolis: University of Minnesota Press, 1980.

Emery, Michael, and Edwin Emery. *The Press and America*. 7th ed. Englewood Cliffs: Prentice Hall, 1992.

Fey, Harold E., and D'Arcy McNickle. *Indians and Other Americans*. New York: Harper and Brothers, 1959.

Fisher, Paul L., and Ralph L. Lowenstein, eds. *Race and the News Media*. New York: Frederick A. Praeger, Publishers, 1967.

Fixico, Donald L. *Termination and Relocation: Federal Indian Policy, 1945–1960*. Albuquerque: University of New Mexico Press, 1986.

Flint, Leon Nelson. *The Conscience of the Newspaper*. New York: D. Appleton and Company, 1925.

Friar, Ralph E., and Natasha A. Friar. *The Only Good Indian . . . The Hollywood Gospel*. New York: Drama Book Specialists, 1972.

Gans, Herbert J. *Deciding What's News*. New York: Vintage Books, 1979.

Gerald, J. Edward. *The Social Responsibility of the Press*. Minneapolis: The University of Minnesota Press, 1963.

Gessner, Robert. *Massacre: A Survey of Today's American Indian*. New York: Jonathan Cape and Harrison Smith, 1931.

Gitlin, Todd. *The Whole World Is Watching*. Berkeley: University of California Press, 1980.

Goldstein, Tom, ed. *Killing the Messenger: 100 Years of Media Criticism*. New York: Columbia University Press, 1989.

Greenberg, Bradley S., Michael Burgoon, Judee K. Burgoon, and Felipe Korzenny. *Mexican Americans and the Mass Media*. Norwood, N.J.: Ablex Publishing Corp., 1983.

Hagan, William T. *American Indians*. 3d ed. Chicago: University of Chicago Press, 1993.

Hauptman, Laurence M. *The Iroquois and the New Deal*. Syracuse, N.Y.: Syracuse University Press, 1981.

Hemingway, Albert. *Ira Hayes, Pima Marine*. Lanham, Md.: University Press of America, 1988.

Henry, Jeannette. Edited by Rupert Costo. *Textbooks and the American Indian*. San Francisco: Indian Historian Press, Inc., 1970.

Hertzberg, Hazel W. *The Search for an American Indian Identity: Modern Pan-Indian Movements*. Syracuse, N.Y.: Syracuse University Press, 1971.

Higham, John. *Strangers in the Land: Patterns of American Nativism 1860–1925*. New York: Atheneum, 1973.

Hilger, Michael. *The American Indian in Film*. Metuchen, N.J.: The Scarecrow Press, Inc., 1986.

Hirschfelder, Arlene B. *American Indian Stereotypes in the World of Children: A Reader and Bibliography*. Metuchen, N.J., and London: The Scarecrow Press, Inc., 1982.

Hoxie, Frederick E. *A Final Promise: The Campaign to Assimilate the Indians, 1880–1920*. Lincoln: University of Nebraska Press, 1984.

———. *Indians in American History*. Arlington Heights, Ill.: Harlan Davidson, Inc., 1988.

Hughes, Helen MacGill. *News and the Human Interest Story*. Chicago: University of Chicago Press, 1940.

Hyde, George E. *Indians of the Woodlands*. Norman: University of Oklahoma Press, 1962.

Hyde, Grant Milnor. *Newspaper Reporting*. New York: Prentice Hall, Inc., 1952.

Indians in the War. Chicago: United States Bureau of Indian Affairs, 1945.

Institute for Government Research, Lewis Meriam, technical director. *The Problem of Indian Administration*. Baltimore: Johns Hopkins Press, 1928.

Iverson, Peter. *Carlos Montezuma and the Changing World of American Indians.* Albuquerque: University of New Mexico Press, 1982.

———, ed. *The Plains Indians of the Twentieth Century.* Norman: University of Oklahoma Press, 1985.

Izard, Ralph S. *Reporting the Citizens' News.* New York: Holt, Rinehart and Winston, 1982.

Jaimes, M. Annette, ed. *The State of Native America.* Boston: South End Press, 1992.

Jones, R. Bruce, ed. *N. W. Ayer & Son's Directory of Newspapers and Periodicals 1953.* Philadelphia: N. W. Ayer & Son, Inc., 1953.

Josephy, Alvin M., Jr. *Now That the Buffalo's Gone: A Study of Today's American Indians.* Norman: University of Oklahoma Press, 1984.

———. *Red Power: The American Indians' Fight for Freedom.* Lincoln: University of Nebraska Press, 1971.

Katz, William Loren. *Black Indians: A Hidden Heritage.* New York: Atheneum, 1986.

Kelly, Lawrence C. *The Assault on Assimilation: John Collier and the Origins of Indian Policy Reform.* Albuquerque: University of New Mexico Press, 1983.

Kopper, Philip. *The Smithsonian Book of North American Indians.* Washington, D.C.: Smithsonian Books, 1986.

Lazarus, Edward. *Black Hills, White Justice.* New York: HarperCollins Publishers, 1991.

Limerick, Patricia Nelson, Clyde A. Milner II, and Charles E. Rankin, eds. *Trails: Toward a New Western History.* Lawrence: University Press of Kansas, 1991.

Lippmann, Walter. *Liberty and the News.* New York: Harcourt, Brace and Howe, 1920.

———. *Public Opinion.* New York: The Macmillan Company, 1922.

Lyden, Fremont J., and Lyman H. Legters, eds. *Native Americans and Public Policy.* Pittsburgh: University of Pittsburgh Press, 1992.

Lyman, Stanley David. *Wounded Knee 1973.* Lincoln: University of Nebraska Press, 1991.

MacDougall, Curtis D. *Interpretative Reporting.* New York: The Macmillan Company, 1938, 1972.

———. *The Press and Its Problems.* Dubuque, Iowa: Wm. C. Brown Company, 1964.

Marling, Karal Ann, and John Wetenhall. *Iwo Jima: Monuments, Memories, and the American Hero.* Cambridge: Harvard University Press, 1991.

Martindale, Carolyn. *The White Press and Black America.* New York: Greenwood Press, 1986.

———, ed. *Pluralizing Journalism Education.* Westport, Conn.: Greenwood Press, 1993.

Marzolf, Marion Tuttle. *Civilizing Voices: American Press Criticism, 1880–1950.* New York: Longman Publishing Group, 1991.

Matthiessen, Peter. *In the Spirit of Crazy Horse.* New York: Penguin Books, 1983, 1991.

Maxwell, James A., ed. *America's Fascinating Indian Heritage.* Pleasantville, N.Y.: The Reader's Digest Association, Inc., 1978.

McNickle, D'Arcy. *Native American Tribalism.* New York: Oxford University Press, 1973.

Mott, George Fox. *New Survey of Journalism*. New York: Barnes and Noble, Inc., 1950.

Murphy, James E., and Sharon M. Murphy. *Let My People Know: American Indian Journalism, 1828–1978*. Norman: University of Oklahoma Press, 1981.

Nabokov, Peter, ed. *Native American Testimony*. New York: Viking, 1991.

National Advisory Commission on Civil Disorders (Kerner Commission). *Report of the National Advisory Commission on Civil Disorders*. New York: Bantam Books, 1968.

Neils, Elaine M. *Reservation To City: Indian Migration and Federal Relocation*. Chicago: University of Chicago Department of Geography Research Paper No. 131, 1971.

O'Connor, John E. *The Hollywood Indian: Stereotypes of Native Americans in Films*. Trenton: The New Jersey State Museum, 1980.

Olson, James S., and Raymond Wilson. *Native Americans in the Twentieth Century*. Provo, Utah: Brigham Young University Press, 1984.

Painter, Muriel Thayer, Edward H. Spicer, and Wilma Kaemlein, eds. *With Good Heart: Yaqui Beliefs and Ceremonies in Pascua Village*. Tucson: The University of Arizona Press, 1986.

Parman, Donald L. *The Navajos and the New Deal*. New Haven and London: Yale University Press, 1976.

Pearce, Roy Harvey. *Savagism and Civilization: A Study of the Indian and the American Mind*. Baltimore: Johns Hopkins Press, 1953, 1965.

Peroff, Nicholas C. *Menominee Drums: Tribal Termination and Restoration, 1954–1974*. Norman: University of Oklahoma Press, 1982.

Peterson, Theodore. *Magazines in the Twentieth Century*. Urbana: University of Illinois Press, 1956.

Philp, Kenneth R. *John Collier's Crusade for Indian Reform*. Tucson: University of Arizona Press, 1977.

———, ed. *Indian Self-Rule*. Salt Lake City: Howe Bros., 1986.

Prichard, Peter. *The Making of McPaper*. Kansas City: Andrews, McMeel and Parker, 1987.

Prucha, Francis Paul. *The Great Father: The United States Government and the American Indians*. Lincoln: University of Nebraska Press, 1986.

———. *The Indians in American Society*. Berkeley: University of California Press, 1985.

Rosten, Leo C. *The Washington Correspondents*. New York: Harcourt, Brace and Company, 1937.

Schrader, Robert Fay. *The Indian Arts & Crafts Board: An Aspect of New Deal Indian Policy*. Albuquerque: University of New Mexico Press, 1983.

Schudson, Michael. *Discovering the News: A Social History of American Newspapers*. New York: Basic Books, Inc., 1978.

Shames, Deborah, ed. *Freedom with Reservation: The Menominee Struggle to Save Their Land and People*. Madison: National Committee to Save The Menominee People and Forests, 1972.

Siebert, Fred S., Theodore Peterson, and Wilbur Schramm. *Four Theories of the Press*. Urbana: University of Illinois Press, 1956.

Siebert, Fredrick S. *Freedom of the Press in England, 1476–1776*. Urbana: University of Illinois Press, 1952.

Sinclair, Upton. *The Brass Check: A Study of American Journalism*. Pasadena: published by the author, 1920.

Slotkin, Richard. *Gunfighter Nation: The Myth of the Frontier in Twentieth-Century America*. New York: Atheneum, 1992.

Smith, Jane F., and Robert M. Kvasnicka, eds. *Indian-White Relations: A Persistent Paradox*. Washington, D.C.: Howard University Press, 1976.

Steiner, Stan. *The New Indians*. New York: Delta Books, 1968.

Stewart, Omer C. *Peyote Religion*. Norman: University of Oklahoma Press, 1987.

Sturtevant, William C., general ed. *Handbook of North American Indians*. Vol. 4, *History of Indian-White Relations*, edited by Wilcomb E. Washburn. Washington, D.C.: Smithsonian Institution, 1988.

______. *Handbook of North American Indians*. Vol. 9, *Southwest*, edited by Alfonso Ortiz. Washington, D.C.: Smithsonian Institution, 1978–1990.

Svirsky, Leon, ed. *Your Newspaper: Blueprint for a Better Press*. New York: The Macmillan Company, 1947.

Talese, Gay. *The Kingdom and the Power*. New York: World Publishing Company, 1969.

Taylor, Graham D. *The New Deal and American Indian Tribalism*. Lincoln: University of Nebraska Press, 1980.

Tuchman, Gaye. *Making News*. New York: The Free Press, 1978.

van Dijk, Teun A. *News Analysis*. Hillsdale, N.J.: Lawrence Erlbaum Associates, 1988.

Versluis, Arthur. *The Elements of Native American Traditions*. Shaftsbury, Dorset, Great Britain: Element, 1993. pp. 46–48.

Vogel, Virgil J. *This Country Was Ours: A Documentary History of the American Indian*. New York: Harper and Row, 1972.

Voices from Wounded Knee, 1973. Mohawk Nation via Rooseveltown, N.Y.: Akwesasne Notes, 1974.

Washburn, Wilcomb E. *The Assault on Indian Tribalism*. Malabar, Fla.: Robert E. Krieger Publishing Co., 1986.

______, ed. *The Indian and the White Man*. Garden City, N.Y.: Anchor Books, 1964.

White, Graham J. *FDR and the Press*. Chicago: University of Chicago Press, 1979.

White, Robert H. *Tribal Assets*. New York: Henry Holt and Company, 1990.

Wilson, Clint C. II, and Félix Gutiérrez. *Minorities and Media: Diversity and the End of Mass Communication*. Beverly Hills: Sage Publications, 1985.

Wolfe, Tom. *The New Journalism*. New York: Harper and Row, 1973.

Wolseley, Roland E., and Laurence R. Campbell. *Exploring Journalism*. 3d ed. Englewood Cliffs, N.J.: Prentice-Hall, Inc., 1957.

Wood, James Playsted. *Magazines in the United States (Second Edition)*. New York: The Ronald Press Company, 1956.

Yost, Casper S. *The Principles of Journalism*. New York: D. Appleton and Company, 1924.

Zimmerman, Bill. *Airlift to Wounded Knee*. Chicago: Swallow Press, Inc. 1976.

JOURNAL ARTICLES, MONOGRAPHS, AND DISSERTATIONS

Bleyer, Willard Grosvenor, "Journalism in the United States: 1933." *Journalism Quarterly* X, no. 4 (December 1933): 296–301.

Burd, Gene. "Minorities in Reporting Texts: Before and After the 1968 Kerner Report." *Mass Comm Review* 15, nos. 2 and 3 (1988): 45–60, 68.

Churchill, Ward, Norbert Hill, and Mary Ann Hill. "Media Stereotyping and Native Response: An Historical Overview." *The Indian Historian* 11, no. 4 (December 1978): 45–56, 63.

Coleman, Cynthia-Lou. "Native Americans Must Set Their Own Media Agenda." *Quill* (October 1992): 8.

Collier, John. "The Indian in a Wartime Nation." *Annals of the American Academy of Political and Social Science* 223 (September 1942): 29.

Copeland, David A. " 'The Sculking Indian Enemy': Colonial Newspapers' Portrayal of Native Americans." Paper presented to the History Division, Association for Education in Journalism and Mass Communications (AEJMC), Kansas City, Mo., August 1993.

Coward, John M. "The Newspaper Indian: Native Americans and the Press in the 19th Century." Ph. D. diss., University of Texas at Austin, 1989.

Downes, Randolph C. "A Crusade for Indian Reform, 1922–1934." *Mississippi Valley Historical Review* 32, no. 3 (December 1945): 331–354.

"E & P Panel Suggests Studies For Press Self-Improvement." *Editor and Publisher.* (March 26, 1949): 5–7, 40–50.

Fedler, Fred. "The Media and Minority Groups: a Study of Adequacy of Access." *Journalism Quarterly* 50, no. 1 (Spring 1973): 109–117.

Gassaway, Bob M. "Press Virus Strikes Navajos." *Quill* (November-December 1993): 24.

Gilmore, Charles W. "The Cherokee Phoenix." *Nieman Reports* 2, no. 3 (July 1948): 13–14.

Hilliard, William. "Stereotypes on the Sports Page." *ASNE Bulletin* (May/June 1992): 20–21.

Klein, Woody. "News Media and Race Relations: a Self-Portrait." *Columbia Journalism Review* (Fall 1968): 42–49.

Koster, John. "American Indians and the Media." *Cross Currents* (Summer 1976): 164–171.

LaFarge, Oliver. "Termination of Federal Supervision: Disintegration and the American Indians." *Annals of the American Academy of Political and Social Sciences* 311 (May 1957): 43–44.

Murphy, James E., and Donald R. Avery. "A Comparison of Alaskan Native and Non-Native Newspaper Content." *Journalism Quarterly* 60, no. 2 (Summer 1983): 316–322.

Olson, Kenneth E. "The Newspaper in Times of Social Change." *Journalism Quarterly* XII, no. 1 (March 1935): 10–11.

Problems of Journalism: Proceedings of the First Annual Meeting of the American Society of Newspaper Editors. Washington, D.C., April 27–28, 1923.

Steiner, Linda. "Construction of Gender in Newsreporting Textbooks: 1890–1990." *Journalism Monographs* 135 (October 1992).

Streb, Edward Justin. "The Rhetoric of Wounded Knee II: A Critical Analysis of Confrontational and 'Media Event' Discourse." Ph.D. diss. Northwestern University, Evanston, Ill., 1979.

Talbot, Steve. "Free Alcatraz: The Culture of Native American Liberation," *Journal of Ethnic Studies* 6, no. 3 (Fall 1978): 83–96.

Watkins, Arthur V. "Termination of Federal Supervision: The Removal of Restrictions Over Indian Property and Person." *Annals of the American Academy of Political and Social Sciences* 311 (May 1957): 55.

Weiss, Richard. "Ethnicity and Reform: Minorities and the Ambience of the Depression Years." *Journal of American History* 66, no. 3 (December 1979): 566–585.

NEWSPAPERS

Arizona Republic
Arizona Star
Chicago Daily News
Chicago Sun-Times
Chicago Tribune
Christian Science Monitor
Daily Oklahoman
Denver Post
Green Bay Press-Gazette
Magee's Independent
Milwaukee Journal
Milwaukee Sentinel
Minneapolis Star Tribune
Muskogee Daily Phoenix
New York Times
Omaha World-Herald
Portland Oregonian
Phoenix Gazette
Rapid City Daily Journal
Santa Fe New Mexican
Shawano Evening Leader
Tucson Citizen
Washington Post

MAGAZINES

America
American Mercury
American West
Asia and the Americas
Atlantic Monthly
Business Week
Christian Century
Collier's
Coronet
Current History
Current Opinion
Editor and Publisher

Esquire
Good Housekeeping
Harpers
Holiday
Ladies' Home Journal
Life
Literary Digest
Look
Mademoiselle
Nation
National Geographic
National Review
Nation's Business
New Republic
New Yorker
Newsweek
The Outlook
Parents Magazine
PTA Magazine
Ramparts
Reader's Digest
Redbook
Saturday Evening Post
Saturday Review of Literature
Scholastic
Scientific American
Seventeen
Sunset
Time
U.S. News and World Report

Index

AIM. *See* American Indian Movement
Albuquerque Evening Herald, 26, 41
Alcatraz Island occupation, 4, 127, 137–40
New Republic on, 139
New York Times on, 139
San Francisco Chronicle on, 140
Time on, 140
"Alcatraz Newsletter," 138
Algonquian tribes, 28
Allotment system, 19–20, 52, 53, 107
All Pueblo Council, 23, 27, 32
American Civil Liberties Union, 102
American Indian Chicago Conference, 128–29, 133
American Indian Defense Association, 20, 32
American Indian Freedom of Religion Act, 154
American Indian Movement (AIM), 140, 141, 142, 162
American Mercury, 87, 91
American Society of Newspaper Editors
and Canons of Journalism, 4–5
on impartiality of newspapers, 6
on the 1920s news media, 22
Anderson, Wallace Mad Bear, 134
Arapaho Indians, 67
Arizona Republic
on ceremonial dance, 66
"filler" story used in, 63–64
on John Collier's meeting with Arizona tribes, 70
on Native American military service, 88
on Navajo rain ritual, 71
on Navajo Tribal Council, 74
on pow wow in Flagstaff, 65
range of coverage of Native Americans in, 57
stereotypical language in, 70
Asher, Carl, 60
Asia and the Americas, 91
Assimilation
articles promoting, 33, 95, 105–6
and ceremonial dances controversy, 29, 32, 33–34
Christian Century on, 95
Dawes Severalty Act and, 19–20
downside of, 106
ideology of, 19, 20
Indian reservations and, 33, 34
Ladies' Home Journal on, 28

official disfavor of, 49
Saturday Evening Post on, 33, 34
termination as updated, 4, 95, 99
Associated Press
on Indian's penalty for intoxication, 63
on Lumbee-Klan conflict, 121
on Menominee wealth, 115
on Navajo rain ritual, 70
on Sen. Watkins's visit to Menominee reservation, 111
on Tlingit banishment practice, 159–60
wire service of, 66, 102
on Wounded Knee occupation, 143–44, 145, 146
Association on American Indian Affairs, 100, 101, 114
Atlanta Braves, 155, 162
Atlantic Monthly, 118
Atwood, Stella, 21, 23
Austin, Mary, 21, 25
Aztec Indians, 28

Banks, Dennis, 141, 145
Bannock Indians, 36
Bellamy, Paul, 22
Bellecourt, Clyde, 162
Bennett, James O'Donnell, 1, 66
Berger, Meyer, 64
Berkhofer, Robert F., Jr., 10, 11, 36
BIA. *See* Bureau of Indian Affairs
Blackfeet Indians, 76
Bleyer, Willard Grosvenor, 53
Boorstin, Daniel, 132
Booth, Alice, 61
Boyle, Kay, 138–39
Bradley, Pharmacist's Mate John, 89
Brisbane, Arthur, 24
Brooklyn *Eagle*, 22
Brown, Dee, 141
Burke, Charles H., 30, 31, 36
Bureau of Indian Affairs (BIA)
boarding schools run by, 20, 32, 51
John Collier and, 20, 49, 50
Indian occupation of headquarters, 127
Indian Reorganization Act and, 129
and Menominee Indians, 107
official quoted in *New York Times*, 33
relocation and, 117
termination and, 101
and Wheeler-Howard bill, 52
Wounded Knee insurgents and, 143
Bursum, Sen. Holm Olaf, 23, 39, 40
Bursum bill
controversy surrounding, 21, 23
framing of stories concerning, 38, 39–41
John Collier and, 21, 23, 38
Nation on, 28
news media on, 24–29
New York Times on, 24, 28, 40
Pueblo Indians and, 4, 21, 23
Santa Fe New Mexican on, 23, 26, 42
Bury My Heart at Wounded Knee (Brown), 141

Caldwell, Earl, 139
Canons of Journalism, 4–5, 6
Central Council of Tlingit and Haida Indian Tribes, 160
Century of Progress world's fair, 1, 66, 73
CETA. *See* Comprehensive Employment and Training Act
Cherokee Indians, 19, 69, 121
Cherokee Phoenix, 104
Cheyenne Indians, 67
Chicago Blackhawks, 155
Chicago Black Panthers, 144
Chicago Daily News
on Ira Hayes, 90
on Navajo abolishment of honorary tribal memberships, 73
on Pueblo Indians' visit to Chicago, 27
on reservation life, 146
on Wounded Knee occupation, 143
Chicago Sun-Times, 1
Chicago Tribune
on Century of Progress world's fair, 1, 66

on Chief Illiniwek controversy, 161–62
editorial cartoon in, 64–65
on Lumbee-Klan conflict, 121
on Menominee culture, 109
New Deal coverage, 54
political bias of, 54, 77
on Pueblos' visit to Chicago Women's Club, 27
on reservation life, 146
on Wounded Knee occupation, 144, 145
Chickasaw Indians, 19
Chief Illiniwek controversy, 1, 160–61
Choctaw Indians, 19, 68
Christian Century, 59, 95
Christian Science Monitor
audience of, 102
on "Indian problem," 105
on Iroquois Confederacy, 119, 120
on Navajo boarding school, 105–6
on "new" Indian, 105
on Pueblo delegation to Manhattan, 42
on termination legislation, 114–15
Civil rights movement, 4, 100, 120, 128, 130
Civilian Conservation Corps, 50
Clearwater, Frank, 143
Cleveland Indians, 155
Clinton, Bill, 154
Cold War, 99, 100, 107
Collier, John
and American Indian Defense Association, 20, 32
and Bursum bill, 21, 23, 38
and ceremonial dances controversy, 32, 35
as commissioner of Indian affairs, 49, 99, 101
on cultural pluralism, 20–22, 50, 90
on Indian enlistment, 90
and Indian New Deal, 20, 86
Indian policy reform efforts of, 4, 50
and *Indians at Work*, 78
influence of, with media, 38, 77
Navajo livestock reduction and, 71
on Pueblo Indians, 25–26, 28
and Wheeler-Howard bill, 75
Collier's, 58
coverage of Native Americans, 59
degraded Indian imagery in, 62
on Native American military service, 87
Columbia Journalism Review, 131
Comanche Indians, 93, 94
Commission on Freedom of the Press. *See* Hutchins Commission
Commonweal, 106, 114
Comprehensive Employment and Training Act (CETA), 153
Cooper, James Fenimore, 1
Cornell, Stephen, 128, 153
Coronet, 118
Costner, Kevin, 1
Council of Progressive Christians, 32
Crawford, Nelson Antrim, 5
Creek Indians, 19, 63
Croatan Indians, 121
Cultural pluralism
articles opposing, 95
articles promoting, 29, 34–38
and ceremonial dances controversy, 29, 32, 34–35, 37–38
ideology of, 3–4, 20–21
and Indian New Deal, 21
implementation of, 50–52
John Collier on, 20–22, 50, 90
New York Times and, 37–38
news media on, 29
Custer Died for Your Sins (Deloria), 133

Daily Oklahoman, 63, 68
Dartmouth College, 155
Dawes Severalty Act, 19–20
Deloria, Vine, Jr., 128, 133–34
Depression era, 50
Dippie, Brian W., 11
Dixon, Sen. Alan, 160
Dodge, Chee, 41–42

Eisenhower, Dwight D., 102, 108
Emerson, Haven, 101
Emmons, Glenn L., 117
Esquire, 134

Essay on Man, An (Pope), 61

Fall, Albert B., 22, 23, 39–40
Federal Board of Indian Commissioners, 60
Fitzgerald, Edward J., 51
Five Tribes, 19, 52, 67
Fixico, Donald, 94
Flathead Indians, 58, 115
Fox Indians, 94
Franklin, Marvin L., 134
Free and Responsible Press, A (Hutchins Commission), 104

Gagnon, Pvt. Rene, 89
General Federation of Women's Clubs, 21
Ghost Dance, 140
Giago, Tim, 155, 162
Gitlin, Todd, 13
Good Housekeeping, 61
Green Bay Press-Gazette, 109, 110–11
Grey, Zane, 21

Hadden, Briton, 58
Harper's, 143
Harvard University, 104
Hayes, Ira Hamilton, 86, 89–90
Hearst, William Randolph, 54
Hedgepeth, William, 138
Hershey, Burnet, 91
Hill, Frank Ernest, 51
Hill, Thomasine Ruth, 136
Hill Indians, 62
Hilliard, William, 163
Honig, Robert, 161
Hopi Indians, 30, 67, 136
Howard, Rep. Edgar, 51
Hubbell, Roman, 70, 71
Hutchins, Robert M., 5
Hutchins Commission (Commission on Freedom of the Press)
  on coverage of minorities, 6–7, 103–4
  Free and Responsible Press, A, 104
  on role of the press, 5

Ickes, Harold L., 49, 87, 90
Illini Indians, 161
Indian Bureau. *See* Bureau of Indian Affairs
Indian Gaming Regulatory Act, 155
Indian New Deal, 4, 21, 52, 86
Indian Reorganization Act (IRA), 49–50, 53, 75, 129
  New York Times on, 76
  Scholastic on, 60
  Time on, 58
Indian reservations
  assimilationist view of, 33, 34
  Chicago Daily News on, 146
  Chicago Tribune on, 146
  Dawes Severalty Act and, 19–20
  history of, 19
  Indian New Deal and, 86
  Menominee, 107
  New York Times on, 145–46
  opponents of, 86
  Pine Ridge Sioux, 140, 141
  Ponca, 153
  poverty on, 100
  relocation from, 101, 116–18, 128
  Rosebud Sioux, 141
  unemployment on, 154
  World War II and, 85, 86, 127
Indian Treaty Rights Committee, 161
Indians at Work, 73, 78
Inter-Tribal Indian Ceremonial, 65
Interior Department, 53
Interpretative Reporting (MacDougall), 54–55
IRA. *See* Indian Reorganization Act
Iroquois tribes, 28, 92, 103, 119–20, 161
Irwin, Will, 8
Izard, Ralph S., 131

Jeep Cherokee, 1
Jicarilla Apache Indians, 135
Johnson, E. Dana, 22
Johnson, Lyndon B., 7, 129, 130
Journalism. *See also* News media
  codes of ethics in, 22, 53
  conventions of, 13–14
  and coverage of minorities, 5, 6–8, 55, 103–4, 130–32, 156–57

form of story, 13; in coverage of Native Americans, 13, 60; feature stories could depict erroneously, 38, 103; news stories lacked cultural sensitivity, 37, 38, 40, 75, 103, 115, 159–60
and framing of stories, 13; in 1920s, 38–39; in 1930s, 53–54; in 1970s, 144; in 1980s, 160
and images, 2
language and tone of story in coverage of Native Americans, 13; describing Indians physically, 27; doubting intellectual ability, 26; generalizing Indian traits, 28, 33, 87–88, 133; judging, 33; labeling by race in crime stories, 62; needless humor, 58–59, 63–64, 105, 133; stereotypical language, 13, 58, 59, 69–70, 115, 120–21; use of first name in second reference, 70
nature of, 2
"new," 132
newsworthiness; and coverage of minorities, 8, 55; and coverage of Native Americans, 73–74, 107, 115, 120, 129–30
organization of story, 13; in coverage of Native Americans, 70–71
and portrayal of Native Americans: historical dimension of, 3, 10–12, 88–89; perpetuation of inaccuracies, 8, 107, 160
role of, 2, 5–6
selection of stories, 13; images of Native Americans and, 10, 13; white definitions of news and, 60, 71–73, 93, 107, 157–58
and stereotypes, 2, 157
texts; on covering minorities, 55, 103–4; in 1920s, 5, 22; in 1930s, 54–55; in 1940s, 103; in 1950s, 103; pre-1970s, 6; study of, 55, 131

Kansas City Chiefs, 155
Kennedy, John F., 129
Kent State University, 144
Kerner, Otto, 7
Kerner Commission, 7–8, 130, 131
Kifner, John, 142
Klamath Indians, 102
Kuehn, James, 131
Ku Klux Klan, 120

Ladies' Home Journal, 25, 28
LaFarge, Oliver, 100, 105, 136
Laird, Rep. Melvin, 108
Last of the Mohicans, The, 63
Lawrence, D. H., 21, 29, 32
Life, 133, 136, 156
Lindsay, Vachel, 21
Lippmann, Walter, 2
Literary Digest, 58
on ceremonial dances controversy, 31
on Navajo tribal police, 73
on 1934 Indian congresses, 56, 57
on Osage oil revenues, 62
Lone Ranger, 12
Look, 137, 138, 156
Luce, Henry, 58
Lucius Nieman Foundation, 104
Lumbee Indians, 120, 121

McCormick, Col. Robert R., 54
MacDougall, Curtis D.
on elements of news stories, 8
Interpretative Reporting, 54–55
Reporting for Beginners, 54–55
Mademoiselle, 133–34, 136
Magee, Carl, 22, 39
Magee's Independent (New Mexico State Tribune), 22, 39
Magazines
circulation of, in 1980s–90s, 156
depth of coverage, 15
as image builder, 14
influence of, 14, 58
interpretative reporting in, 58, 78
in 1930s, 58–59
Markham, Edwin, 21
Masters, Edgar Lee, 21
Maya Indians, 28
Means, Russell, 141, 142, 145

Medill School of Journalism, 54
Menominee General Council, 108
Menominee Indians
  images of, in news media, 109
  lawsuit filed by, 107
  legal status of, in 1950s, 111
  per capita payments to, 107–8, 115
  reservation of, 107
  resistance of allotment by, 107
  termination and, 102, 107–8, 109, 110
Menominee Restoration Act, 108
Menominee Termination Act, 108, 115
Milwaukee Journal
  on distribution of Menominee per capita payments, 116
  on Menominee living standards, 109
  on Sen. Watkins's visit to Menominee reservation, 111
Milwaukee Sentinel, 112
Minneapolis Star Tribune, 162
Minnesota Twins, 162
Mohawk Indians, 128
Murphy, James E. and Sharon M., 131
Muskogee Daily Phoenix
  on Mae West's search for Indian costar, 66
  political bias of, 76
  range of coverage of Native Americans, 15, 57
  on Wheeler-Howard bill, 52, 67–68, 68–69

NAJA (Native American Journalists Association), 159
Nation, 58
  on the Bursum bill, 28
  coverage of Native Americans, 59
  on Pueblo culture, 28
  on Wheeler-Howard bill, 51
National Congress of American Indians (NCAI), 91, 127–28
National Council of Churches, 142
National Indian Youth Council (NIYC), 128–29
National Industrial Recovery Act (NIRA), 53
Native American Church, 30, 136
Native American Educational Services College, 161
Native American Graves Repatriation Act, 154
Native American Journalists Association. *See* NAJA
Native Americans. *See also* Indian reservations; *names of specific tribes*
  activism of: Alcatraz Island occupation, 4, 127, 137–40; American Indian Chicago Conference, 128–29, 133; American Indian Movement, 140, 141; early, 4, 128; National Indian Youth Council, 128–29; newsworthiness of, 129–30; protest of Indian images as logos and mascots, 155; "pseudo-events" in, 132; results of, 4; Super Bowl demonstration, 162; traditionalists and, 129, 141; Trail of Broken Treaties, 141; World Series demonstration, 162; Wounded Knee standoff, 127, 140–42
  allotment system and, 19–20, 52, 53
  assimilation and. *See* Assimilation
  as "bad" Indian, 11, 12. *See also* News Media, Native American images in
  ceremonial dances controversy and, 29–32
  coverage of, before World War II, 9
  and cultural pluralism. *See* Cultural pluralism
  energy resources of, 154
  as exotic relic, 12, 26–27. *See also* News Media, Native American images in
  gambling enterprises of, 154
  as "good" Indian, 11. *See also* News Media, Native American images in
  government boarding schools and, 20, 32
  images of, 1, 2, 10, 12; in the news media. *See* News media, Native American images in; origins of,

3, 10–12; in the press. *See* News media, Native American images in; themes of, 10
influence of, 16
legal status of: in 1920s, 85; in 1940s, 85; in 1950s, 102, 114
and local press coverage: in 1920s, 15, 39, 42; in 1930s, 52; in 1940s, 92; in 1950s, 109, 111, 118–19; in 1960s–70s, 146–47
military service of, 85-86, 90–91
New Deal reforms and, 49; Indian Reorganization Act (IRA), 49–50, 53; Wheeler-Howard bill, 50–53
as noble savage, 11, 12. *See also* News media, Native American images in
public interest in, 127, 128
reactions of, to media images, 12, 148, 156–57, 158–59
religious freedoms of: in 1920s, 21, 31, 32, 37, 38; in 1970s, 154
relocation of. *See* Indian reservations
self-determination of, 128–29, 153, 154
self-government powers of: in 1930s, 52, 53; in 1950s, 102
termination of federal services to. *See* Termination
traditionalists among, 129, 141, 154
treaty rights of, 114, 154
tribal nationalism of, 128–29, 153, 154
as "vanishing race," 19. *See also* News media, Native American images in
Navajo Indians, 60
abolishment of honorary tribal memberships, 72
boarding school for children of, 105–6
ceremonies of, 34, 93, 158
disease incorrectly linked to, 158–59
and Indian Reorganization Act, 53
life expectancy of, in 1950s, 107
lifeways of, 64
livestock of, 71–72
military service of, 85, 86, 93
per capita income of (1980s), 153
rain ritual of, 70
Tribal Council of, 71–72, 74
uranium mining of, 154
NCAI. *See* National Congress of American Indians
Neuberger, Richard L., 87, 90, 91
New Republic
on Alcatraz occupation, 139
coverage of Native Americans, 59
on Native American enlistees, 90
on Native American military service, 87
on Pueblo ceremonies, 35
on termination legislation, 114
News media. *See also* Journalism; *names of specific publications*; Newspapers; Magazines; Radio; Television
on Bursum bill, 24–29
and Canons of Journalism, 4–5
constraints on, 8–10, 159
and coverage of minorities, 5, 6–8, 55, 103–4, 130–32, 156–57
on cultural pluralism, 29
First Amendment and, 5, 53
history of Native American coverage, 12
ideal of, 2
and images, 2
investigative reporting and, 132
Kerner Commission on, 7
mission of, 3, 6
Native American images in, 2
in 1920s: "bad" Indian, 26; child of nature, 34; degraded Indian, 26; exotic relic, 27–28; "good" Indian, 24–26, 105; intellectually inferior, 26; noble savage, 24; rich Indian, 115; "vanishing race," 28
in 1930s: "bad" Indian, 59, 61–65; child of nature, 61; exotic relic, 56–57, 59, 65–66; "good" Indian, 59, 60–61; involved Indian citi-

zen, 59, 67–69; object of ridicule, 58–59, 63
in 1940s: eager enlistee, 90–91; exotic relic, 87, 92–94; good Indian warrior, 87–89; loyal patriot Indian, 91–92
in 1950s: conformist, 104–5; degraded Indian, 105–6, 107; exotic relic, 106, 119; improvident, 115, 116; involved Indian citizen, 107, 109; rich Indian, 116; victim of urban society, 118
in 1960s–70s: degraded Indian, 134–35, 146; exotic relic, 135–36; heroic warrior, 142; militant, 136–37; prophet and savior, 133; renegade, 144–45, 146; savage and warlike, 139–40; shrewd capitalist, 134; Western movie warrior, 144
in 1980s–90s: degraded Indian, 157, 158, 159; exotic relic, 157; legitimate protester, 162
Native American voices in: in 1920s, 41–42; in 1930s, 59, 67, 77, 78; in 1940s, 86; in 1950s, 114, 117; in 1960s–70s, 132, 133, 147; in 1980s–90s, 156, 158–59
"new journalism" and, 132
news as defined by, 8; in 1920s, 22, 38; in 1930s, 53–55, 74, 77; in 1950s, 102–4, 120; in 1960s–70s, 130–32; in 1980s–90s, 155–57
origins of, 3, 10–12
political bias in, 76–77
"pseudo-events" and, 132
role of, 2, 5–6
and stereotypes, 2, 157
white viewpoint in, 8, 12, 24
Newspapers
concerns of, during Roosevelt administration, 53–54
circulations of, in 1980s–90s, 155–56
dual nature of, 53
"filler" articles in, 66–67
interpretative reporting in, 54–55, 77–78
local, and coverage of Native Americans: influence of, on images, 55; in 1920s, 15, 39, 42; in 1930s, 52; in 1940s, 92; in 1950s, 109, 111, 118–19; in 1960s–70s, 146–47
national versus local, 55–58
objective reporting in, 54, 131–32
Newsweek
on American Indian Chicago Conference, 133
on artifacts as fashion, 135
on Comanche war ceremonial broadcast, 93
on Creek tribe election, 63
interpretative reporting in, 58
on Super Bowl protest, 162
on tribal religions, 136
on urban Indians, 135
New Yorker, 156
New York Evening Journal, 24
New York Herald Tribune, 62
New York Times
on Alcatraz occupation, 139
articles deemed newsworthy by, 74
on Blackfeet Indians, 76, 134
on Bursum bill, 24, 28, 40
on casting of *The Last of the Mohicans*, 63
on cocktail party benefit, 135
and cultural pluralism, 36–37
"fillers" in, 66
on Indian New Deal, 60
on Indian Reorganization Act, 76
on Iroquois Confederacy, 119–20
on Jim Thorpe, 70
on Lumbee-Klan conflict, 121
on Menominee wealth, 115
on Miss Indian America, 136
on Native American enlistment, 90, 91
and Native American images, 15
on Native American military service, 87–88
on Native American protest of treaty rights abrogation, 114
on Native Americans as uncivilized, 33

on Navajo Indians: abolishment of honorary tribal memberships, 72; rain ritual, 71; tribal police, 73
"new journalism" in, 139
op-ed column in, 157–58
on Osage oil revenues, 62
on Paiute struggle against white cattlemen, 36
as paper of record, 102
on Pueblo Indians: ceremonial dances of, 35–36; delegation to New York, 27; at a Senate hearing, 26
on relocation, 117
on reservation life, 145–46
on Super Bowl protest, 162
on termination legislation, 113–14, 114–15
on Tlingit tribal recognition, 160
on Wheeler-Howard bill, 75
on Wounded Knee occupation, 142–43, 145
New York Times Magazine
on All-Pueblo Council, 27
on attitudes toward Native Americans, 32–33
on Navajo Indians, 34, 64
on Wheeler-Howard bill, 51
Nieman Fellowships, 104
Nieman Reports, 104
NIRA. *See* National Industrial Recovery Act
Nisqually Indians, 137
Nixon, Richard M., 129
NIYC. *See* National Indian Youth Council
Northwestern University, 54

Oakes, Richard, 137, 139
Office of Indian Affairs, 73
Olson, Kenneth E., 54
Oneida Indians, 94
Onondaga Indians, 92
Osage Indians, 28
Dawes Severalty Act and, 19
as degraded Indian, 62
John Collier's meeting with, 68

The Outlook, 27, 40

Paitano, Frank, 42
Paiute Indians
as degraded Indians, 36, 38
termination and, 115
Papago (Tohono O'odham) Indians, 92
Parents Magazine, 65
Parrish, Maxfield, 21
Parsons, Elsie Clews, 21
Peattie, Donald Culross, 90
People, 156
Peyote, 30, 136
Pine Ridge Sioux reservation, 140, 141
Plains Indians
as "bad" Indians, 25
popular image of, 121
Sun Dance of, 30, 67, 93
warfare tradition of, 93
Ponca Indians, 153
"Poor Lo," 61
Portland Oregonian, 162–63
Pow wow, 28
Press, the. *See* Journalism; News Media
Publick Occurrences, Both Forreign and Domestick, 12
Pueblo Indians
All Pueblo Council of, 27, 32
attributes of, praised by whites, 24, 61
as "bad" Indians, 26
Bursum bill and, 4, 21, 23
ceremonies of, 35
Council of Progressive Christians and, 32
as "good" Indians, 24–26, 61
John Collier's view of, 21
spirituality of, 35
as "vanishing race," 28
Pyle, Ernie, 93, 94

Quill, 159

Radio, 55
Raleigh, Sir Walter, 121
Ramparts, 137

Rapid City Daily Journal
on American Indian Movement (AIM), 146–47
James Kuehn and, 131
on 1934 Indian congresses, 56
range of coverage of Native Americans, 57
on Wounded Knee occupation, 143, 146–47
Reader's Digest
circulation of, 1980s–90s, 156
coverage of Native Americans, 59
on Inter-Tribal Indian Ceremonial, 65
on Native American deficiencies, 134
on Native American enlistment, 90
on Native American military service, 87
on relocation, 117
on termination, 100–101
Reagan, Ronald, 153
Relocation, 101, 116–18, 128
Renehan, A. H., 26
Report of the National Advisory Commission of Civil Disorders (Kerner Commission), 7–8, 130, 131
Reporting for Beginners (MacDougall), 54–55
Reporting the Citizens' News (Izard), 131
Ripley, Josephine, 115
Rogers, Maria L., 51
Romero, Antonio, 41
Roosevelt, Franklin D.
on interpretative reporting, 54
and John Collier, 20, 49
and Wheeler-Howard bill, 75
Roosevelt, Theodore, 28, 42
Rosebud Sioux reservation, 141
Rosenthal, Joe, 86
Rousseau, Jean-Jacques, 11

Sac and Fox Indians, 70, 94
Sacramento *Bee*, 22
St. Louis Post-Dispatch, 160–61
Sandburg, Carl, 21
San Francisco Chronicle
on Alcatraz occupation, 140
John Collier and, 25–26, 28
on Pueblo Indians' artistic superiority, 25–26
San Francisco State College, 137
Santa Fe Kiwanis Club, 32
Santa Fe New Mexican
on Bursum bill, 23, 26, 42
on ceremonial dances, 32
E. Dana Johnson and, 22
on Navajo abolishment of honorary tribal membership, 72
on Navajo rain ritual, 70
on Pueblo self-government, 68
range of coverage of Native Americans, 15, 22
on Santa Fe Kiwanis Club spoof, 32
stereotypical language in, 70
Saturday Evening Post
on assimilationist philosophy, 33, 34
on Indian enlistment, 90
on Indian New Deal, 60–61
on relocation, 116
Scholastic, 60
Schudson, Michael, 131, 132
Schultz, Terri, 143
Scientific American, 65
Seminole Indians, 19, 62, 154
Seneca Indians, 103
Sergeant, Elizabeth Shepley, 35, 87, 89
Seymour, Flora Warren, 60, 77
Shawano Evening Leader
on Indian dancing contest, 118–19
on Menominee community activities, 112–13
on Menominee per capita payments, 116
on Menominee response to termination, 109
on Sen. Watkins's visit to Menominee reservation, 110, 111
Shoshone Indians, 36
Siebert, Fredrick S., 5
Simon, Sen. Paul, 160
Sinclair, Upton, 22
Sioux Indians
enemy of, 161

honorary tribal memberships, 73
land claims of, 74
Sun Dance of, 93
and Wounded Knee (1890), 141
and Wounded Knee II, 140, 142, 143
Smith, Faith, 161
Society of Professional Journalists, 159
Spicer, Edward, 37
Sports Illustrated, 156
Springfield Republican, 74
Stanford University, 155
Steiner, Linda, 6
Stephens, Mitchell, 8
Sunset Magazine, 35

Taft, William H., 42
Taos Indians, 136
Tax, Sol, 128
Television, 55, 102, 155, 156
Termination. *See* Indian reservations
American Civil Liberties Union and, 102
Commonweal on, 106
Dwight Eisenhower and, 102
Flathead Indians and, 115
Klamath Indians and, 102
legislation for, 101–2, 108, 113–14
Menominee Indians and, 102, 107–8, 109, 110
opponents of, 100, 101
origins of, 4, 99
Paiute Indians and, 115
promoters of, 99, 100, 114
rationale for, 99–100
relocation and, 116, 128
results of, 4
Richard Nixon and, 129
Ronald Reagan and, 153–54
Teters, Charlene, 155
Thomas, Edward, 160
Thorpe, Jim, 70, 139
Time
on Alcatraz occupation, 140
on artifacts as fashion, 135
founding of, 58
on Indian Reorganization Act, 58
on militant movement, 136–37
on "Navajo Flu," 158
on 1934 Indian congresses, 56–57
on Wounded Knee occupation, 144, 146
Tinker, Maj. Gen. Clarence L., 86
Tlingit Indians, 159, 160
Tohono O'odham (Papago) Indians, 92
Tonto, 12
Tuscarora Indians, 92, 128

United Press International, 102, 119, 120, 121, 161
University of Illinois, 1, 155, 160
University of Minnesota, 54
University of Wisconsin, 53
U.S. News and World Report (United States News), 58, 134, 144
USA Today, 156, 158

Vestal, Stanley, 88
Villard, Oswald Garrison, 95
Vorse, Mary Heaton, 60, 78

Wampum, 28
Warner, Glenn (Pop), 70
Washington, George, 119
Washington Indians, 137
Washington Post, 5, 158–59
Washington Redskins, 155, 162
Watkins, Sen. Arthur V., 100, 108
on termination, 100, 114
visit of, to Menominee reservation, 109, 110
Webb, Alvin, 121
West, Mae, 66
Wheeler, Sen. Burton K., 51
Wheeler-Howard bill, 50–53, 72, 75
Franklin D. Roosevelt and, 75
Muskogee Daily Phoenix on, 52, 67–68, 68–69
Nation on, 51
Native Americans and, 50–53
New York Times on, 75
New York Times Magazine on, 51
White, Owen P., 62
White, Robert H., 158
White, William Allen, 21

Wiedrich, Bob, 144
Wilson, Richard, 141
Woodlands tribes, 28
Work, Hubert, 33, 34
Wounded Knee, South Dakota
  Indian massacre at, 19, 140–41
  Indian occupation of, 4, 141–42; Associated Press on, 143–44, 145, 146; *Chicago Daily News* on, 143; *Chicago Tribune* on, 144, 145; framing of stories concerning, 144; *New York Times* on, 142–43, 145; *Rapid City Daily Journal* on, 143, 146–47; *Time* on, 144, 146; *U.S. News and World Report* on, 144

Yaqui Indians, 36–37, 39
Yellowbank, James, 161
Yost, Casper S., 6
Your Newspaper (Nieman Fellows), 104

Zah, Peterson, 158–59
Zimmerman, William, Jr., 101

About the Author

MARY ANN WESTON is Associate Professor at the Medill School of Journalism, Northwestern University. She specializes in multicultural issues in journalism, journalism history, and reporting and writing.

ISBN 0-313-28948-4
90000>
EAN
9 780313 289484
HARDCOVER BAR CODE